FELLOWSHIP OF LOVE

FELLOWSHIP OF LOVE

METHODIST WOMEN CHANGING AMERICAN RACIAL ATTITUDES 1920–1968

Alice G. Knotts

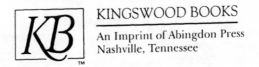

KINGSWOOD BOOKS
An Imprint of Abingdon Press
Nashville, Tennessee

FELLOWSHIP OF LOVE: METHODIST WOMEN
CHANGING AMERICAN RACIAL ATTITUDES, 1920–1968

Copyright © 1996 by Abingdon Press

All Rights Reserved.

This book is printed on acid-free recycled paper.

Library of Congress Cataloging-in-Publication Data

Knotts, Alice G.
     Fellowship of Love : Methodist women changing American racial
attitudes, 1920–1968 / Alice G. Knotts.
        p.   cm.
     Includes bibliographical references and index.
     ISBN 0–687–02719–5 (pbk. : acid-free paper)
     1. Methodist women—United States—History—20th century. 2. Race rela-
tions—Religious aspects—Methodist Church—History—20th century. 3. United
States—Race relations—History—20th century.
     I. Title.
     BX8345. 7.K56   1996
     261.8'348'008827—dc20

96–30274
CIP

Scripture quotations are from the Revised Standard Version of the Bible, copyright ©1946, 1952, 1971 by the Division of Christian Education of the National Council of Churches in the USA. Used by permission.

Hymn in preface, "In Christ There Is No East or West," by John Oxenham, 1913, *The Methodist Hymnal*, 1935.

Portions of this text were previously published in *Methodist History*, July 1989 XXVII:4 230-40, "Southern Methodist Women and Interracial Relations in the 1930s"; October 1990 XXIX:1 37-43, "The Debates Over Race and Women's ordination in the 1939 Methodist Merger"; July 1988 XXVI:4 199-212, "Race Relations in the 1920s: A Challenge to Southern Methodist Women." Used by permission.

Portions of this text were previously published in *Black Women in United States History*, ed. Darlene Clark Hine, vol. 16, *Women in   the Civil Rights Movement: Trailblazers and Torchbearers, 1941–1965*, ed. Vicki Crawford, "Methodist Women Integrate Schools and Housing, 1952–1959," 251-58 (Brooklyn, NY: Carlson Publishing, Inc., 1990). Used by permission.

98 99 00 01 02 03 04 05 —10 9 8 7 6 5 4 3 2

MANUFACTURED IN THE UNITED STATES OF AMERICA

To my parents
J. Ross Knotts and Marjorie Cooley Knotts,
who faithfully live the gospel

and to my shalom sisters,
Jeanne G. Knepper and Jean Miller Schmidt,
working to create a shalom community.

Contents

ABBREVIATIONS
OF ORGANIZATIONS

ACLU	American Civil Liberties Union
AFL	American Federation of Labor
ASWPL	Association of Southern Women for the Prevention of Lynching
BMCR	Black Methodists for Church Renewal
CIC	Commission on Interracial Cooperation
CIO	Congress of Industrial Organizations
CME	Colored Methodist Episcopal [Church]
CORE	Congress of Racial Equality
CSR	Christian Social Relations
CSR/LCA	Christian Social Relations and Local Church Activities
EUB	Evangelical United Brethren
FEPC	Fair Employment Practices Commission
FOC	Fellowship of the Concerned
FOR	Fellowship of Reconciliation
HUAC	House Un-American Activities Committee
ILD	International Labor Defense
MEC	Methodist Episcopal Church
MECS	Methodist Episcopal Church, South
MFSA	Methodist Federation for Social Action
MFSS	Methodist Federation for Social Service
MPC	Methodist Protestant Church
NAACP	National Association for the Advancement of Colored People
NACW	National Association of Colored Women
NCC	National Council of Churches
PCCR	President's Committee on Civil Rights
SCHW	Southern Conference for Human Welfare
SCLC	Southern Christian Leadership Conference
SNCC	Student Nonviolent Coordinating Committee
SRC	Southern Regional Council
STFU	Southern Tenant Farmers Union
WCC	World Council of Churches
WCTU	Women's Christian Temperance Union
WFMS	Woman's Foreign Missionary Society
WHMS	Woman's Home Missionary Society
WMC	Woman's Missionary Council (of the MECS)
WSCS	Woman's Society of Christian Service (of the MEC)
WSG	Wesleyan Service Guild
YMCA	Young Men's Christian Association
YWCA	Young Women's Christian Association

11

Preface

In Christ there is no East or West,
In Him no South or North;
But one great fellowship of love
Throughout the whole wide earth.

In Him shall true hearts everywhere
Their high communion find;
His service is the golden cord
Close binding all mankind.

Join hands, then, brothers of the faith,
Whate'er your race may be.
Who serves my Father as a son;
Is surely kin to me.

In Christ now meet both East and West,
In Him meet South and North;
All Christly souls are one in Him
Throughout the whole wide earth.[1]

—John Oxenham

During the time period covered in this volume, "In Christ there is no East or West" served as the theme song for race relations. Many Protestant churches in the U.S. celebrated Brotherhood Sunday every February by singing this hymn and frequently it was used at interracial and ecumenical gatherings. Every monthly meeting of Methodist women in churches large or small began with devotions consisting of scripture, singing, and prayer. The purpose of these missionary society meetings fit so closely with the words of "In Christ there is no East or West" that these frequently sung words left an indelible mark on the identity of Methodist women.

The poem describes "one great fellowship of love / Throughout the whole wide earth" that transcends geography and race. This fellowship

13

of love brings together as family people who serve a loving God by demonstrating love in all their relationships.

The vision of Methodist women, who felt they were part of "one great fellowship of love," explains why faith and action became inextricably joined for them. The women at the heart of this story refused to wall off citizenship and social responsibility from what it meant to follow God and Jesus. God called them to be tolerant of difference and loving agents of change, inviting persons participating in unjust social systems to shift their weight and lend their aid to do what is good. For these women, being a faithful Christian meant being a good neighbor and working to overturn injustice.

Acknowledgments

Many people have helped bring this book into being. Faculty at the Iliff School of Theology and University of Denver provided guidance: Dr. Jean Miller Schmidt, my dissertation advisor, and Drs. Will B. Gravely, Dana W. Wilbanks, and Vincent G. Harding. I am grateful to friends and strangers who provided interviews and librarians who helped find obscure books and records. Friends who patiently listened to researched stories helped me know which ones to tell. I especially appreciate the encouragement and family support I received from Jeanne Knepper, Andrea Knepper, and Laura Knotts.

I wish to thank the General Commission on Archives and History of The United Methodist Church for awarding this book the 1991 quadrennial Jesse Lee Prize in Methodist History. The suggestions made by the committee chaired by Dr. Robert W. Sledge and the recommendations made by an anonymous scholar have tremendously enhanced the book.

If peace is to come to the peoples of the earth, it will come because "men of good will" have faith in its realization and work constructively toward its achievement. Toward this end Methodist women are committed to accept their full share of responsibility.

—A Call to Methodist Women
Journal of the Woman's Division
(September 9, 1952), 36

Introduction

When the curtain falls on the twentieth century and social analysts and historians summarize its qualities and characteristics, there will be some who note that the fanfare surrounding major international conflicts and scientific developments overshadowed a major issue of the times—human relations. While the earth's population increased from one billion to six billion and nations built bigger bombs to enhance national security, some leaders learned that peace is not a condition but a process. Central to that process is the need to overcome barriers to communication based on assumptions about race, gender, religion, and national origin and to cross these boundaries to share economic and political power.

With the conviction that the world has a choice about its future, that people could live with a sense of hope and fulfillment rather than despairing both their present and their future, and believing that improved human relations contribute to peace and a foundation for that future, I chose to write about a model for changing attitudes about human relations. I wanted to explore a movement for renewal and change set within my own religious tradition in order to see whether there is evidence that significant and radical social change can be nurtured within a large, middle-of-the-road, socially accepted organization. I also believed that investigation would show that religious heritage and authority have a powerful capacity to surmount other human differences and evoke commitment both to self-examination, the precursor to change, and to human relations, that is, to social commitments beyond oneself.

An Underreported Churchwomen's Movement

The southern Methodist women who set out in the 1920s to provide an example to the whole world of what Christians might accomplish in race relations followed an ambitious vision untamed by awareness of

17

limitations. They were convinced that they could accomplish anything with God's help. Yet they were, perhaps, closer to the heart of the process of working for peace than they realized. It was no coincidence that a major commitment of many Americans to address problems of human relations surfaced immediately following World War I. While the United States spent billions of dollars and thousands of lives on military equipment and national defense during the twentieth century, the ledgers of history reveal bottom-line progress in human relations made by an organization of churchwomen in coalition with many other voluntary organizations concerned about human rights.

Why would this be so? There are several reasons. Methodist women were linked by religious beliefs and by structures which allowed freedom of opinion and dialogue on controversial issues. Discussion and disagreement within a framework of voluntary commitment and connection provided a healthy environment that enabled persons to re-evaluate their attitudes and uproot their prejudices. Growth and development are nurtured more easily when fear does not contribute to the erection and maintenance of barriers. Methodist women worked for race relations earlier than other mainline denominational groups precisely because they adhered to a gospel message which some of them interpreted as transcending race, class, and gender. They also came from a religious tradition that, since its earliest roots, understood that spiritual life is related to all aspects of life. Consequently, because Methodists were concerned about social issues, Methodist women accepted as their Christian and civic responsibility the task of influencing the quality of human relations of their communities and their nation.

Several mileposts marked my own journey in the writing of this book. In 1972 I attended a United Nations Seminar on Southern Africa sponsored by the Women's Division of the General Board of Global Ministries of The United Methodist Church. Theressa Hoover, head of the Women's Division, invited me to her home for an unforgettable dinner. Exposed to dynamic leaders and new insights, I became aware in a new way of the concern of these churchwomen to be on the cutting edge of social issues. Later, in reading Thelma Stevens' book, *Legacy for the Future*, I came across a tantalizing line to the effect that women "did more than make coffee" in their support for the civil rights struggle. I wanted to know what they had done and whether they had made a difference, since women's work in the civil rights movement had been unreported. Widespread reading of even secondary sources did not provide much to indicate the role of women in the struggle.

In 1983 I turned to interviews for leads. Diane Nash, a leader in the Nashville wing of the movement in the 1960s, gave me an important tip. She urged me to explore what ordinary people did during those active years of the civil rights movement. All over the South, the movement emerged because the time was ripe. I wondered what had happened to convince people that this was the time to end segregation. This book explores the step by step process by which the Woman's Division of the Board of Missions of The Methodist Church (henceforth abbreviated as Woman's Division) led churchwomen to reject segregation and embrace the ideal of an American culture without racial barriers.

My book is about one of the largest, longest, most far-reaching and underreported aspects of the civil rights movement in the United States, involving an organization of 1.2 million members: Methodist women's work for civil rights. From 1920 through 1968 and beyond, this work has been underreported because the organization was denominationally based and female in a time when, by and large, neither church business nor women's activities made news. The double barrier of silence meant that no one paid much attention and as time passed, even many women have forgotten these events, since the significance of telling the story was lost when its importance was denied.

This book limits its focus to an exploration of developments in African American/white relations in the South even though Methodist women worked to broaden the understanding and practice of civil rights of all races and ethnicities throughout the nation. Leaders of Methodist women directed their work toward breaking down all racial barriers. Specific efforts by Methodist women on behalf of Asian Americans, Native Americans, Hispanic Americans, and other ethnic minority groups were smaller and received less publicity and visibility. Methodist women's success stemmed from two qualities: first, membership in one of the few truly nationwide Protestant denominations in the U.S. and second, leadership brought by women from the Methodist Episcopal Church, South.

Persistence and genuine human caring characterized the process used by these churchwomen. Although they met resistance, they made limited, demonstrable, and significant advances for human rights. Methodist women exercised authority based on religious beliefs and democratic principles. These shaped their sense of accountability, organizational strengths, and interpersonal qualities, thereby increasing empathy for civil rights work. In other words, Methodist women made changes in their own lives and their organizational structure at the same time that they worked for broader social change.

Stereotypes of churchwomen's organizations as dull groups of older women might mislead people to surmise that the work of Meth-

19

odist women was not broad and influential. It is true that the vision of local groups was often myopic. National leaders opened windows on the world to local women, thus connecting local actions to global issues. The progress of Methodist women in transforming race relations, in spite of the achievements claimed here, is not a finished task but an ongoing process. United Methodist Women continue their work with program priorities on human and race relations.

In this volume the term "civil rights movement" indicates intentional efforts between 1940 and 1968 on the part of both African American and white leaders to establish equality of all races as a basic human value. The civil rights movement, a part of the larger African American freedom struggle, worked to overcome attitudes of racial prejudice and to establish, both in custom and in civil law, equal and fair treatment for all. African American women influenced a predominantly white culture and white organizations in three ways: they organized and strengthened local community groups working on civil rights, they reformed the way organizations held interracial meetings, and they constantly reminded people that racial segregation must end.

Both 1920, when the interracial movement emerged following World War I, and 1940, when war involvement was used as an excuse to deny citizenship rights of Japanese Americans, provided turning points in the consciousness of African Americans and some key Methodist women's missionary society leaders. This book explores the efforts of Methodist women who changed the values of white women, increased public support for civil rights for African Americans, and prepared a growing segment of the nation to either endorse or accept the practices of busing and desegregation of public schools. The objective of the African American freedom struggle was to realign the relationship between races in the United States, a task not yet completed. This book cannot report an overall goal accomplished, but it does note positive achievements.

This book is about a grassroots movement of women in local church groups who helped change attitudes, practices, and even federal policies relating to race relations and civil rights. It shows that the U.S. probably experienced less violence than might otherwise have occurred between 1960 and 1965 because churchwomen raised local consciousness about racial injustices, belonged to local citizen's committees, and sent their children to integrated public schools.

Methodist women organized societies long before massive sit-ins and continued do so after the 1965 Voting Rights Bill was passed. Working for civil rights and improved race relations was only a portion of their agenda. Although they comprised a surprisingly powerful

20

church-related movement, individual women's commitments proved to be fragile when social structures were challenged in the 1960s.

The civil rights movement was indebted to churches for hosting rallies and housing voter-registration workers; to Christian sources for the stirring gospel music of the movement and the empowering theology and rhetoric of Martin Luther King, Jr.; and to others who responded to injustice and violence with love and nonviolence. This book moves beyond the obvious connections between churches and social activists to explore how the Woman's Division of Christian Service of the Board of Missions of The Methodist Church changed racial perspectives of moderate white women.

The power and role of the church affected the grassroots character of the movement. The gospel message linked Methodist women with each other and with Christians and Jews who heard in the appeal for civil rights a call to include all persons in the human family and demonstrate God's love and justice in tangible ways.

Institutions and movements engage in social reform differently. Institutions may compromise and become indecisive in times of crisis. Movement organizations act more quickly, take more risks, involve masses of people and obtain more immediate results than do institutions. Movements disperse more quickly when a crisis is over. Charismatic leaders or a handful of movement leaders have great influence, which is lost if they die or leave, while institutions may sustain an effort over a long time, ultimately making significant progress.

The Woman's Division used the strengths of both. It nurtured Christian and ethical perspectives that, over a long period of time, changed attitudes of many women about civil rights. The Woman's Division also carried out a specific campaign to end the racially segregated jurisdictional system of The Methodist Church. With the exception of some well-educated and thoughtful leaders, most organized Methodist women were not able to modify their views and practices as quickly as change occurred under the impact of the active years of the civil rights movement from 1954 through 1968. Yet, had it not been for the earlier work of these Methodist women, public resistance to the civil rights movement and to integration of schools and public facilities would have been far greater than it was. Although many Methodist women were not prepared for the far-reaching changes they experienced, some were able to counsel others to accept the new ways and adapt to them. Bonds of faith and organizational structure maintained connections among people, who, in other circumstances, might have parted company when their attitudes were so different.

The Organization and Structure of the Woman's Division of Christian Service, 1940–1968

The structure of the Woman's Division had features which proved to be an asset to making long-term progress in the area of civil rights. At the highest level, the leadership of the Woman's Division was shared. Departments of Foreign Missions, Home Missions, and Christian Social Relations and Local Church Activities (CSR/LCA) each had an executive secretary who worked in a collegial relationship with the other two executive secretaries, coordinating and implementing the programs set by the officers of the Woman's Division. The position of chair of the Woman's Division's staff meetings rotated on an annual basis among the executive secretaries.

Mutual cooperation and participation provided the basis of planning and goal setting, living out a commitment to democratic principles. The staff of the Woman's Division recommended goals and objectives, initiated program ideas, drafted resolutions, and planned conferences and seminars. All of these ideas came as recommendations for discussion and action to the officers of the Woman's Division, approximately fifty women elected to represent Methodist women.

The Woman's Division represented ordinary grassroots women from the entire nation. The Methodist Church, which claimed to have churches in every county of the forty-eight contiguous states, had one or two local women's missionary groups in nearly every local church. Fulltime homemakers belonged to the Woman's Society of Christian Service (WSCS). Employed women joined the Wesleyan Service Guild (WSG) which held evening meetings, in contrast to the daytime meetings of the WSCS.

Local societies had close organizational ties with district, conference, jurisdictional, and national officers. In addition to having a president, vice-president, secretary, and treasurer, each level had program officers who related to national staff. This book focuses especially on the work of the secretary for CSR/LCA. Other program officers included a secretary for Foreign Missions, a secretary for Home Missions, and secretaries of Children's Work, Youth Work, and Young Adult Work. Large societies had committees to assist each secretary in her work. The Methodist women's groups assumed responsibility for much of the mission education done in the local church, educating not only the women, children, youth, and young adults, but often providing information to the pastor and rest of the congregation as well. Thus, in the local church, organized Methodist women were very influential.

The Woman's Division staff expected accountability. The Department of CSR/LCA not only launched initiatives asking officers to carry out particular activities, but also expected quarterly reports from local church, district, conference, and jurisdiction leaders giving details about each group's activities. The accountability built into the structure of the Woman's Division provided direction. These were not free-wheeling friendship groups. They raised all their own funds and remained financially independent from the church. Regular accountability helped hold the organization together in times of controversy and emphasized the need for action as well as study and reflection.

The Woman's Division of Christian Service had its own communication channels. It published its own magazine to which most officers and many local Methodist women subscribed. _The Methodist Woman_ provided informative articles about the work of the Woman's Division, discussed mission themes and social issues, and presented monthly columns of information and guidance to help each officer know how to implement her responsibilities.

The vast connectional network of officers in the WSCS and the WSG gave the organization qualities of both a grassroots organization and a national organization. Each local society or guild had freedom to interpret the national program and adapt it to specific local needs. Individual members also were free to act according to their own beliefs whether or not they agreed with perspectives of the national staff. The structure provided room for creative tension between different points of view. The staff led and guided, but the membership did not always follow. Ideological gaps developed most frequently around social issues and race relations. Members of the WSCS valued their membership even if they disagreed with Thelma Stevens, the executive secretary of the Department of Christian Social Relations, who, on social issues, was the most outspoken leader in the organization. The stability of the organization enabled attitudes to change gradually.

An Overview of the Chapters

This book shows how the activities of this Methodist women's movement for civil rights developed decade by decade, rarely in the public eye, shaping and being shaped by events and public opinion. Beginning with the early twentieth century, the organizational assets that proved most reliable for transforming race relations were already present: (1) Methodist emphasis on God's ability to help transform society as well as individual lives; (2) long-standing recognition of the

23

injustice of segregation; (3) communication between black and white church leaders on the subject of race relations; (4) women's experiences of gender-based discrimination and elementary sensitivity to racial discrimination; and (5) the semi-autonomous status of the Methodist women's missionary societies.

The social gospel provided important theoretical and pragmatic influences on this women's movement for civil rights. Methodist women believed that people were inherently good and that moral suasion could influence people to do good for those less fortunate. The second chapter adds historical and theoretical background to the Methodist women's strong ecumenical ties and the interracial WCTU network it inherited. In the 1920s, African American women sought and cultivated white churchwomen as allies in their struggle. They laid an organizational foundation for their work.

By the early 1930s, social pressure mounted for more fairness in education, the criminal system, and the availability of public utilities and services. Clearly, problems were not merely local. Women organized a crusade against lynching that brought them into community leadership and the public arena. As we see in chapter 4, by the later 1930s, gender, education, and economic issues broadened the political agenda of those working on race relations. Programs designed to work in tandem but carried out separately by white or black groups lost power and usefulness.

As the Methodist Episcopal Church, South, moved toward the 1939 merger that created The Methodist Church and a racially defined jurisdictional system, organized Methodist women took a position between those of African American leaders and other church leaders. Southern white women and African American women from the Methodist Episcopal Church brought to The Methodist Church experienced interracial leadership. Chapter 6 provides biographies of key leaders from the Department of Christian Social Relations who helped guide the Woman's Division of Christian Service in all its programs related to race between 1940 and 1968.

Chapter 7 describes changing views among African Americans and white liberals, and demonstrates how the Truman administration leadership set a new context after World War II. Organizations such as National Association for the Advancement of Colored People, Fellowship of Reconciliation, Congress of Racial Equality, the Southern Regional Council, and the Methodist Federation for Social Service increased pressure to end segregation. Methodist women participated in this interracial network of cooperating organizations. They provided overlapping leadership and shared information, strategies, and ideas. The network influenced the attitudes and positions of social institutions and government.

In the 1940s, Methodist women found a theological voice for their work. They articulated a vision of a social order without racial barriers. Chapter 8 explains how they incorporated social science and democratic principles into a foundation for a Christian-based movement for civil rights. The new rationale and cultivation of leaders pressed Methodist women into a dramatic new engagement with politics at the national level. This is described in chapter 9, which examines specific ways Methodist women worked to change race relations and end segregation in church and society.

The 1950s, introduced in chapter 10, presented a more hostile climate for race relations work. Although attitudes polarized and resistance grew, a few Methodist women engaged in more direct action than in the past. Chapter 11 explicates how, based on their new concept of mission related to a broader understanding of human rights, Methodist women pledged to end segregation in church and society. They used workshops, training events, and various other activities to help other Methodist women overcome prejudices.

During the tumultous 1960s, described in chapters 12 and 13, Methodist women made great efforts to reduce racial tensions in the South and overturn segregation through legislation and voting rights. Chapter 13 tells how they proceeded with interracial mergers culminating with the desegregation of The United Methodist Church. Finally, chapter 14 names additional forms of growth in identity, self-understanding, and spiritual life that came as Methodists learned from their experiences. Methodists invited people to change their attitudes about race and learn to create a worldwide fellowship of love. The appendices provide a wealth of information; footnotes add sources, detail, stories, and humor for those who wish to read further.

The field, of all others, for the care and labor of Southern women is the mission to the colored people, because in the nineteenth century, if there is a people to whom they should be grateful, it is these people. . . . Bishop, *give us work: we can do it*, not at once perhaps, but let us begin.

—Letter from Mrs. E. C. Dowdell to
Bishop James O. Andrew of the
Methodist Episcopal Church, South, (1861)

CHAPTER 1

Ingredients for a
Civil Rights Movement:
A National Church, an Autonomous
Agency, and Discrimination

The story of the Methodist women's campaign for civil rights begins with intertwined stories of racial and gender discrimination in the nineteenth and early twentieth centuries. Methodist women had founded women's missionary societies specifically because gender discrimination had barred the door to their participation in the full life of the church. Through these societies, Methodist women grew spiritually as they transformed their less powerful social position into a gift employed in Christian living.

Discrimination provided a wake-up call to Methodist women: God calls people of faith to learn to live with respect for one another. Racial discrimination was not obvious to people who had been living in a culture whose social norms reinforced public obliviousness to injustice. Methodists found it easier to object to segregation in principle than to dismantle the social conventions that perpetuated it. Yet Methodist women had gifts for this larger task. They belonged to the only nationwide church in the U.S. and to an autonomous organization.

Early Methodism, Race Relations, and the South

Early in American history Methodist circuit riders and Baptist preachers plied their trade in the South, surpassing the success of religious leaders of other persuasions. Religious homogeneity of the region consolidated by the 1830s, contributing to its cultural identity, and establishing a base for a Methodist-led movement.[1] Eighteenth-century Methodist preaching in the South underscored the development of personal piety and an individualistic approach to salvation while it also played an important role in establishing patterns for social order and social stability among the scattered farms of the South of the 1700s.[2] The historic concern of the Methodist Episcopal Church (MEC) to make a social witness to the gospel and that denomination's experience as a national church prior to 1845 helped shape the expectations of Methodist women in the twentieth century.[3]

Three major Protestant denominations—Methodists, Presbyterians, and Baptists—divided over the issue of slavery. Northern and southern branches of Methodism, the first of these denominations to reunite, in 1939 formed the largest Protestant church in the United States at the time. Among Protestant groups in the South, Methodists, with a national identity and a Wesleyan emphasis on social issues, held the most influential position to deal with issues of African American/white race relations.[4]

Methodist controversies over racial issues date back very early in the MEC, which organized in the United States in 1784. Clergy in the new church attempted to establish an anti-slavery norm. Although some colonial Methodists owned slaves, by 1798 the Conference adopted a rule that no Methodists were permitted to buy, sell, or hold slaves. Within six months this standard had been challenged and relaxed.[5] In 1808 the church allowed pastors, exercising some caution, to admit to membership persons who held slaves for the purpose of emancipating them when state laws and circumstances allowed.[6] The official stance of the MEC was modified so that each annual conference had the power to make policies regarding the buying and selling of slaves. The new position enabled the MEC to establish policies in keeping with state laws which prohibited the emancipation of slaves. By arguing that their ability to win new church members would be seriously curtailed if membership requirements were not compatible with state laws, southern Methodists persuaded the church to allow exceptions in the South.

In 1844 the slavery issue divided the MEC. By 1845, the Methodist Episcopal Church, South, (MECS) formed as a denomination composed of conferences south of the Mason-Dixon Line that voted for separation from the MEC.

After the Civil War, in some places the northern branch of Methodism treated the southern states as though they were occupied territory available to be evangelized by the church of the victors.[7] Northern Methodists asserted the right to establish northern congregations across the street from southern ones, creating animosity between the two churches. Nevertheless, in due time after slaves had been freed, the

28

northern church concluded that the primary obstacle to reunion no longer existed. Three northern delegates arrived at the 1874 General Conference of the MECS, bearing fraternal greetings. From this first encounter until 1938, these two branches of Methodism debated their relationship and reunion.

Between 1894 and 1916 a joint Commission on Federation considered proposals for church unification. The MECS responded to one 1914 proposal with a recommendation that "the colored membership of various Methodist bodies be formed into an independent organization holding fraternal relations with the . . . united church."[8] In 1870 this had been the southern solution for dealing with its own African American members and had resulted in the formation of the Colored Methodist Episcopal Church (CME). The 1916 General Conference of the MEC responded by proposing to organize the "colored membership" of the new church into one or more jurisdictional conferences, leaving the reorganized General Conference integrated. The Joint Commission on Unification formed in 1916 worked on these and other proposals over the next twenty-two years without debating racial attitudes, meanwhile searching for ingenious political strategies to satisfy both northern and southern white constituencies.

Delegates to the General Conference—always men until women were added in 1904 and 1922 in the northern and southern branches, respectively—focused their attention on the politics of unification rather than race relations. However, beginning in 1912 in the South, white women and African American women addressed human relations by opening tentative conversations on race relations and working together to address inner city problems.

Religion was used to justify both slavery and segregation. While the initial reason for importing Africans in bondage to the American colonies was to provide labor for the developing tobacco industry, southerners found another reason to justify importing approximately 358,000 Africans as slaves.[9] Southern white slave owners claimed that it was their religious duty to bring these "heathens" to Christianity and to provide for their salvation. White slave owners believed that they were morally and biologically superior to persons of African descent.[10] Using the stories of Ham (Gen. 9:20-27), Joseph (Gen. 37–50), and Onesimus (Phil. 1:10-16), slave owners argued that the Bible supported slavery.[11]

Segregationists found instances where the Bible told of separation and used these to assert that God endorsed racial segregation. They believed that Noah's sons started two distinct racial groups, and that the African American race was sent to live in Africa. They claimed that at the Tower of Babel God separated people by languages as a penalty for racial integration. Segregationists used the prohibition in Leviticus 19:19 against mixing two kinds of cattle, seed, or cloth to infer that mixed marriages were sinful. Social Darwinism's teaching that some life species and genetic features were superior to others provided handy endorsement of white racial supremacist views and was used to claim that black and white races were not meant to mix.[12]

Pro-slavery arguments were based on the principle of social inequality. Indeed, some whites asserted racial paternalism, the notion that the white race had God-given responsibility to protect, support, and control the black race in return for service.

A Background of Segregation

In the post-Civil War Reconstruction of the South, the position of African Americans rose dramatically, then plummeted in betrayal.[13] Between 1867 and 1868, African Americans were elected to serve in state legislatures and held numerous elected positions as sheriff, justice of the peace, and county commissioner.[14] These interracial governments were soon suppressed, however, and the legal status of African Americans was undermined when segregation (Jim Crow) laws were adopted. Turmoil reigned while federal and state agencies jockeyed to redefine relationships between races. A policy of federal authority over affairs of race began to take shape with the Thirteenth Amendment (1865) that granted freedom to slaves. The Fourteenth Amendment (July 1868) was intended to protect personal rights with "due process." In 1870 the Fifteenth Amendment gave African American men the right to vote. An 1875 Civil Rights Act granted "all persons full and equal enjoyment of the accommodations, advantages, and facilities . . . of inns, public conveyances . . . theaters, and other places of public amusement." In civil rights cases of 1883, the Supreme Court overturned federal laws and upheld segregation in schools and public transportation.

Yet federal policies deferred to regional folkways. Court decisions permitted businesses to select or segregate their customers. Courts allowed school districts to operate two separate school systems with substandard and inadequately funded segregated schools for African Americans. Color lines limited job opportunities.

Soon whites passed new laws discriminatory against blacks and found ways to take away voting rights. With increasing finesse, local and state governments passed bills for poll taxes, criminal disqualifications, and literacy requirements that prevented most African American people from voting. Grandfather clauses exempted sons and grandsons of pre-1867 voters (when very few blacks voted) from most of the same restrictions. White-perpetuated acts of force, brutality, terror, and intimidation kept African Americans from registering and voting. In Louisiana alone, between 1896 and 1904, the number of registered African American voters dropped from 130,334 to 1,342.[15] New segregation laws were still being written in the 1930s, such as a 1935 Oklahoma law that separated people by race when they went fishing.[16]

By 1896 the U.S. Supreme Court, in *Plessy v. Ferguson*, launched the era of "separate but equal" which selectively enforced the first component of the principle but not the latter one. The court enabled states to make laws requiring segregated railroad facilities for African Americans. As never before, segregation became the sanctioned way of life in the South with the blessing of the Supreme Court. Indeed, by January 14, 1899, the Boston *Evening Transcript* noted that the Republican Party, with President William McKinley in the White House, had taken the South's race policy as its own.[17] Northern opposition to southern racial laws and customs had been muted. Policies of racial supremacy co-opted federal and national public support. In the South, sectionalism and racism flourished under a banner that recalled the horrors of Reconstruction.

Whereas northerners had taken pride in their part in ending slavery, now the social climate permitted racial hatred to fester and conspired with mob racial violence, terrorizing African Americans and enforcing racial status. Between the years 1885 and 1915, 2,850 persons were lynched.[18] By 1906 the conservative Charleston *News and Courier*, finding that segregation was inadequate to deal with racial problems, recommended mass deportation of African Americans.[19]

Years of economic hardship and legal entrenchment of segregation contributed to a period in race relations which Rayford W. Logan has described as "The Dark Ages of Recent American History." During the period before World War II, Logan noted, "second-class citizenship for Negroes was accepted by presidents, the Supreme Court, Congress, organized labor, the General Federation of Women's Clubs—indeed by the vast majority of Americans, north and south, and by the 'leader' of the Negro race."[20]

The pre-war migration of African Americans out of the South fueled the nation's growing racial antagonism, raised resentment that effectively closed the doors of many labor unions to interracialism, and established once and for all the national scope of America's racism.

31

Decade by decade after 1910, people sought greater freedom in the North—initially 300,000; then 1,300,000 in the 1920s; 1,500,000 in the 1930s; and 2,500,000 in the 1940s.[21] For the first time, the African American population in the South was surpassed by that in all other parts of the nation. By the 1960s, only one-third of African Americans lived in the South.

All the while, African Americans found ways to protest. Various African American leaders provided an array of options based on different social analyses. An examination of the different positions of five African American leaders provides a cultural backdrop for understanding racial perspectives that attracted Methodist women.

Booker T. Washington (1856–1915), spokesperson for a new age in African American/white relations, concluded that education and economic self-help programs were among the most effective African American responses to the harsh setbacks of segregation. In an 1895 speech that came to be known as the Atlanta Compromise, Washington spoke of races functioning as separately as the fingers on the hand, but inevitably joined together in one nation. Disclaiming the value of political leadership in a time when African Americans could not win elections, Washington nevertheless convinced several American presidents of their need for African American leadership in certain political situations. He also funneled major financial commitments from white northern philanthropists to southern African American schools and institutions. Washington's choice to make the best of a bad situation through self-help rather than confrontation suggested to many a policy of submission for African Americans that, though not intended, appeared to be "an invitation to further aggression."[22]

Bishop Henry McNeal Turner (1834–1915) of the African Methodist Episcopal Church, immediately opposed Booker T. Washington's position. "The colored man who will stand up and in one breath say that the Negroid race does not want social equality and in the next predict a great future in the face of all the proscription of which the colored man is the victim, is either an ignoramus, or is an advocate of the perpetual servility and degradation of his race variety."[23]

John Hope (1868–1936), a professor at Roger Williams University in Nashville in 1886, also dared, as did few African American leaders, to defy Washington's view. "If we are not striving for equality, in heaven's name for what are we living? I regard it as cowardly and dishonest for any of our colored men to tell white people or colored people that we are not struggling for equality. . . . Why build a wall to keep me out?"[24] Child of an interracial marriage, Hope married a daughter of an interracial union. Turner and Hope used the socially

32

forbidden words: they demanded nothing less than social equality. Hope later became the president of Atlanta University, and his wife Lugenia brought these views to her active interracial work with the Young Women's Christian Association (YWCA) and churchwomen.

In his 1903 book, *The Souls of Black Folk*, **W. E. B. DuBois** directly challenged Booker T. Washington, who had become the narrow funnel for interracial contacts whose money controlled the African American press and whose opinion and actions obstructed the rise of an African American civil rights movement. DuBois and like-minded leaders concerned with civil rights gathered at Niagara Falls in 1905. DuBois lashed out at Washington's abandonment of political power, higher education, and civil rights, and his inordinate confidence in the notion that an elite "talented tenth" would lead the race. Instead, DuBois demanded the African American right to vote, "civic equality" and "education of youth according to ability."[25] After the passage of time made these ideas more reformist than radical, the Methodist women's campaign for civil rights was to follow this direction under the leadership of Thelma Stevens. In 1909 supporters of the new movement for African American civil rights founded the National Association for the Advancement of Colored People (NAACP), a group dedicated to using the legal system to advance human rights. In 1911 the National Urban League organized to help African Americans adjust to city life.

Marcus Garvey led a number of African Americans along yet another path toward separatism rooted in the principle of self-government and self-control. Garvey accentuated pride in African heritage and culture, offered hope, and extolled black beauty. "We are not seeking social equality . . . we do not seek intermarriage. . . . We want the right to have a country of our own and there foster and reestablish a culture and civilization exclusively ours," he wrote.[26] Enticing thousands with the lure of a return to Africa, Garvey led the Universal Negro Improvement Association, which may have had a million members at its peak in the mid-1920s.

The social analysis of racial problems and solutions changed slightly in each decade. The breadth of African American views interacted with the range of white responses and opinions on race relations. The women in this book chose various courses of action found to the left of the middle of the road, but never more radical than the liberal left African American leaders of the protest movement. White arrogance and attitudes of superiority maintained a social distance between whites and African Americans who cooperated interracially.

Out of the unique American blend of democracy, Christianity, racial issues, and problems of modernization came a conviction articulated from many quarters that African Americans deserved more fair treatment than they were receiving in the twentieth century. Thus a young newspaper reporter, Ray Stannard Baker, after a race riot in the Brownsville quarter of Atlanta, in 1906 wrote: "Christianity and humanity demand that we treat the Negro fairly. He is here, and here to stay . . . it is our Christian duty to protect him."[27] White Methodist women, who began with a similar paternalistic stance, gradually enlarged their fellowship of love.

The Influence of Gender Issues in Women's Work

Methodist women came to hold a position of advantage for addressing problems of race relations and civil rights. This book examines how they attained this leverage and what they did with it. For reasons bigger than their own intentions, they maintained an autonomous women's missionary organization in the context of a national church. Both The Methodist Church (1939–68) and the Woman's Division of Christian Service obtained these strengths by an indirect route in which discrimination on account of race and gender played a part.

It is against the backdrop of segregationist views of southern Methodist church leaders that the race relations efforts of Methodist women of the Woman's Home Missionary Society (WHMS) and the Woman's Missionary Council, the southern predecessors of the Woman's Division, stand out in fuller meaning. Segregation by gender in church and society led to the formation of women's missionary organizations.

The origins of separate missionary societies for Methodist women and ultimately their engagement with the issue of race relations derived from the women's dissatisfaction with the treatment they received as women. Some Methodist women came to identify with the frustration and anger African Americans felt under segregation.

Foreign and home mission work provided a channel for women to engage in social service and to enter the public sphere. Churchwomen, ready to expand the influence of their Christian living beyond the four walls of their homes, claimed the world as their household.[28] While nineteenth-century culture extolled the virtues of women, glorified motherhood, and limited women's sphere of influence, Christian women expanded on the strengths of their prescribed role, namely, caring for home and family,[29] and interpreted in universal terms the acceptable gender-role expectations of women to care for children and one another. Within a few short years after 1869, northern Methodist women had established missions in China, India, Liberia, Brazil, and other nations. American women brought the missionary message to women in India and China who, secluded in their homes, would not otherwise have heard it. Efforts directed toward helping and saving "heathen women" of other races justified interracial contacts on the grounds that God's promise of salvation was for all people.

In both northern and southern branches of Methodism, white women launched home mission work with southern African American women. Northern women of the MEC first organized mission work with black Americans in New Orleans in the early 1870s under the leadership of Jennie C. Hartzell. In 1880, women who organized to support Hartzell's mission work formed the WHMS.

As early as 1861 issues of race and gender mingled for women of the MECS, who felt that because of their proximity to slaves, God called them to assume responsibility for these neighbors of theirs. In 1861 Mrs. E. C. Dowdell, of Alabama, wrote to Bishop James O. Andrew with an appeal that he take action to organize a women's missionary society to aid in the work of the Alabama Conference Missionary Society of the MECS. She proposed that women take a more active role in the mission outreach of the church by extending charity toward African Americans. According to Dowdell, the fundamental reason for southern women to engage in mission to African American people was to repay the kindness of African American women who had cared for white children, nursed the sick, and spared white women from arduous and dreary tasks.

Gender issues continued to influence women's understanding of their mission tasks. In the South this led to the 1878 formation of the WFMS with Juliana Hayes as president. Hayes claimed that women could engage in work for the benefit of other women, "uplifting" heathen women from degradation brought on by ignorance, sin, and superstition.[30] Women's home missionary work of the MECS, which formally organized in 1890 under the leadership of Lucinda Helm, appealed to women to aid other women by raising funds to provide housing for pioneer preachers and their families.

Women of the CME organized in 1894, initially serving as an auxiliary to the bishops. Enlarging their understanding of home and family, in 1918 CME women formed the Connectional Woman's Missionary Society. Responsibility for the care of home and family provided an early link between white women and African American women.

By 1920 many men and women, white and African American, held to the widespread belief that women had certain inherent qualities by virtue of their gender. Women were perceived as nurturing, "naturally" having a religious spirit, being a moral influence on the home, and having a positive influence on their men. Southern women may have been more submissive than their northern contemporaries, but they developed a protected sphere within which they influenced husbands, children, and politics. Suzanne Lebsock, who studied free northern black women, observed that "No one objected to a woman's acquisition of power as long as she did not ask that it be made obvious, official, or general."[31] The presumed innate qualities of women contributed to a notion, which had circulated among both African American and white southern women, that white southern women were in a prime position to make changes in racial attitudes. White women could identify with African American women in the experience of womanhood in caring for home and family, and comprehending the yearning for fairness which African American women had for their children, their husbands, and themselves. White women believed that they could influence their husbands along the lines of undertaking Christian responsibility toward this neighboring race.

At first the women's missionary organizations were small, but as women founded schools and colleges, homes and settlement houses, they invested in land and assets. By 1910 the WFMS of the MECS, supported ninety-five active foreign missionaries, the WHMS supported ninety-nine deaconesses and city missionaries, and their combined budgets exceeded one million dollars.[32]

The good business sense of the women attracted the attention of church leaders on the Board of Missions. Yet the women were taken by surprise in 1906 when, without being consulted, they heard the General Board of Missions recommend to the General Conference the immediate unification of the Woman's Home and Foreign Missionary Societies. All mission work would be united under one Board of Missions. Such an action would provide the MECS with a large home missions program where, apart from salary support to small churches, virtually none existed. Control of the combined new budget would shift from women to men. Belle Harris Bennett, president of the WHMS, reported that her counter-proposal, that the new mission board include equal representation of men and women, was greeted with laughter.

In 1906 the General Conference established a study commission to report its findings to the 1910 General Conference. The commission proposed to unite women's home and foreign mission work in a Woman's Missionary Council which would be a programmatic agency accountable to an expanded Board of Missions with administrative oversight for expenditure of funds. Women were granted membership on a church board for the first time and given one-third of the voting positions, yet the presence of thirteen additional non-voting bishops who were "accustomed to an absolute domination of the Parent Board," left the women with only token power.[33] From the trauma of the merger was born the women's laity rights movement in the MECS, which seated the first women delegates to General Conference in 1922.

Not only did the Board of Missions acquire authority over designation of funds but they also ended the women's missionary publication *Our Homes* edited by Mary Helm, thereby silencing the voice of an independent women's journal which had subscribed to the cause of uplifting the Negro race. In 1911 the Woman's Missionary Council paid tribute to Mary Helm by resolving to expand its mission work among African American people.

The connection between the social inferiority attributed to gender and that ascribed to race was not lost on the leaders of the Woman's Missionary Council. White southern missionary women were concerned about the status of women. It related to their mission emphasis and was critical for their own political status. Leaders of the Woman's Missionary Council entered the 1920s with an understanding that behind the struggle for women's rights and their concern for better race relations, notions of superiority and inferiority, hierarchy and subordination, had to be replaced by a profoundly new social order based on the social teachings of Jesus.

It shall be the duty of the Department of Social Service to promote the study of conditions and needs among the Negroes, locally, throughout the South; also to arouse the women of our auxiliaries to a sense of this personal duty as Christian Southerners to meet the needs and ameliorate the conditions of this backward race who are in our midst by personal service and sympathy. We recommend the giving of this sympathy and service in any or all of the following ways: . . .

(8) By creating in the local white community higher ideals in regard to the relation between the two races; by standing for full and equal justice in all departments of life; . . . by standing, in short, for the full application to Negroes and to ourselves of the Mosaic law of justice: "Thou shalt love thy neighbor as thyself."

—*Annual Report of the Woman's Missionary Council*
Methodist Episcopal Church, South
cited in Lily Hammond
In Black and White (1914), 201–2

CHAPTER 2

The 1920s:
Interracial Cooperation

Both the social gospel and the Women's Christian Temperance Union (WCTU), shaped early Methodist women's ventures into interracial cooperation, inviting women to transform their surrounding social conditions. Just as the social gospel sowed a broad field in urging Christians to consider the application of salvation to society as well as to individual souls, the WCTU helped enlarge the scope of women's work from home to the world. In addition, the WCTU created an ecumenical network of women engaged in home missions which provided social services and worked politically for change to alleviate dehumanizing social conditions.

This chapter traces the formation of foundational concepts that guided Methodist women as they opened hearts and minds to interracial work. African American women sought and cultivated professional relationships with white Methodist women, pointed out directions for cooperative work, invited them to risk new experiences, and accompanied them in interracial work.

Like a rose in bud, the fullness of their work opened slowly, delicately, and showed itself to be multifaceted. Carrie Parks Johnson's gentle leadership frustrated black women who longed for political and civil rights, but persuaded thousands of white women to risk becoming involved in race relations work of the day.

The Social Gospel Influence

The American social structure faced crises in the late nineteenth century brought on by rapid industrialization, modernization, urbanization, and immigration. The social gospel offered a religious response to massive social problems that profoundly challenged American Christians' reliance on sacraments, preaching, conversion, and personal faith. Rampant poverty, unemployment, racial and ethnic discrimination, industrial greed, exploitation of workers and child labor, low wages, starvation, lack of educational opportunities, a powerful liquor industry, corporate and political crime all indicated that not only individuals but also society itself stood in need of conversion.

A Baptist minister and spokesperson for the social gospel, Walter Rauschenbusch, claimed, "The fundamental purpose of Jesus was the establishment of the kingdom of God, which involved a thorough regeneration and reconstitution of social life."[1] Rauschenbusch elaborated, "Approximate equality is the only enduring foundation of political democracy. The sense of equality is the only basis for Christian morality."[2]

Bordon Parker Bowne, professor of philosophy at Boston Theological School from 1876 to 1910, taught that individuals are circumscribed by social conditions around them. One's environment provides both opportunities and constraints which radically affect the available choices. He believed that the gospel entreats Christians to create a social setting which cares for both the physical and spiritual well-being of its members.

The social gospel placed a new emphasis on ethics and justice in making real God's reign on earth. It stressed progress and the ability of people and social institutions to make inroads "against the entrenched forces of evil and economic exploitations."[3] Urban pastors began to struggle with the gap between the good news they preached and harsh realities of life. Methodist women's deaconess and urban home mission work in social settlements, orphanages, hospitals, and institutional churches placed women on the front lines of the social crisis in this country.[4] Southern Methodist women were reading noted social gospel authors: Josiah Strong, Washington Gladden, Walter Rauschenbusch, Shailer Mathers, Charles Stelzle, and Richard Ely.[5] Exposure to the social gospel began to change Methodist women's understanding of religion and to help them re-define their responsibility. John Patrick McDowell wrote of these women:

> The women cared less about figuring out how God and human beings cooperated than about calling people to assume responsibilities. They disdained complacency; they celebrated human effort, most particularly in the growth of [God's] kingdom on this earth.[6]

The social gospel prepared Methodist women to live out their faith by engaging with social issues. Already they had a model for action.

The WCTU Network: Ecumenical and Interracial

Thousands of American women became involved in the temperance movement, and Methodist women formed the core. Concerned with social reform, not just alcohol, the temperance movement gained ascendancy between the rise of the abolitionist movement and the civil rights movement, in parallel with the maturation of the women's suffrage movement and the emergence of women's missionary societies and the deaconess movement. In 1892 the WCTU, the largest organization of women in the United States up to that time, was headed by Frances Willard (1839–98), a Methodist educator and talented orator. Frustrated by gender discrimination in her career as a college administrator, Willard found an opportunity to apply her religious values and skills in a campaign that empowered women. The WCTU provided Willard a front for enlarging the role of women and mobilizing their leadership in the reformation of American society. King alcohol was directly implicated in manifest social ills such as broken homes, abandoned families, loss of employment, poverty, physical and emotional abuse of women and children, rape, murder, and other crimes. If the saloon was a threat to the home, women could legitimately enter the public sphere of politics to defend the arena of their responsibility. While Willard did not appeal directly to women to change their philosophy of separate gender spheres of responsibility, WCTU activities expanded the place of women in American life.

Alcohol-related social problems crossed racial and national lines, and so did the WCTU, as it grew to over two million members worldwide. During her 1881 organizing and speaking tour of the South, Willard addressed African American, Native American, and white audiences. She insisted that the WCTU welcome Jews and Catholics.[7] Although she wore a black suit, kept her tone of voice and gestures modest, and did not advocate women's suffrage, she attracted crowds, criticism, and praise because she was the first woman that most people in her audiences had heard speak in public.[8] Across the South, WCTU organizers Sally Chapin and Georgia McLeod cultivated the formation of local WCTU unions that, in the 1880s, were integrated. Gradually southern unions segregated by race. Resisting this trend, North Carolina's state chair of African American unions wrote, "[We do not want] to exclude any white sisters who might wish to work with us. . . . We believe all men are created equal."[9]

Officers and leaders in the WCTU, drawn from the ranks of widely representative denominational women's missionary societies, included a strong and predominant core of Methodist women. By gathering

41

ecumenical cooperation of women from missionary societies, the WCTU served as an organizing model for later civil rights work of churchwomen through the Committee on Interracial Co-operation and the Association of Southern Women for the Prevention of Lynching (ASWPL), although the latter group decided to exclude African Americans. In each case, Methodists provided more members and leaders than any other group, probably due to: first, the leadership network initially developed and cultivated by Frances Willard; second, the strength of Methodism in the South; and third, the appeal of the social gospel and its fertile ground within Methodism. These same factors shaped Methodist women's work in race relations.

Early Visions of Race Relations in the Woman's Missionary Council

In the early 1900s, the Woman's Missionary Council (WMC) of the Methodist Episcopal Church, South, (MECS) launched two forms of institutional outreach to African Americans. The first program offered college education for black women. In 1906, the WMC funded and provided staff for Paine College Annex, a women's program at Paine College. This Colored Methodist Episcopal college in Augusta, Georgia, had historic ties to its parent denomination, the MECS, stemming from 1877, when the MECS agreed to provide mission funding to the new denomination whose members were exiting the MECS. Supporters espoused three different purposes. Paine College president, Dr. Walker, desired to develop a co-educational campus; potential students dreamed of obtaining a quality liberal arts education; and white middle- and upper-class women of the Southern Methodist Episcopal Church, South, hoped the new women's program would train excellent domestic workers. After the leaders of the missionary society had prayerfully reached a decision to financially underwrite Paine College Annex, Tochie MacDonell, a member of the WMC executive committee, reported, "There were many who feared that the undertaking would be unpopular, but all were willing to follow God rather than man."[10]

The second program was implemented in 1912 when the WMC started its first Bethlehem Center, a social settlement among African Americans adjacent to the Paine College campus in Augusta, with Mary DeBardeleben as director. Louise Young, the dean of students at Paine who later taught sociology at Scarritt College for many years, supervised student volunteers at the Bethlehem Center. The following year the WMC backed Sallie Hill Sawyer, a member of Capers Chapel Colored Methodist Episcopal Church in Nashville, as she started another Bethlehem Center close to Fisk University. Estelle Haskin, director of field education at the nearby Methodist Training School, developed a training program at the Bethlehem Center for students from both institutions. Both in Augusta and in Nashville, the proximity of the Bethlehem Center to the campus and the interchange of campus and community resources created a pocket of human resources for leadership in interracial issues.

A Committee on Social Service established by the WMC in 1913 enhanced its commitment to race relations. The term "social service," used by the emerging academic discipline of sociology and applied to social work in the nation's burgeoning cities, included charitable work for ethnic minorities.[11] The Council urged churchwomen's groups to study and remedy practical conditions for Negroes, including public schools, recreation facilities, jails and courts, housing and sanitation. The WMC took a courageous and pioneering stand by adopting a resolution that condemned lynching. Even so, new programs and new attitudes about race generally failed to materialize among white women. With the exception of a few deaconesses, home missionaries, and members of the boards of Bethlehem Centers who worked or met interracially, the new commitments of the WMC failed to help white women cross racial lines. For attitudes to change, grassroots Methodist women needed to listen and learn.

Changes in Racial Ideology

A few key writers began to change racial ideology among Methodists. Bishop Atticus G. Haygood's 1887 volume, *Our Brother in Black*, took an approach toward "racial uplift" that paralleled that of Booker T. Washington. He claimed that African Americans must grow from within to be ready for citizenship. Haygood offered a four-point plan for whites:

(1) Make way for change. Don't let prejudice get in the way. Provide both moral and intellectual education.
(2) Encourage and motivate African Americans.
(3) Offer self-help opportunities so that African Americans can become self-supporting.
(4) Due to massive poverty, give help for at least a generation. Provide separate public school systems.[12]

Haygood believed that God called southerners to a new mission:

working out God's plan for African Americans and whites to live together in freedom.

A network of religious leaders who exchanged lectures, literature, and ideas brought social gospel teachings about race and sociological methods that had started in the North.[13] Belle Harris Bennett, Tochie MacDonell, and Mary Helm, key leaders of Woman's Home Missionary Society (WHMS), valued occasional opportunities several times a year when they gathered in the MacDonell home to read and share ideas about the theological and practical implications of the social gospel.[14] The MacDonell children, overhearing the women's sessions that brainstormed plans for Methodist women, teasingly named them the "triumvirate." The three women challenged each other to grow and develop in their understandings of race and their directions for leadership on this issue. The experience broadened their views and shaped the direction of women's missionary literature on race.

Mary Helm, editor of the Methodist women's home missions publication *Our Homes*, espoused concepts of development and change in her mission study book, *The Upward Path: The Evolution of a Race*. Although she claimed that providence placed African Americans where they could be aided by white Christians, she introduced social gospel beliefs:

(1) The divine presence in all persons places a value on human life and assures that people and societies can grow and change for the better.
(2) Sin has collective and communal, as well as individual and private, dimensions.
(3) Christian love is expressed in justice, and consequently opposes ignorance, poverty, helplessness, oppression and injustice.
(4) Unmended injustice reaps an evil harvest.

Helm wrote, "Justice perverted becomes retributive, and no man or country can fail to receive sooner or later the evil result of injustice."[15] Helm called for a higher moral perspective in race relations. She paved the way for an even stronger appeal from Lily Hammond.

Lily Hammond's Appeal to White Women

In 1914, Lily Hammond, a Methodist woman from Georgia, wrote *In Black and White*, a comprehensive appeal to white women to change their racial attitudes. Her more radical departure from traditional white views led white southerners to criticize her. Hammond's husband,

44

John Dennis Hammond, was forced to leave the presidency of Paine College because of her boldness. Hammond, a daughter of slave-owners, had been an active leader among southern Methodist women (MECS) from the early years of the home mission movement.[16] She called for interracial communication. This significant development helped open the door to interacial experiences in the 1920s.

Hammond urged Methodist women to move beyond charity and explore interracial friendships. "It is impossible to serve the best interests of either race without this personal communication between the two."[17]

Hammond directly challenged prejudice. Yet in the same book she claimed that supremacy of social position is a strength to be used for service.[18] She observed that whites often based their claim of superiority on their observation that African Americans did not advance much in fifty years after they won freedom from slavery, then added, "If there were no encouraging signs after our management of him [African Americans] for fifty years, the difficulty might lie with the management."[19] In other words, oppression limited development of human potential.

Citing discrimination, intolerable injustices, and double standards practiced under segregation, Hammond pointed to places where whites needed to make adjustments in race relations. First among these, the horror, brutality, fear, and terror of lynchings must go, she said. Not only were people mutilated and killed by mobs, but because lynchings could erupt anywhere, anytime, without rational foundation, they maintained an oppressive fear among African Americans. "This sense of evil possibly impending, with the deep distrust engendered by it, colours all the Negro's relations with us."[20]

Hammond excoriated the peonage system, tenant farming, and sharecropping for perpetuating debt. She berated the double standard in train fares. African Americans, who paid the same price for abominable accommodations as whites paid for greater comfort, subsidized white passengers' travel! Observing that segregation seemed to be a response to "a natural desire of races to affiliate with their own," she opined that the central issue for African Americans was not an urge to integrate but concern for a fair share of safety, cleanliness, and comfort.[21]

"Everybody on earth is human first and racial afterwards," Hammond declared. Her call for justice was based on divinely granted human equality. "We must see in the Negro first of all, deeper than all, higher than all, a man, made in the image of God as truly as ourselves."[22] Without justice, people are not safe. She declared:

45

The only basis of living between man and man, whether low or high, which is safe for either is justice. And where there is less than justice, the danger is ever greater for the oppressor than the oppressed. If white civilization is to endure in the South or anywhere else, it must strike deep roots into the soil of our common humanity, and reach down to that bed-rock of justice which makes the framework of the world.[23]

Hammond believed that the unifying catalyzer that had the power to overcome diversity and separation was the power of God's love and care for all represented in the death of Jesus for the entire human race. All races, she believed, come together for service of the human race which reaches toward the light of God.

Hammond advocated four points: First, that race relations between whites and African Americans should be based on the theological affirmation that all persons are made in the image of God. She emphasized qualities common to all humans, rather than those that were diverse. Second, she believed that growth and development are basic characteristics of human life, both for the individual and the social community. This meant that while conditions such as poverty or ignorance were statistically correlated with race, they were not qualities actually in persons of a particular race, but were related to their circumstances. Hammond used the concept of "environmentalism," a notion that people's abilities and capacities are shaped by their cultural and social environment, to argue against the more popular understanding of racial inferiority determined by biological factors commonly believed to be linked to race. Third, she established an ethic of justice as the norm for human relationships. She warned white oppressors of the lack of safety in their reliance on authority and claimed that the use of oppression jeopardized the durability of white civilization. Fourth, she embraced a doctrine of Christian reconciliation which evoked sympathy and called people to work for the good of the whole human race.

Hammond did not challenge segregation or white supremacy. Neither did she call for integration. Had she done so, she would have lost her white audience. For her time, she was pressing for dramatically liberal views. She attempted to separate morality based on justice and law, such as universal rights granted to every person, from morality based on social distinctions, a given that deserved to be maintained.[24] She felt that privileged women had responsibilities for the moral condition of their communities.

Mary Helm and Lily Hammond helped bring social gospel beliefs in the goodness and improvability of humanity together for Southern

46

Methodist women with the issues on their minds: gender, class, and race privilege; social justice; and a fledgling sense of responsibility for the social order. Hammond paid tribute to the women of the MECS for being the only white churchwomen's group in the South organized to work on behalf of African Americans.[25] Indeed, Methodist women were helping to form a new movement.

In several ways Hammond encouraged whites to take responsibility for the social injustices being perpetuated against African Americans. Beginning with the presumption that all people were interrelated, prejudice was not appropriate. Neither were labels, for they were too simplistic and confining.[26] Hammond acknowledged her role in a slave-owning family. The fact that her parents opposed slavery did not change the reality of their participation in that system. In the same way, she and other whites participated in the system of segregation, even if they personally opposed it. She blamed whites for their lack of knowledge about the black race because of their choice to withdraw into a world of their own.[27] She challenged white-owned corporations to be more fair and responsible. She felt that whites needed to change their attitudes, acknowledge their complicity, and grow in their ability to relate to other races. The bottom line for her was that the Christian faith offered a model of love as the vital connecting force between people. She appealed to Christians to make interracial interpersonal connections.

Hammond's own conversion to the cause of race relations, though unique, was based on the discovery of jarring incongruities. As a child, riding one day in a cart driven by her cousin, she noticed a poverty-stricken mother and child in the doorway of a dilapidated one-room log cabin. Lily Hammond told her own story:

> "Why must they live like that?" I demanded. "Why do I have everything, and they nothing?"

> My elderly cousin laughed a little, and then, realizing my excitement, spoke soberly. "Don't take other people's troubles too seriously, my dear."

> [After pondering, Lily asked:] "Why didn't God make them another way . . . ? It would have been just as easy."[28]

Hammond's questions continued when, at age fifteen, she investigated tenement houses in a northern city, over protests by her father. Slum conditions reminded Hammond of southern poverty, and both situations appeared to Hammond to be an impediment to full human development that God intended for all persons.[29] Issues of class and race merged for Hammond. Were justice issues for the racially oppressed and the underprivileged not the same? But Hammond could not set aside her own class status and white privilege:

> The privileged South has at last opened its doors of counsel and invited the underprivileged to enter in and talk over, men with men, the needs and duties which confront them both in making the land a home of justice and opportunity for all.[30]

Who would rise to the great challenge of the times? The people uniting would be women; women standing together for all the women of the world.[31] Jacquelyn Dowd Hall has observed that Hammond's analysis of race relations was "of particular importance in shaping the consciousness" of the next generation of white churchwomen engaged in interracial work. Hammond's appeal for face-to-face interracial contact and cooperation had a significant influence.

Women's understanding of race was grounded in an understanding of individual rights based on membership in a group. In this case, Methodist women were expanding the concept of group from race to humanity. This contrasted with nineteenth-century arguments based on individualism, that an individual deserved freedom from slavery or that a woman deserved rights equal to those of a man. Slavery and female gender excluded people from the benefits of individual rights. Subordination of women was, therefore, similar to slavery.

If differences of gender did not provide sufficient reason for subordination, then it followed that neither did differences of race. Physical attributes were "not reason enough to exclude a group of persons from rights that in principle belonged to all persons."[32] Men had used the argument of physical difference to claim that they deserved rights from which women were restricted.

Racial prejudice established biological categories that divided humans into groups, but liberalism, grounded on doctrines of dignity and liberty of the individual, attempted to establish social conditions where people could "develop their capabilities to the fullest."[33] Recognition of these truths provided incentive for women to join hands across racial lines to work on common concerns, even though their analyses of problems varied.

Methodist women based the new movement for interracial cooperation on "cooperation between the better classes of both races for the uplift of the Negro poor."[34] Class cooperation across racial lines, but within the framework of segregation, shaped interracial work in the 1920s.

Methodist women continued to participate in an unjust economic class system. Instead of a two-part segregation with whites on top and

African Americans on the bottom, Methodist women cooperated with vertical segregation. They supported the idea that people of different races might have equal class-differentiated standing.[35] They gave little consideration to the more demanding platform of civic equality described by W. E. B. DuBois. Some key African American women hoped that this would change.

African American Women Seek Allies

A select network of women from an emerging black middle class introduced some liberal white middle-class churchwomen to the ideas of W. E. B. DuBois and Booker T. Washington. In the first and second decades of the twentieth century a network of educated, civic-minded upper middle-class African American women applied their energy and abilities to the project of "racial uplift." Some were educators. Others were community organizers, administrators, social workers, churchwomen, or community volunteers. Many met through the Young Women's Christian Association (YWCA), although by the 1920s the most common tie was membership in the National Association of Colored Women (NACW). Women of exceptional talent and energy gave leadership.

Several prominent black women invited and guided white Methodist women. One of these women was Lugenia Burns Hope, who started the Neighborhood Union, a settlement house and community organizing project in Atlanta, in 1906. The wife of John Hope (mentioned earlier for his outspoken opposition to Booker T. Washington), who served as president of Morehouse College and later of Atlanta University, Lugenia was highly respected and an excellent organizer. In her Atlanta neighborhood, garbage was burned on the unpaved streets due to lack of garbage service, and the city refused to provide street lights or access to the municipal water supply. Motivated by these urban slum conditions, she created a community organization that was financed, controlled, and operated by African American women. Hoping to stabilize the neighborhood, women of the Neighborhood Union engaged in activities to reduce crime and help the poor. These efforts attracted criticism and placed them in conflict with local white leaders— the school board, Sanitation Department, and merchants.[36]

Mary McLeod Bethune, another outstanding member of the NACW, established and led the National Council of Negro Women and the Southeastern Federation of Colored Women's Clubs. Founder and president of Bethune-Cookman College in Daytona Beach, Florida, she established ties with the MECS to help fund the college. Her MECS membership opened opportunities for national leadership through MECS organizations in the 1940s. Of all the women involved in the civil rights work of this period, as director of the Division of Negro Affairs of the National Youth Administration from 1936 to 1943 she came to hold the highest government position.

Leaders of Bethune's caliber believed that by working with upper middle-class white women they could secure additional support for their agenda for African Americans in communities across the South. Other women in this network included Lucy Craft Laney; Janie Porter Barrett; Charlotte Hawkins Brown; Eva Bowles, field secretary for the YWCA; Margaret Murray Washington; Elizabeth Ross Haynes; Katharine Du Pre Lumpkin, student secretary for the Southern Division of the National Student Council and later, author of *The Making of a Southerner*; Juliette Derricotte, YWCA National Student Council leader in interracial work and later Dean of Women at Fisk University; Grace Towns Hamilton, a co-founder of the Neighborhood Union and, later, the first African American woman elected to the Georgia legislature; Mrs. M. L. Crosthwaite; Marion Raven Wilkinson; Nettie Langston Napier, a president of NACW; and Mrs. H. A. Hunt, president of the Georgia Federation of Colored Women's Clubs.[37]

Before asking the WMC for support, African American women approached the YWCA because some of them were active leaders in it. Organized in 1870 in the South, the YWCA had developed programs and activities for the spiritual and physical well-being of young women in many southern communities. The roots, constituency, and programs of the YWCA were explicitly Christian, and because of its community-based contacts with the poor, immigrants, African Americans, college students, and church leaders, the YWCA also was influenced by the social gospel. The YWCA was a logical choice to begin women's interracial work. But segregation and racism impeded and frustrated the African American women as they tried to work through organizational channels.[38]

Jacquelyn Dowd Hall, in her book *Revolt Against Chivalry: Jessie Daniel Ames and the Woman's Campaign Against Lynching*, described how the African American women's caucus decided to expand their approach for allies. "By cutting across the boundaries of existing organizations, they hoped to bring the strongest black women leaders together with the most progressive whites in an organization specifically devoted to improving race relations."[39] The women's caucus concluded that "the time was ripe [to] go beyond the YWCA and any other organization and reach a few outstanding white and Negro women, Christian and with well-balanced judgment and not afraid."[40]

This strategy proved to be effective, possibly because, compared with YWCA leaders, Methodist women (MECS) had stronger southern roots, closer affinity with social gospel teachings, and a tradition of social concern. Among white women allies, the YWCA gave significant leadership to the interracial movement, second only to the strength provided by Methodist women. The time ripened for interracial cooperation.

A Movement for Interracial Cooperation Begins

Monumental events gave birth to a new movement for interracial cooperation in the 1920s.[41] World War I sensitized African Americans to the discrepancies between the realities of their lives and the ideologies of democracy and freedom that the U.S. defended. Under segregation black veterans were denied that for which they had fought. In 1919, bloody race riots erupted in Charleston; Longview and Gregg counties in Texas; Washington, D.C.; Chicago; and Elaine, Arkansas. Seventy-six African Americans were lynched. Under stressful domestic conditions, African American leaders pushed open doors of communication with white leaders.

In 1919, John and Lugenia Hope prodded and guided Will Alexander, a white southerner, to help them begin to organize a massive attack on racial problems in the South. Alexander, who had just wrapped up a position coordinating YMCA war relief work, brought YMCA funds and a network of white civic leaders to the task, founding the Commission on Interracial Cooperation (CIC), a group of approximately twenty select leaders.[42] The CIC, as their use of the term "interracial" indicated, committed themselves to improve relations between races. They were not at this point seeking equal rights, balance of power, an end to segregation, or racial integration. After a year of meetings, the white leaders decided it would be appropriate to include African American leaders! Another year passed before they decided to admit women to their membership. Many of the men in the CIC were husbands, relatives, and friends well known to the women's caucus of the CIC. The CIC's approach remained paternalistic and failed to give all of its members equal recognition, voice, and power.[43]

Black women seeking allies in race relations work had kept an eye on the WMC of the MECS, its Bethlehem Centers, and its stand against lynching. When slow-grinding wheels of progress in the YWCA made going difficult, Lugenia Hope approached Will Alexander and suggested that he use his Methodist connections to approach the leaders of the WMC and put them in contact with the women's caucus.[44]

In 1920, in response to appeals from Dr. Will Alexander and Belle Harris Bennett, then president of the WMC,[45] the WMC tabled its customary plans for Negro work and appointed a Committee on Race Relations to spend a year investigating living conditions and needs of southern blacks.

Estelle Haskin and Carrie Parks Johnson, two executive committee members of the WMC, began their research by attending the national meeting of the NACW. Expecting to be honored guests, they were taken aback when they were seated near the rear of the auditorium at Tuskegee Institute. As they observed the conference, they were astounded to discover hundreds of able, talented, professional African American women who ran a quality organization. Their previous exposure to domestic servants and their own southern upper middle-class white stereotypes of the abilities of African Americans meant that they were unprepared for what they witnessed. They were shocked to discover a mature parallel culture in their midst.

Ten members of the NACW met in July 1920 at Tuskegee Institute in the home of Margaret Washington, widow of Booker T. Washington, with Estelle Haskin and Carrie Parks Johnson. The club women, all educated and representing the new African American middle class, included noted educators who had founded and operated their own secondary schools, a college, and an institution for juvenile delinquents. Their names read like a *Who's Who* in African American history: Janie Porter Barrett, Mary McLeod Bethune, Charlotte Hawkins Brown, Lugenia Hope, Lucy Laney, Mary Jackson McCrorey, Jennie Moton, Margaret Washington, Marion R. Wilkinson, and Mrs. M. L. Crosthwaite.[46] The white women very likely were unaware that they were sitting with and being led by some of the South's most gifted civic leaders whose talents matched or exceeded their own. The meeting opened with prayer because faith united where race divided.

Carrie Parks Johnson and Estelle Haskin did not know how to overcome the well-founded suspicion that their primary concern was to obtain more reliable domestic servants. Gradually the African American women revealed some of their concerns which, after the meeting, were incorporated into a position paper that summarized the needs they had begun to articulate. The paper dealt with domestic service, child welfare, travel, education, lynching, suffrage, and the bias of the white press. One Methodist woman wrote, "The Colored Women's

Statement had a broad appeal because of its practical suggestions, its very humanness, and its simplicity. . . ."[47]

Following the meeting, Haskin and Johnson faced a difficult task. They wanted to persuade white southern Christian women to broaden their view of race relations, a very delicate subject on which feelings ran high and on which women were not agreed. They convened an interracial conference in Memphis in October 1920. Nearly one hundred white women from many denominations assembled, including Methodist secretaries of social service, who gathered expecting to discuss race relations. They had no social preparation for the shocking arrival of four black women in their midst—Margaret Washington, Elizabeth Haynes,[48] Jennie Moton, and Charlotte Hawkins Brown—who described what it was like to be African American, female, and concerned about their race.[49] The two-day conference, flying in the face of deeply held interracial taboos, was emotional, informative, and mind changing.

In its December 1920 annual report, the Commission on the Church and Race Relations of the Federal Council of Churches of Christ in America predicted that the Memphis Woman's Interracial Conference "in its deliverance will do more to bring the womanhood of the South into active service in behalf of the race than any other yet held." The leaders of the WMC and members of the NACW, in cooperation with the newly formed CIC, were hailed as "the strongest force yet organized in the nation in behalf of the colored race."[50]

A Continuation Committee was formed in Memphis to carry on communication between white and African American women and became the Woman's General Committee of the Commission on Interracial Concern. Within a year it garnered leadership from civic and religious women's organizations, African American and white, representing a constituency of more than a million southern women.[51] From the outset, the white and African American members of the CIC Woman's Committee held different views. Some, daughters of interracial unions, opposed sexual abuse of women and hoped to counter the inaccurate sexual mythologies used to undergird racism. White CIC women, however, disapproved of interracial sex. Unprepared to challenge the racial caste system, they desired to bring together "the best type of white women and the best type of colored women."[52]

The WMC moved from voluntary to professional leadership for its interracial work when it employed Carrie Johnson as chairperson of the Commission on Race Relations (1921–26). The CIC also hired Johnson as a director of Woman's Work and to be responsible for the Woman's General Committee. Johnson set out to inform white southern churchwomen about conditions in the African American community across the South and to organize groups of women, white or African American, at every level so that they could work together to improve race relations. Groups formed in rapid succession.

Attitudes would need to change, Johnson knew, for this ambitious program to succeed. Drawing from the perspective of Lily Hammond, Johnson thought that this could best happen through increasing personal contact of white women with African American women, and by introducing white women to noted African Americans whose lives and achievements demonstrated the human drama, ambitions, desires, and abilities of persons of color.

From the start, Johnson secured Methodist support for her CIC work and used CIC to provide resources for the Methodist work. She set up interracial conferences in each southern state with a sizeable African American population and invited local and district social service leaders. As a result of this intertwined coordination of Methodist women's and CIC interracial work, Methodist women comprised over half of all the women involved in interracial dialogues and studies of race relations during the first decade of the interracial movement.[53] Among the Methodist Woman's Missionary Societies, state and local interracial committees were formed. The organizational network emphasized local action.

Interracial projects usually involved minimal interracial communication and often supported segregation. One white Methodist women's auxiliary in South Georgia reported a wide variety of interracial activities conducted in one year. The women secured community concessions: a public rest room,[54] a clinic, and a public health nurse. The community built a playground for black children. The same South Georgia women's group ostensibly assisted African American missionary societies, participated in a rally with African American citizens to improve race relations, planned a new school building, provided day care, and worked on sanitation problems. All of these services to the African American community were designed to keep the races separate while improving conditions.[55] Some goals, such as securing an African American public health nurse, might have been accomplished by having white women persuade white public office holders to designate tax money for such an expenditure, thus requiring minimal interracial contact. Other goals included interracial mingling in a public setting, such as white women attending an African American PTA meeting. The variety of projects undertaken and their adaptation to the local situation indicate that African American women were suggesting to white women avenues for interracial activities.

Interracial work, though not initially "hands on," grew at an astounding rate. Johnson reported the formation of a total of 110 auxiliary interracial committees in 1922, 445 in 1923, and 571 in 1924. Even where there were no formal committees, many Methodist missionary societies began interracial work. Maud Henderson, a Methodist who succeeded Johnson as director of Woman's Work for CIC, reported in 1926 that over eight hundred interracial committees were working in the South "to form day nurseries, to establish parks and playgrounds, to secure better housing, better sanitation, and better educational privileges."[56]

In 1928, Johnson's successor in the WMC brought demanding new challenges. Bertha Newell found that the greatest obstacle to interracial work was not "antagonism to the idea of working with Negroes," although there was plenty of it, but widespread indifference.[57] Newell suspected that among white Methodist women's groups more interracial work was being reported than was actually occurring. She differentiated between work done by white groups for African American women and children and interracial activities involving African Americans and whites working together. In place of promoting charitable but condescending actions on the part of white women toward black women, Newell urged white women to work with African American people, helping them organize and lead their own community groups. Black communities founded groups that worked for better schools, sponsored PTAs, started branches of the YMCA and YWCA, obtained and equipped playgrounds and libraries, and started school clinics and baby clinics.[58] Bertha Newell pressed Methodist Woman's Missionary Societies to engage in more local interaction between white women and African American women. These cooperative interracial tasks required more sustained effort than charitable activities and began to engage women in consultation and systematic communication across racial lines.

In spite of the fact that the leaders of the WMC failed to call for an end to segregation or for changes in segregation laws, they were changing grassroots race relations in the South, especially in cities and towns. These white women, who expressly opposed "social equality of the races" and interracial marriage, were participating in and leading a portion of the interracial movement.

White women's participation in the interracial movement gained immediate success and grew rapidly. It was led by upper middle-class southern women and attracted others who enjoyed and benefitted from that affinity and who desired to cope with the uneasiness they felt about race relations. Neither the leaders nor the grassroots membership of the Methodist women's missionary societies were prepared to end segregation, but the leaders knew they were undermining it and accepted this task as their social responsibility.

Methodist women began a new spiritual journey. Social transformation is, at its heart, spiritual. Speaking through the voices of social gospel prophets, and crying with the pain of the brutalities that segregation and prejudices inflicted on African Americans, God called white Methodist women to a higher vision. The white leaders believed that they were children of God, and that African Americans were also God's children. In spite of prejudice, they responded to the invitations and concerns of black women. They risked new behaviors that began to undermine their understandings of race. They were about to discover that an inequitable social system perpetuates lawlessness and genocide.

We believe that we have a great opportunity to help to solve the race problem in America in a Christian way through strengthening the church ties between white and colored Methodists. We believe that such a Methodist connectionalism transcending race and nation and economic class will be better able to create in us the mind which was in Christ Jesus who taught us of one God who is the Father of all and in whom we are all brothers one of another.

—*Twenty-seventh Annual Report*
of the Woman's Missionary Council, 1937, 143

CHAPTER 3

The Early 1930s:
Concern for Fairness

Social, economic, and political changes in the 1930s gave birth to new ideological understandings, social analyses, and organizational networks. African American leaders increased pressure to end racial inequities and segregation. With black migration out of the South, black/white racial issues became less regional and more national. Links between racial and economic justice became more clear. Economic, race and labor isues challenged an established social system that had long benefitted southern upper-class whites. Again the federal government became involved in the South, this time developing farm support policies. Radical white allies of a growing African American civil rights movement began to call for an end to segregation. Southern liberals and moderates engaged in discussion about how to accomplish desegregation.

With the formation of the Association of Southern Women for the Prevention of Lynching (ASWPL) led by Jessie Daniel Ames, Methodist women now headed three key women's organizations with overlapping Methodist membership. Together they could make great strides in interracial work, turning it gradually into interracial experiences that changed women's understanding of race and of the links between racism and sexism.

Mounting Pressures and Political Changes

African American leaders in the 1930s applied pressure for change in areas of economic, political, and legal rights. With a sensitive political consciousness and a desire to vote, they opposed white primaries, poll taxes, and literacy requirements for registration. The system of farm tenancy, now proven to be no exit from poverty, continued to collapse under cotton crop failures, urban and northern migration, unscrupulous landowners, and extra-legal pressures from segregationists. Masses of skilled and unskilled laborers were shut out of union membership because of race. Unions themselves often had their hands tied by effective coalitions of management, laws favoring corporations, and law enforcement officials. Forty-three trades unionized by the American Federation of Labor (AFL) excluded African Americans entirely, and twenty-seven others welcomed only token members, according to a 1902 study conducted by W. E. B. DuBois.[1] Little had changed in thirty years.

African American protest centered in the National Association for the Advancement of Colored People (NAACP) which had already begun its legal struggle against disfranchisement and Jim Crow laws. In 1915, the Supreme Court found grandfather clause limitations on the right to vote to be unconstitutional, and began its attack on white primaries in the 1920s. Then, in 1935, NAACP began its concerted legal attack on discrimination and segregation in education, a campaign designed and coordinated by NAACP legal counsel Charles Hamilton Houston.

When Robert R. Moton, president of Tuskegee Institute, spoke out against racial injustice in his book *What the Negro Thinks* (1929), the days of accommodation and gradualism appeared to be numbered as the center of this ideology joined with the stronger protests of the NAACP. Drawing from socialist and Marxist interpretations that political power was rooted in economic power, A. Philip Randolph called for the emergence of a radical new movement that would unite white and African American workers against the capitalist class. This, he perceived, was the path toward social justice.[2] Randolph appealed for workers to join unions. Frustrated by hostile racial attitudes in the AFL, Randolph organized the Brotherhood of Sleeping Car Porters in 1925.

On the national scene, labor organizers, distraught by the policies of the AFL, formed the Congress of Industrial Organizations (CIO) in 1935. From the start, the new labor giant opposed "any and all forms of discrimination between one worker and another based upon considerations of race, creed, color, or nationality" and condemned discrimination in hiring and working conditions.[3] The CIO's forthright approach placed them on public record for a variety of issues surrounding racism and prejudice. Support for anti-poll tax laws, anti-lynching laws, and a federal Fair Employment Practices Commission were balanced by opposition to discriminatory southern practices and politicians and denial of the right to vote.

Big changes were under way economically, politically, and demographically. Community-based social institutions provided some hope for African Americans who flocked north and to cities in search for a livelihood. August Meier and Elliott M. Rudwick have observed that African American migrants brought to their new urban surroundings traditional cultural anchors—the church and the matrifocal family.[4] Home and church nurtured hopes, and kept alive aspirations and community structures essential to survival and protest. These social institutions proved to be elemental to the rise of grassroots protests in the 1950s and 1960s.

A few votes could sway an election in the South's predominantly one-party white primary system. With voter registration limited by poll taxes, educational and property requirements, and racial discrimination, few people voted. Votes were purchased, lost, and manufactured in fraudulent schemes. Effective control of southern politics remained in the hands of landowners, bankers, and corporations.[5] Limited voting made politics more vulnerable to control by people of wealth, the Ku Klux Klan (KKK), religious groups, or fringe groups.

Economic struggle, political consciousness, and pressure for the rights of groups emerged in new ways in the 1930s. Liberal southern journalists expressed dissatisfaction with southern white solidarity which clearly benefitted demagogues and intolerant radical right ideology.[6] A 1930 debate between twelve leading southern journalists and the Nashville Agrarians, who represented a conservative longing to return the South to an agriculture-based economy, clarified in the public eye that rural poverty was systemic and many southern problems had an economic base.

CIC Executive Director Will Alexander's timely investigation of a 1930 lynching in Sherman, Texas, opened his eyes to the relationship of the national economic catastrophe to racial problems. Convinced that lynching was not case-by-case violence, but that its roots related to poverty, "limited education and economic insecurity," as well as racism, Alexander began to explore broad-based solutions. As the decade passed, the CIC, federal leaders, liberal journalists, African American leaders, white allies, moderates, liberals, and radicals came to a consensus that the South's regional problems needed a region-wide solution and national economic assistance.

The New Deal of Franklin Delano Roosevelt's 1932 presidential victory brought new approaches to continuing problems. The Farm Security Administration channeled federal funds for crop reductions to address the plight of sharecroppers and tenant farmers. Unscrupulous landowners retired their own debts rather than pass the money along to tenant farmers whose livelihood depended on fewer acres planted.[7] The CIC organized a Southern Policy Committee in 1935 to promote region-wide solutions to the South's economic problems. With Will Alexander in the lead, the Southern Policy Committee documented the ineffectiveness of New Deal agricultural policies and prepared the Bankhead-Jones Farm Tenancy Bill of 1935 to help people buy land. Alexander took a position as deputy administrator of the Farm Resettlement Administration. A year later Alexander was appointed to head the Resettlement Administration, then renamed Farm Security Administration, to underscore new attempts to keep farmers on their land. Southerners, ever alert to the strings attached to federal policies or aid, accepted farm programs while vigorously opposing proposals for federal anti-lynching bills. In 1942 Jessie Daniel Ames commented on the integral relation between federal farm relief programs and lynching.

> And here it is that the Federal Government enters the campaign against lynching, not with a flashing sword of vengeance but with promise of a better day for the rural farm laborers of the South. Work relief from the Federal and State Governments put these people to work and reduced idleness and boredom and, equally as important, gave them a little cash money to spend with white merchants. . . . The Farm Security Administration offered them a chance to own something of their own for the price of the labor they had been doing for practically nothing in the past. . . . The Federal Government, in its entire agricultural program of work, home ownership, proper diet, and health clinics, entered the field against lynching.[8]

The CIC's Southern Policy Committee brought together southern liberals representing regional organizations, education, and business for a major conference in Birmingham to provide guidance for regional development. Seeing an opportunity to gather political support in the South, Franklin Roosevelt lent his support to liberal southern leaders who planned the 1938 Southern Conference on Human Welfare (SCHW). Aimed at gathering ideas and momentum for regional solutions to southern problems, the liberal leadership of the conference alienated and excluded radical leaders from participation while also drawing the ire of hardline segregationists. Twelve hundred delegates to the 1938 SCHW, from sharecroppers to capitalists, raised suspicions on many sides as they debated whether to condemn segregation in order to work for economic democracy.[9] By integrating seating, delegates defied city code for two days until city police arrived. Forced to segregate, they re-seated separately left to right according to race instead of the usual front to back. Eleanor Roosevelt astutely and defiantly placed her chair in the aisle between the two groups, fueling the anger of segregationists.

Eleanor Roosevelt gave a stirring address in which she called for greater emphasis on public education. The adopted resolutions closely match the 1930s agenda of Methodist women. SCHW called for more playground facilities for African Americans, abolition of the poll tax, an end to race discrimination, and they agreed to set future meetings only in cities where the conference would not be segregated.[10]

The SCHW attracted criticism from both Right and Left. The KKK and segregationists saw it as a White House ploy to help re-elect FDR. Senator Martin Dies, an anti-communist sleuth, charged that secretly the conference had been planned and dominated by Communists. The planners, however, deliberately did not invite Lillian Smith, an influential writer whose pen helped change attitudes about race. She objected to the conference's failure to firmly oppose segregation.

Follow-up activities of the SCHW diminished over the next four years. Its one surviving arm, the Southern Conference Education Fund, tended by radicals Anne and Carl Braden, influenced the later civil rights movement but did not secure the cooperation of Methodist women. Methodist women struggled with which ideological and political choices to make among confusing options. They listened to many voices, including those of radical and liberal white allies.

Radical and Liberal White Allies and Southern Regional Solutions

In 1930 an odd assortment of white radicals, working at interracial tasks, cultivated white radical analyses of the race and class issues troubling the South. These white radicals were mostly Methodists and intellectual heirs of the radical social gospel and they developed an economic and racial social critique that informed leaders of Methodist women.

In the 1930s over half of African American labor union members belonged to the United Mine Workers. In 1932 labor unrest at Fentress Coal and Coke Company in Wilder, Tennessee, involved African Americans who struck for better working conditions and higher pay. The United Mine Workers strike radicalized Howard and Alice Kester, Don and Constance West, and others who, already seminary-trained in the teachings of the social gospel, organized a variety of economic and political responses to southern problems. Howard Kester and Don West, students of Alva Taylor at Vanderbilt University School of Theology, linked with students of Harry F. Ward and Reinhold Niebuhr at Union Theological Seminary in a support network of young white radicals devoted to changing the South.

Other white radicals belonged to the same network. Myles Horton, aided by James Dombrowski, founded and ran Highlander Folk School. Highlander educated common people in an interracial setting, cultivating the inner life and outer skills needed to engage in social change. Claude Williams became the director of Commonwealth College in Mena, Arkansas, an interracial educational center where the curriculum included labor organizing. Writers Lillian Smith and Paula Snelling educated white girls in the ways of independent critical thinking at a camp on Old Screamer Mountain in Georgia and edited the radical journal *South Today*.

Scholars have used different systems of social analysis to define and evaluate southern liberal and radical forces in the 1930s. Anthony Dunbar (*Against the Grain*, 1981) distinguished radicals from liberals in that radicals tried to achieve economic power through organizing unions and forming cooperatives. In developing a third category for moderates, John Kneebone (*Southern Liberal Journalists*, 1985), found racial issues at the heart of the matter and concluded that moderates worked for greater equality within the system of segregation while liberals rejected segregation. Anthony Lake Newberry ("Without Urgency or Ardor," Ph.D. dissertation, 1982) and Jacquelyn Dowd Hall both noted that southern liberals embraced "environmentalism," the idea that human surroundings can limit or expand the opportunities for people to fulfill their potential. Newberry found two varieties of mainstream liberals in the 1940s and 1950s: gradualists who supported advancement within segregation, and liberals who opposed segregation in publications, speeches, or with political or legal action.

Because attitudes have changed from one decade to another, this book uses behavior, repercussions, and the relation of these to sources of power as a guide to help define liberals and radicals, rather than establishing a particular stance on an issue as definitive.

 Liberals are people who set themselves apart from the predominant mores of their culture by their support for the human and civil rights of groups of persons who are being treated with prejudice. Liberals tend to push those in power to make changes faster than otherwise would occur, but not so fast as to lose the support of officials. Radicals' support for the rights of groups of people leads them to take actions that threaten the power base of an apathetic or biased political

64

or economic system which permits the perpetuation of human rights violations. Radicals want justice now.

When otherwise liberal acts, such as walking in a protest march, are countered with illegal reprisals, threats, violence, or death, the acts have become radical. Often radical actions create economic threat to an established political or corporate power base. Union organizing and cooperative farming have been radical actions. Occasionally ideas themselves raise the spectre of change and are attacked for being radical primarily because they call for immediate change without delay or compromise. Lillian Smith, who disseminated her social analyses of the southern race, class, gender, and economic issues through publications, neither campaigned to overthrow capitalism nor participated in a sit-in; yet her house, office, and manuscripts were destroyed by arson. The terms "liberal" and "radical" are relative to their context. Movements by either of these descriptions were weak in contrast to the system of segregation in the South in the 1930s.[11] When women began to speak and act for themselves in opposition to lynching, they threatened a taproot of both sexism and racism that held segregation in place. Ordinary activities became radical.

The Association of Southern Women for the Prevention of Lynching, 1930

As never before, white churchwomen engaged in working for a regional solution to the problem of lynching during the 1930s. The anti-lynching movement, from its inception, was a double-edged movement directed to changing social attitudes regarding women and lynching. In 1929 Jessie Daniel Ames succeeded Maude Henderson as director of Women's Work for the Commission on Interracial Cooperation. A leader at her best when attention could be focused on a single issue, she used her position to convene women across ecumenical lines and founded the Association of Southern Women for the Prevention of Lynching (ASWPL) in 1930. She was assisted by Bertha Newell, head of the Bureau of Social Service of the Woman's Missionary Council. Ames' opportunity came after CIC had formed an all-male committee to oppose lynching, did not add women to it, and failed to respond to protests from Mary McLeod Bethune and Mrs. J. W. Downs of the Woman's Missionary Council (WMC). Ames observed to a friend, "The men were out making studies and so the women had to get busy and do what they could to stop lynchings!"[12]

65

Arthur Raper, research director of the CIC, author of *The Tragedy of Lynching* and co-researcher with Gunnar Myrdal on *An American Dilemma*, in an interview once described the power of women in the anti-lynching movement:

> Women had been sort of shut out of the church: they couldn't become preachers. They were shut out of the courts: they couldn't be judges. They were shut out of the sheriff's office. They wanted to do something. . . . So here, now, was this lynching thing, and . . . Jesse Daniel Ames just grabbed onto it . . . , "This we will do." . . . They were women that had ability. . . .
>
> [They would say:] We don't need anybody to protect our virtue. And if you get up in the Congress of the United States and say that you are lynching to preserve our virtue, we're going to call you down.[13]

Although African American women in CIC for a long time had claimed that lynchings could only be ended when white women organized to prevent them, they objected when Ames excluded them from membership in ASWPL.[14] Until this time, African American women had been leading the fight against lynching through an NAACP group formed in 1922 called the Anti-Lynching Crusaders. The Crusaders wanted to include white women in their program to support the Dyer Anti-Lynching bill. About nine hundred white women did join, but no mass movement came from the effort. Nevertheless, African American women had developed an analysis of racial violence and sexual exploitation of women that ASWPL slowly, but reluctantly, adopted.[15]

Moderate   Ames hoped to attract women who represented the "middle" of southern political thought, people not otherwise involved in race relations or civil rights work. Without tackling the ticklish subject of interracial leadership and interracial meetings, she could appeal to women's sensibilities and horror over gruesome lynchings and perhaps gain the support of white segregationists for this long-overdue reform.

White women who founded ASWPL believed that they could end lynchings. Many felt that their attitudes could influence those who lynched or approved of lynchings—husbands, sons, fathers, uncles, cousins, sons-in-law, and friends. Women knew sheriffs, judges, police officers, mill owners, merchants, and landlords. Always before a lynching, there was talk: conversation that women could influence. Angry white men would take the law into their own hands. Those with the most to lose economically had the most investment in "keeping niggers in their place," but often their dirty work was done by poor whites who were angry about their own struggles to make ends meet. Municipal and county law enforcement officials, joining with local abrogations of the law and human rights, conspired with silence, failed to perform their duties, or outright joined in mob brutalities.

The ASWPL mounted its arguments. The women of its constituency had benefitted economically from the lynchings. In order to end lynchings, they must be willing to surrender future privilege based on the evil of lynching and the fear it created.

Members of CIC's Woman's Department were drawn initially from the leaders of the WMC and its state organizations, from the National Association of Colored Women, and from church and civic organizations that had existing networks of women's groups with their own budgets and programs.

In 1930 the CIC Woman's Department, which had lost momentum under Maude Henderson's leadership, set out to reactivate women's work of the CIC.[16] The Women's Committee made a new commitment to equal racial representation in its membership. Equal racial representation was virtually unheard of in the South at this time. Jessie Daniel Ames and Bertha Newell, Ames' close confidante and best friend, set up an Advisory Committee of six women, three white and three black.

The Women's Committee of the CIC secured the leadership of equal numbers of white and black members, thirty-six in all, representing all major African American or white Protestant denominations and women's organizations in the South. These were churchwomen, educators, clubwomen, social workers, and YWCA secretaries.[17] The roster of African American leaders shows both expansion and continuity with the previous decade: Charlotte Hawkins Brown, Janie Porter Barrett, Jennie B. Moton, Mary McLeod Bethune, Juliette Derricotte, Lugenia Hope, Nannie Burroughs, Mattie E. Coleman, Mary Jackson McCrorey, Sallie Stewart, and Marion Wilkinson among others.[18]

In 1933 at a Church Woman's Conference sponsored by the Woman's Department of CIC, white and African American women once again were represented almost equally in a discussion of what churchwomen could do about race relations. Ten black women represented nine denominations and the YWCA. Seven white women represented four denominations: three white women came from MECS, two came from the Presbyterian Church in the United States, and one each came from the Southern Baptist Convention and the National Council of Jewish Women. Frank discussion of ways to increase local interracial religious fellowship, to enhance appreciation of the abilities of both racial groups, and to ensure legal justice led to hopes that many states would plan similar conferences of concerned churchwomen.[19]

Grassroots interracial work of the 1930s that laid foundations for the 1950s civil rights movement in the South depended substantially on Methodist women. CIC engaged primarily in research while depending on women for local action and support. CIC did not have men's committees related to YMCAs or the MECS which focused on interracial work.

Three cooperating organizations strengthened each other: the Woman's Missionary Societies (local units headed by the WMC), the ASWPL, and the Department of Women's Work of the CIC. The network, interracial and interfaith, drew its core from Methodism. This formula was so successful that it was repeated in the 1950s. The interracial leadership core at CIC guided ASWPL, provided strategy, focus, and interfaith strength. The Methodist woman's missionary societies endowed the effort with clarity about God's call, and the ASWPL provided enthusiastic women who were willing to respond. This philosophy and strategy invited women to be forward thinking.

White women who guided Methodist women in the interracial movement and the anti-lynching campaign held top positions in the WMC, the Woman's Department of the CIC, and the ASWPL.

Along with Jessie Daniel Ames, who headed both the Woman's Department of CIC and the ASWPL, white Methodist leaders who were also leaders in CIC and ASWPL included Bertha Newell, superintendent of the newly reorganized Bureau of Social Relations of the Woman's Missionary Council; Estelle Haskin, editorial secretary of the Board of Missions of the MECS; Louise Young, chair of the Committee on Interracial Co-operation of the WMC; and later Dorothy Tilly, who became secretary of the Committee on Rural Development of the WMC and eventually succeeded Ames as director of the Woman's Department of the CIC. In this manner, southern Methodist women became involved in the top echelons of leadership of a movement of white allies seeking southern regional solutions to the race problems of their day.

The overlap in leadership between ASWPL, the CIC Women's Committee, and the WMC led to many forms of mutual cooperation. The WMC requested that conference women's missionary societies endorse the ASWPL and designate their conference superintendents of Christian Social Relations and representatives of Christian Citizenship and Law Observance as members of the state associations of ASWPL. Louise Young and Bertha Newell organized state associations of ASWPL in North Carolina and Tennessee. Newell urged Methodist women "to give all assistance in their power to Mrs. Ames during her organization meetings in their respective states . . . ," which, Newell reported, they did.[20]

In time, the "southern regional solution" fell largely into the hands of women and a narrowly focused organization. As the decade passed,

Overlapping Leadership

the CIC became more of a research organization and less of a movement. Staff member George Mitchell gathered sociological data for the CIC. Will Alexander and Arthur Raper spent more and more time in Washington, D.C., coordinating the Farm Security Administration. Eventually Jessie Daniel Ames, whose thrust and attention on ASWPL had pre-empted other work of the Woman's Committee of the CIC, often was the only full-time staff member of the CIC in the Atlanta office. In 1941 Ames, who had headed a whites-only ASWPL, turned to Gordon Blaine Hancock, dean of Virginia Union University, to gather a concensus from economically advantaged black leaders for an interracial agenda that sympathetic white leaders would be able to support. The new agenda encountered women with a growing awareness of gender discrimination.

Awareness of Racism and Sexism

Methodist women became aware of issues of power and privilege inherent in racism, especially through their experiences on account of gender. When studying racism, white women recognized parallels with the second-class treatment they received in the name of being proper and appropriate. They began to question and cross traditional social boundaries of gender and race.

In the 1930s, leaders of the WMC advocated changing their mission emphasis from work *for* to work *with* women of color. The WMC's program of interracial work quickly reflected the objectives of the ten-year program of the revitalized thirty-six member Women's Committee of the CIC. Methodist women developed sustained race relations programs characterized by committee work and local efforts. Of the many race-related activities of Methodist women in the 1930s, the anti-lynching effort proved to be the largest, best supported, and most sustained. It moved churchwomen into political action.

Women learned about racism. In one ASWPL discussion participants concluded, "[t]he white race dominates and determines almost exclusively the expenditures for improvement provided by public and private funds for both races." Discrimination effectively shut off "opportunities vital to the spiritual and mental growth of people."[21]

Racism had close parallels with the discrimination white women experienced because of their gender. A study commission of the WMC issued a 120-page *Report of [the] Commission on Woman's Place of Service in the Church* in 1930. Using facts and figures from church statistics, the

69

report documented discrepancies and inequalities that women faced. Clearly, women were angered by unequal treatment within the church in appointive and elective positions, salaried positions, and barriers to full and equal ministerial standing. The church took their money but did not give them equal rights. Women first were seated in the General Conference in 1922, yet most local church committees excluded women. Regular ordination and clergy credentials were denied women until 1954, although in 1924 the General Conference granted women limited ordination as local pastors. The report examined women's economic, educational, and political status and the bearing of these on church status. It concluded that genuine equality must be economically based and that the church should serve all people:

> Securing laity rights in the church and political enfranchisement in the state by no means ended the struggle for equal opportunities of women with men. . . .

> After all the fundamental question is woman's economic emancipation, without which the purpose of life may be frustrated or destroyed. . . .

> Changes must come in the whole situation until that time when the church shall adjust its duties to its members, whether men or women, without regard to sex, and shall enter upon its full program of service to all people.[22]

 In 1933 the Committee on the Status of Women of the WMC noted that the question of the place of women in church and society assumed that man's place was the norm and woman's place, therefore, was a variant. The committee concluded, "A better understanding of the values contributed to society by women will produce a more normal estimate of the relative place of men and women."[23] This revelation concerning social standards for women paralleled the understanding of the ethnocentricity of southern culture emerging about the same time from the interracial meetings. It is possible that the two informed each other.

Methodist women found that their Christian responsibility engaged them in pressing for social change on two fronts simultaneously, toward breaking down barriers of race and gender. Torn by the difficulties of working interracially, white women chose to work separately through their missionary societies and the ASWPL. At the same time, through experiences with summer Christian Leadership Schools and local Bible study/community organizing groups for African American women, white southern Methodist women realized the need to work with African American women if their Christian beliefs were to be practiced.

70

Behind the many social pressures of the 1930s, the emerging controversy over segregation, and the development of women's organizations addressing racial issues lay a deep-seated human concern for fairness. The theological message of the leaders of the interracial movement was making an impact. God provided the basis of human equality among people of different races. In spite of attempts to rationalize injustice, the cry for fairness grew louder. African American leaders; white political leaders; radical, liberal and moderate white allies; and white Methodist women and other Christian churchwomen became part of an interracial network openly concerned about fairness. White allies were about to use the problem of lynchings to lay a broader groundwork for the transformation of social attitudes about race. There was nothing fair about lynchings. The 1930s alliance of leaders of the ASWPL, the Women's Committee of the CIC, and the WMC launched a new phase in Methodist participation in the women's anti-lynching campaign.

The gospel is the most tremendous engine of democracy ever forged. It is destined to break in pieces all castes, privileges, and oppressions. Perhaps the last caste to be destroyed will be that of sex.

—Anonymous
Twenty-seventh Annual Report
of the Woman's Missionary Council, 1937, 160

CHAPTER 4

The Later 1930s:
A Multifaceted Movement Emerges

What could women do to change racial policies in the U.S.? Undaunted by the immensity of the problems at hand and the seemingly endless task of changing attitudes one person at a time, Methodist women searched for truth. Riveted by the case of the nine Scottsboro, Alabama, teens accused of raping two white girls, Methodist women set out to gather facts about interracial incidents. Repeatedly, evidence revealed brutal acts by lawless white men.

Methodist women became concerned about the quality of life in their communities, for they felt that God called people to live together in harmony. Neither unsupportive husbands nor critical neighbors could stop Methodist women from following God's higher calling. This call to work for fairness in their own communities led them into an increasingly political arena. They became involved locally with schools, rural development, voting rights, and employment conditions of domestic workers. Religious issues became political, and political issues became local.

Public issues directly impacted the women's personal lives. Although they worked to change public opinion and to help others less fortunate, those who had come to help received unpredicted gifts.

Expanding the Anti-lynching Movement

As local missionary societies began to study lynchings and their causes, an interracial incident consumed national attention. Nine youths, ages thirteen to twenty, riding a boxcar near Scottsboro, Alabama, were accused of raping two young white women, Ruby Bates and Victoria Price, on March 25, 1931. Hitching a train ride was enough to get any of them in trouble. The young women's accusations of rape may have been intended to spare themselves arrest, but many people had special interests to protect. The International Labor Defense (ILD), the legal arm of the Communist Party, immediately seized this opportunity to defend the rights of African Americans. The National Association for the Advancement of Colored People (NAACP) soon secured attorneys for the defense, but failed to declare, as the ILD had done, that the nine were innocent. Convinced that innocence or guilt should be determined through due process of law, the NAACP awaited the outcome of a trial. Segregationists and the majority of white southerners remained unflapped by revelations that the young women were experienced prostitutes: the honor of white women must be defended, preferably in court. If not, a minority stood ready to protect the women's honor by lynch law. Liberal whites hoped to prove that the American legal system could discover the truth without regard to race and administer justice. In a hasty trial just two weeks later, the Scottsboro boys, already condemned by the press and by a mob waiting outside the courthouse, were found guilty. Circumstances were compounded by inept legal counsel for the defense.[1]

For two years the ILD courted the young defendants and their families and gathered national publicity for the Communist Party. Disorganization, poor communication, and errors in judgment left the NAACP in the dust. In a see-saw effort to wrest the case from the ILD, the NAACP secured Alabama's top legal counsel, and eventually Clarence Darrow as well.[2] The NAACP filed legal motions intent on taking the Scottsboro case to the U.S. Supreme Court. African American popular support, however, backed the ILD. In the end, the ILD exclusively handled the defense, which, with appeals, dragged on until 1938. The young men were convicted by all-white juries. The Supreme Court, however, determined in 1935 that public officials must not exclude persons on account of race from rolls of potential jurors.

The high drama of the Scottsboro case provided the backdrop to the women's anti-lynching campaign. Leaders of the Woman's Missionary Council (WMC) opposed "legal lynching," the perversion of justice that assumed the guilt of those charged and arrested for a crime. Some Methodist women, failing to consider the possibility that individuals might not have committed the crimes of which they were accused, argued that all potential lynching victims should be punished by the judicial system. In 1931 Bertha Newell received letters from the Women's National Association for the Preservation of the White Race and the Woman's Georgia Committee for Law Enforcement criticizing her defense of "criminal negro men, at the expense of innocent white girls."[3]

Their religious convictions about race led Ames, Newell, and other leaders of the WMC to stand outside the accepted norms of southern society. Their posture, cultivated by awareness of racism and sexism, fostered independence from the Methodist Episcopal Church, South, (MECS) and nurtured interdependence among women's organizations.

In this volatile climate, the Bureau of Christian Social Relations urged that women vigorously circulate the ASWPL pledge against lynching in every community. The Bureau developed and promoted a plan asking that one missionary society in each county seat organize the anti-lynching campaign for that county, "securing signatures of county officials, preachers and teachers in the county and of officers of all organizations, civic and religious in the county."[4] By 1933 several thousand women had signed the pledge. Methodist women approached leading citizens and police officers, obtaining many new signatures for the pledge against lynching. Women interviewed candidates for governor in various states concerning their attitudes toward lynching.

Dorothy Tilly, a Methodist from Atlanta, was unlike most southerners who retreated when rumors of a lynching circulated. She and a few ASWPL members would descend on the troubled area by car, bus, or train. Willing to confront angry mob leaders, Tilly and other Methodist women and churchwomen from ASWPL would talk community leaders into preventing a lynching on the grounds that courts and systems of justice would punish offenders.

Dorothy Tilly once described the instance of a small town pastor who was told by his maid that there was to be a lynching that night. The pastor, not knowing what to do, did nothing, and the lynching occurred.[5] Tilly and other women were angered.

Churchwomen celebrated their effectiveness in preventing lynchings. In 1934 the ASWPL announced that there had been fourteen lynchings and fifty-five lynchings prevented.[6] Between 1930 and 1938, prevented lynchings ranged from a low of forty-four to a high of ninety per year, with the higher prevention rates in states where the ASWPL was active.[7]

The widely publicized case of the lynching of Claude Neal on October 26, 1934, helped to convince many previously apathetic citizens that prompt federal anti-lynching legislation was needed. Neal was taken from a jail in Brewton, Alabama, and lynched in Marianna, Florida, in a carefully orchestrated episode "involving unspeakable cruelties and barbarity and witnessed by several thousand persons. . . ."[8] The lynching created headlines nationwide and publicized the incongruity between a nation proud of its democratic principles and its Christian faith, yet showing broad public support for racism as a law unto itself.

Women involved in the anti-lynching movement acted courageously. In 1936 Charles S. Johnson, CIC member and African American sociologist from Fisk University, wrote that churchwomen had
taken "the boldest stand of any group in the South against mob violence
and lynching." Johnson credited them with being "the chief support of
the active interracial committees."[9]

Bertha Newell made bold claims about the significance of Methodist women's interracial work. "The Church women are the main de-
pendence for awakening the women of the South on the menace of
lynching," she wrote in her 1936 annual report to the WMC. Newell
knew that most of the active workers in the ASWPL were superintendents of social service in local and conference Methodist women's
groups. She claimed that she had "positive proof that both women and
men who had signed the pledge against lynching were the factors that
protected the accused from mobs and insisted that the law should not
be hindered."[10] Methodist women were, indeed, making a difference
in law enforcement.

Disagreement within liberal ranks weakened women's effectiveness
toward the end of the decade. The ASWPL opposed federal anti-lynching legislation, but in 1938 the WMC broke ranks with ASWPL. African
American women members of the CIC Charlotte Hawkins Brown,
Lugenia Hope, Nannie Burroughs, and Mary McLeod Bethune all
argued with Jessie Daniel Ames in an attempt to convince her to support
the federal anti-lynching legislation.[11] Ames reasoned that lynching was
a folkway that would not end until people were persuaded that lynching
was morally wrong. While the WMC agreed with Ames, they believed
that moral actions could be hastened by civil rights legislation. Moral
behavior could and should be legislated. Thus southern liberals found
themselves in an uncomfortable position: both defending the South
and its progress against national pressure to change more quickly, and
simultaneously fending off attacks from southern segregationists who
protested all cracks and changes in the system of white supremacy.

Methodist women's concern for fairness provided a first-hand
education by immersion in political processes. The women lobbied,
wrote letters, and learned about needs for new legislation. Across the
South, Methodist women's circles discussed the Costigan-Wagner bill
and "great interest [was] aroused in proposed Federal legislation."[12]
When, in 1938, the U.S. Senate was close to a vote on the Dyer
Anti-lynching Bill, a few southern senators effectively used a filibuster
to stop its passage. Methodist women responded by lobbying for the
end of filibusters. They continued to work with the ASWPL for stronger
state laws and a mandatory change of venue for the accused.[13]

The anti-lynching program gradually changed Methodist women's theology of Christian mission. Although God called Christians to alleviate problems of injustice, they knew that serving God meant cultivating public attitudes that fostered bonds of community across racial lines and working for laws that provided equal rights for all. Methodist women were discovering that as churchwomen they had a responsibility to change public policies that obstructed justice. Not everyone welcomed their new commitment.

Critics and Husbands

Methodist women worked in a climate of opposition to interracial work. Bessie Alford, state Methodist women's chair of Christian Social Relations in Mississippi and a powerful speaker, met with obstinate resistance of groups. For five years she tried to persuade her annual conference to adopt an anti-lynching stance.[14]

Methodist women could be evasive and Methodist men recalcitrant on racial issues. In her 1935–36 annual report, Bertha Newell quoted a woman from Tyler, Texas, as saying "'to her certain knowledge' many of the women involved in her mission study course on race relations had relatives who lynched."[15]

Some husbands were openly supportive; others were not. Bessie Alford's husband supported her race-related activities while her sister, Montie B. Greer of Potts Camp, Mississippi, had a husband who opposed her work. Greer hid from her husband the threats she received while she engaged in the investigation of lynchings.[16] Other husbands were closeted supporters. Historian Jacquelyn Dowd Hall told a story she heard from Louise Young:

> . . . Louise Young asked an older co-worker why southern men allowed ther wives to engage in such 'outrageous' activities.
>
> "Let them, child," the woman replied. "Why they're so proud of them they don't know what to do. . . . They're glad that . . . the women can do things their husbands couldn't get away with."[17]

Leaders of Methodist women pushed socially acceptable boundaries for women. Hall noted that middle-class white women had privileges and immunities as long as they stayed within permissible bounds that allowed them to "engage in unconventional activities without endangering either their husbands' jobs or their own standing."[18] Thus

77

the most outspoken Methodist women leaders of interracial work either were single or had supportive husbands whose livelihoods were not at risk. They successfully engaged many women in a wide variety of interracial activities.

Schools, Rural Development, Voting Rights, Domestic Workers, and Christian Leadership Schools

Methodist women's interracial work became more local, active, and diverse in the 1930s. Within the WMC, the Committee on Interracial Co-operation secured assistance from the Commission on Rural Development and the Committee on Christian Citizenship and Law Observance in addressing racial problems. White women studied African American experiences. Some societies sent white volunteers to help lead a Bible study in the neighboring African American church. Each week when the Bible study adjorned, white and African American women convened as a community club to plan and coordinate efforts to improve community services and reduce racial tensions. The volunteers reported back to their missionary society and enlisted the assistance of white women with community improvement projects. Where these interracial linkages continued over a period of time they built bridges between otherwise estranged groups. Direct contacts helped dispel misconceptions held by white women.

Schools

In 1933, Bertha Newell invited Methodist women to focus attention on improving African American public schools. Newell and Young, as members of the Administrative Committee of the CIC, were actively involved in planning school surveys being conducted interdenominationally throughout the entire state of Alabama.[19] White women discovered large discrepancies in the public funds available to schools for white children and African American children. Schools and homes lacked or had inadequate toilets and sanitation facilities. Louise Young, chairperson of the WMC Committee on Interracial Co-operation, reported that one committee member had served on a state committee "to examine public school text books with a view to appraising the accuracy and adequacy of their treatment of the Negro." Upon finding many omissions and inaccuracies, the committee recommended using supplementary materials.[20] An exemplary women's auxiliary from South Georgia reported in 1938 that they had been busy with interracial activities.

Early in January we visited a Rosenwald School. We furnished books, maps, pictures, kitchen equipment, and other helps. Had a country doctor talk on mosquitoes and malaria control. Met with colored mothers to speak on care of sick, control of flies, and home beautification. Discussed many problems of plantation life. Furnished church school literature and helped in their teaching plans.[21]

During the depression, MECS women turned their attention to rural development. The region depended on the labor of tenant farmers, both African American and white, who were generally poor and powerless. Tenant farmers suffered from depressed market values of crops and lack of control over rents or the prices of feed, seed, and farm implements. Many farm families had inadequate housing, sanitation, food, health care, and education.

Although Methodist women were not as economically daring as radical activists who challenged the South's racial and economic systems by forming the Southern Tenant Farmers Union (STFU), their leaders paid attention to this movement. In 1934 Sherwood Eddy purchased the two thousand-acre Rochdale Farm in Mississippi as an experiment in resettling both white and African American tenant farmers.[22] Local residents shunned and harassed the farmers and their families. The pastor of the Marked Tree MECS, the Reverend Agner Sage, accused the sharecropper movement of having Communist members, promoting revolution, and siding with African Americans. Sage organized white sharecroppers to oppose the STFU, and may have been responsible for purchasing machine guns for an attack on a union rally in 1935.[23] Arkansas alone had 3,931 destitute sharecropping families evicted in 1937 for attempts to organize. White terrorist activity mounted in response to the economic strength created by uniting the poorest of the South's poor. By 1938 the farmers relocated to Providence Farm in Holmes County, later known as the Delta Farm Cooperative.

Methodist women took a serious look at the possibility of starting an experimental cooperative farm for sharecroppers. In 1937 Louise Young, Bertha Newell, Mabel Howell, Mrs. J. W. Downs, and Mrs. Lee Britt served as a WMC research committee who investigated this option.[24] The WMC's failure to launch a cooperative points to the threat that such economic leadership presented. Later, in the 1960s, as racial incidents reached inflammatory proportions, Methodist women were to become involved with the Mississippi Delta Project.

Instead, the WMC addressed rural development by cooperating with the President's Committee on Farm Tenancy; the Farm Security Administration, headed by Dr. Will Alexander of the CIC; and with

Dorothy Tilly, who served on the National Rural Administration. In 1947, Dr. Arthur Raper and Dr. Charles S. Johnson led a WMC-sponsored School of Christian Living course on farm tenancy.[25] Town or city woman's missionary societies yoked with rural missionary societies and worked out programs for mutual benefit. Of 1554 rural societies, one-third reported cooperation with sister societies by 1940 and 674 indicated that they were doing rural community work such as establishing curb markets, securing better housing for tenants, and, most frequently of all, promoting community health through clinics and campaigns.[26]

Politics Methodist women became more active in local electoral politics. In 1934 some local groups began to make studies of the white primary, which excluded African American voters from primary elections, and the extent to which restrictive voting requirements or procedures limited African American voter registration. Leaders admonished local groups to correct abuses of justice.

Voting Rights This first venture of the WMC into the area of voting rights indicated that attitudes were changing. That which had been so "dangerous" that Carrie Parks Johnson removed it from the statement prepared by ten African American leaders in 1920 had now come to be a form of injustice recognized by the leaders of the WMC.

Domestic Workers In 1934 the Committee on Interracial Co-operation sought to study employment practices regarding domestic workers. They especially wanted Methodist women to scrutinize the situation in their own homes. No longer would the study be anonymous or generalized.

Now Methodist women were to examine their own terms and contracts with employees. How many hours of work were expected for how much pay? Was the pay adequate? Were the hours excessively demanding? Could a family be supported on the basis of pay given for household work? A guide for this study, including specific questions and a tally sheet, was distributed in the educational packets on race relations and industry.

The new study was based on standards of domestic service established by the CIC and the YWCA, organizations which had collected massive data in the preceding years from domestic workers and housewives.[27] The results of the study of domestic service persuaded the WMC that throughout the South, standards needed to be raised. They recommended that "Conferences, auxiliaries, and missionary women cooperate with the federal WPA [Works Progress Administration] and NYA [National Youth Administration] training projects for household servants [and join] with Junior Leagues, YWCAs, and Women's Clubs in improving conditions of household employment."[28]

Methodist women continued to support Christian Leadership Schools, another channel of communication between African American and white women. These summer continuing education events, taught by leaders of the WMC, helped provide leadership training for members of Colored Methodist Episcopal (CME) women's missionary societies. When both black and white women lived and studied together for a week, it gave white leaders opportunities to hear the concerns of educated African American Christian women who were leaders in their own communities and conferences. The relationship was not reciprocal, however. The WMC did not invite CME women to teach in their summer leadership schools.

Local women's societies also benefitted from the Leadership Schools. White auxiliaries contributed toward the expenses of African American women sent from their communities and invited those who attended to present reports in person to the white auxiliaries.[29] Bertha Newell, superintendent of the Bureau of Social Relations of the WMC, commented that the follow-up local contacts between women who had attended these schools and the white auxiliaries had been "one of the finest products of our experiments in interracial cooperation."[30] The process of supporting a local African American delegate to attend these schools, then studying community needs with her and her associates, and gradually working together on local projects linked women across racial lines in Christian service. Interracial contacts generated by the leadership schools for CME women touched the spiritual lives of white women who testified that they "came to help and were helped."[31]

From 1940 to 1961 the Woman's Division, successor to the WMC, continued to cooperate with the CME Church and the Executive Committee of the Woman's Connectional Missionary Council in planning summer leadership schools. Cooperation between the Woman's Division and the Woman's Connectional Missionary Council began as an innovative and useful venture, and phased out when other interracial activities surpassed it in value. The demise of the summer leadership schools led to greatly diminished contact among women of two branches of Methodism that shared historical roots. In its peak in the 1930s, the leadership schools provided a "safe" place for black women to help white women understand that they had responsibilities for shaping public social policies.

Expanding Political Dimensions of Social Responsibility

Methodist women in the 1930s shouldered new political and social responsibilities. Additional women became involved as the missionary societies expanded their experiences in race relations with interracial contacts, became politically active, and participated in the anti-lynching campaign.

Missionary societies defied southern segregation customs, using the Bible to appeal to women to extend Christian hospitality. The WMC Committee on Interracial Co-operation encouraged white women's missionary societies to extend invitations to African American church-women to participate in local schools of missions and World Day of Prayer meetings. Without making an issue of segregation or integration, leaders emphasized what was happening: women were meeting interracially and establishing new expectations for southern hospitality.

Gradually Methodist women came to believe that churchwomen should help shape public opinion. As superintendent of the Bureau of Christian Social Relations, Bertha Newell convinced southern Methodist missionary society women that it was their responsibility to use their influence and Christian values in the public arena. In her 1936 annual report to the WMC, she related personal integrity to public moral good. Each person has personal responsibility for a share in making public opinion, Newell declared. She knew that, "every public issue with a moral content *has a direct bearing on our personal lives.*"[32] Not only were Methodist women to integrate personal and public claims for moral consciousness in their own lives, but women should convince others to engage in "making public opinion."

Newell's report substantiates the claim that the WMC intentionally set out to change race relations in the South. Although the council's work in race relations extended to other races and other regions of the country, its work on African American/white relations in the South was more sustained because of the proximity and intensity of the issues. White southern Methodist women found that they were in a position where they could make a difference and where their faith called for change.

The WMC was beginning to understand its Christian mission in terms of human relations. Where attitudes created barriers, the Methodist women believed that God called them to open lines of communication and channels for people to experience a more abundant life without poverty and discrimination. White women responded to the invitation to assume Christian responsibility, and in doing so, discovered the moral poverty that stems from racial discrimination. Those who had come to help, received. They found their own lives enriched. The new lines of communication they were opening and the friendships they were developing were nudging them into positions of greater leadership in church and society.

Will the feature of racial segregation tend to be permanent, or is it possible to keep ourselves so aware of its ethical imperfections on the basis of Christian brotherhood that we will desire to reconsider this aspect of church organization from time to time, working ever toward a more brotherly union?

—Twenty-seventh Annual Report of the
Woman's Missionary Council, 1937, 142

CHAPTER 5

Interracial Leadership for The Methodist Church

In the 1930s, the Methodist Episcopal Church, South, (MECS) prepared to merge with the Methodist Episcopal Church (MEC) and the Methodist Protestant Church (MPC). The most difficult of all the negotiations was the question of race. In 1844, the MEC and MECS had divided over the issue of slavery. Initially the MECS refused to reunite if church union meant accepting nearly 326,000 black church members. Ultimately a compromise plan was negotiated that created a reunited church with five regional jurisdictions plus one Central Jurisdiction for African American churches and pastors, annual conferences and bishops. The Woman's Missionary Council (WMC) lobbied for full inclusion of people of all races without segregated church structures.

As had happened in 1910 when women's concerns were set aside by the MECS, the 1939 merger that formed The Methodist Church, and with it a system of six racially segregated jurisdictions, increased Methodist women's concerns about the status of women in the church. Instead of extending women's clergy rights beyond those of ordained local pastors, The Methodist Church refused full conference membership even to women who previously had held this privilege in the MPC.

Methodist women worked to make the most of their new multiracial segregated church. The WMC had groomed Thelma Stevens for leadership on racial issues in the new church. She brought together women, black and white, to set a new agenda.

The WMC Opposes the Central Jurisdiction

In reality, both the northern and southern branches of Methodism were racially segregated. MECS and northern Methodist mission programs concerned with race emphasized institutional charity. Awareness and criticism of the church's own participation in racism was low. Consequently, the WMC provided leadership not only to women but also to the larger church. Although the MEC sponsored numerous African American colleges, a nurses' training program and medical school, the MECS had done little to strengthen individuals or institutions in the African American community. In 1939, the MECS did not consider enrolling African American students in Methodist colleges and universities such as Vanderbilt, Duke, and Emory, nor did Scarritt Training School for Christian Workers, a school owned and operated by the WMC, admit African American students. Another twelve years passed before Scarritt was to open its programs to persons of all races.

Methodist women tended to be a few steps ahead of the rest of the church in study and action on racial issues. One instance of this occurred in 1939 when, as part of the new Race Relations Sunday observance, southern Methodist women agreed to learn about schools and colleges within their conferences, which had been founded by other branches of the newly united Methodist Church.[1] This gave white women an opportunity to interact with people in nearby African American Methodist churches.

In 1937, the WMC took a position in opposition to the proposed formation of segregated jurisdictions. The merger Study Group report called upon the church to be a reconciling agency and by example to preach a universal gospel. Of all the white groups in the MEC and MECS speaking on the subject of unification, the WMC most nearly reflected the views of the African American Methodists. The report advised the church to refuse to surrender the claims of Jesus to the comfort of traditional patterns. It asserted that Methodist women's experience of cooperation with CME women in leadership schools provided a model for enabling pastors and congregations, committees and annual conferences to engage across racial boundaries in common tasks of Christian mission. The WMC claimed:

> We believe that such a Methodist connectionalism transcending race and nation and economic class will be better able to create in us the mind which was in Christ Jesus who taught us of one God who is the Father of all and in whom we are all brothers one of another.[2]

The WMC attempted to articulate a vision of society dominated by Christian teachings of human equality under God and to move the church to model these values for the larger society. With heartfelt conviction, leaders of Southern Methodist women knew that structural segregation within the new denomination would deprive them and other Methodists of a dimension of religious experience which had come to them from working with African American Methodist women. Southern Methodist women had gleaned from Jesus' teachings a set of relational values which, in 1937, the Committee on Research and Study of Status of Women identified as follows:

(1) The supreme worth of the individual;
(2) his direct responsibility to God;
(3) the obligation of unselfish service laid on all irrespective of sex;
(4) human brotherhood; and
(5) Divine fatherhood.[3]

The divine fatherhood of God implied the claim that all people equally were children of God regardless of race.

Portions of the statement from the WMC were picked up by the religious press. Perhaps surprised by the openness of such a large organization of southern women to the possibility of an interracial church without a racially segregated jurisdictional system, the *Christian Century* considered the possibility that, had other representatives formed the Commission on Unification, the MECS might have accepted some other plan of union.[4] The WMC Study Group raised doubts as to whether the plan of unification was the best possible plan, wondering whether its "ethical imperfections" would become permanent or if people would be able, within its framework, to continue "working ever toward a more brotherly union."[5]

In spite of careful preparation of this report, the WMC represented a minority opinion and was out-voted in General Conference. Methodist women, whose feelings were discredited and points of view denied by this action, expressed concern about the status of women.

The WMC found support for an inclusive gospel in Jesus' attitude shown toward women. The story of the Samaritan woman at the well spoke to them of both gender and racial inclusiveness. In this encounter, "one of the earliest declarations of the wideness of the gospel message," Jesus spoke "to a woman of bad reputation and of a despised race, thus giving great emphasis to the idea of the universal fatherhood of God and the universal sisterhood of women."[6]

Lobbying for Ordination of Women

Full ordination rights remained a painful struggle for women. Women in the MECS were barred from full ministry by an 1896 episcopal decision. Yet they concurred with the authors of *Woman and the Church*:

87

The most important contribution to humanity is that every human personality, whether Jew or Gentile, bond or free, male or female, has an infinite value to God and therefore a right to respect and consideration from man. . . . No one is going to listen to a church if it is teaching a principle, the right application of which has not been worked out in the relation of its own members, within its own body. . . . If it is the case of the church which involves the slight to the personalities or any difference to the rights of women, who constitute one-half of its members, can that church hope to offer to the world, distraught through the neglect of this very principle, a message which will carry any weight at all?[7]

Once women exercised laity rights, starting in 1922 in the MECS, organized Methodist women increased pressure for women's clergy rights. The fact that women in the MEC gained limited ordination as local pastors in 1924 and that women in the MPC could be fully ordained encouraged the MECS women.[8] Starting in 1926 and continuing at each successive General Conference of the MECS the WMC submitted a memorial calling for women clergy to be granted full ordination and conference membership. The margin of defeat was narrow enough that in 1931 hopes were high that at the next conference authority would be given for full ordination and conference membership for women.[9] Instead, full clergy rights for women, although the subject of appeal by Methodist women at every succeeding General Conference, were not granted until 1956. One bargaining chip for the 1939 merger was an agreement that women would not be eligible for full clergy rights in the new denomination. This provision withdrew the right of full conference membership to women from the MPC tradition who desired to continue in ministry after the merger.

The WMC closed its third decade with a constituency of 312,000 women,[10] a figure similar to the 323,347 African American members of the MEC[11] whose presence had been the subject of extended unification talks. If the white women compared their political strength with that of their African American brothers and sisters they may have noticed that there were two African American bishops, Bishop Robert E. Jones and Bishop Matthew W. Clair, who entered the united church, but not one woman minister with full credentials. There were guarantees for representation of African American men in high offices of the church, but no constitutional rights ensured for women. The WMC organized in twenty-one annual conferences and elected fifty-four women delegates to the Uniting Conference.[12]

The WMC protested the church's discrimination against women who made up approximately two-thirds of the church membership, "yet have very limited representation on Conference Boards and Commissions. . . ."[13] The Council's memorial to the 1940 General Conference argued, "We believe . . . the Church . . . [needs] to conserve to the Church the genius, power and inspiration of faithful called and prepared women. . . ."[14] The memorial, asking General Conference to enable women to be full members of annual conferences and thus have full clergy rights in The Methodist Church, was defeated on the grounds that the church had enough to do regarding the merger. Women's rights would have to wait.

In 1939 the Committee on Christian Social Relations of the WMC, thirty-five strong, included in its ranks four women who had maintained on-going interest and leadership in race relations: Bertha Newell, Dorothy Tilly, Louise Young, and Estelle Haskin. They, along with their predecessors Mary Helm, Belle Harris Bennett, Lily Hammond, and Carrie Parks Johnson, and a contemporary, Jessie Daniel Ames, constitute an honor roll of leaders in the pre-1940 years of the Methodist women's campaign for southern civil rights.

'cloud of witnesses'

Southern Leaders and Interracial Strength Move North

In preparation for the merger, the WMC wanted to train a new person to lead the program of the Bureau to carry the strength of the southern women's leadership into the new church structure. In 1938 the WMC chose Thelma Stevens, head resident of the Bethlehem House in Augusta, Georgia, to be the new superintendent of the Bureau of Christian Social Relations. She accepted on a part-time basis and for one and a half years divided her time between the two positions.

The impending merger and new leadership of Thelma Stevens brought forth a new dimension of concern for interracial leadership. Stevens' former professor of sociology at Scarritt College, Louise Young, proposed an interracial weekend New Year's Fellowship Conference for Methodist women. This was held from December 30, 1938, to January 1, 1939, at Paine College.[15] Its aim was to cultivate closer interracial contact between women of the CME Church, the MEC, and the MECS. Women evaluating the conference concluded, "it became clear that . . . we were seeking a greater awareness of our common needs and resources and building confidence among ourselves and a belief in the ultimate triumph of the power of God."[16]

New Years' Fellowship Conference

Unlike the CME leadership schools in which white women led and African American women participated, this weekend event mixed the racial balance of both leaders and participants and served to establish foundational friendships on which the new united women's organization would build leadership and programs. Susie (Mrs. David D.) Jones of Greensboro, an active lay member of the MEC, came to know Thelma Stevens at this conference. Their interracial friendship stimulated Methodist women's work in the years to come. Thelma Stevens noted a change in the work of the WMC:

> More and more emphasis is given to social legislation, education, voting, health, public safety, delinquency, and recreation and less emphasis placed on the "number of old magazines collected" or some similar welfare project that sometimes has very little if any permanent educational value.[17]

As Louise Young reported, one practical result of the New Year's Fellowship Conference was the compilation of a list of fifty African American women representing the MEC with whom the Southern Methodist women's representatives in each annual conference might cooperate.[18] Difficulties of cooperative efforts were compounded by the fact that boundaries of white annual conferences did not match the boundaries of African American annual conferences.

In 1939 the Bureau also launched its first summer school, a six-week leadership training program in Christian Social Relations (CSR) held at Scarritt College, for ten carefully selected women.[19] Two shorter seminars were held for conference superintendents of CSR at Lake Junaluska and Mount Sequoyah to facilitate study and planning for conference CSR programs.[20] The summer schools of mission eventually became an important vehicle for motivating concern and action relating to race relations. Systematic leadership training developed strong leadership to implement programs.

The fall 1939 meeting of the Bureau of CSR articulated three concerns for the work which lay ahead: women needed (1) to be reminded of their roots and the fundamental Christian principles undergirding their work, (2) to receive training to be able to carry out their programs, and (3) to have practical interracial experiences in order to confront and deal with their own prejudices and inconsistencies.[21] The Bureau expressed concern that past interracial studies had focused narrowly on the "American Negro" to the detriment and at least partial exclusion of other minority groups. The understanding of interracial activities was broadened to include many racial groups.

Although the merger was voted in July 1939, the women's missionary organizations took a year to make their structural transition. The merger brought together nine different missionary boards and organizations, six of them composed of women. The Women's Missionary Council came from the MECS, the MPC added a Woman's Foreign Missionary and a Woman's Home Missionary Society, and the MEC contributed three groups: the Woman's Foreign Missionary Society, the Woman's Home Missionary Society, and the Ladies' Aid Society. Each denomination's Board of Missions also participated in the merger. All across the uniting churches, the church year 1939–40 was a time for the formation of new boards, committees, and commissions. For churchwomen of the MPC and MEC who were unaccustomed to being part of the Board of Missions, the new arrangement represented a concession of power. Under the new structure, women managed the Woman's Division of the Board of Missions and Church Extension, and ← comprised one-third of the total membership of the Board. Funds contributed by the combined women's missionary programs nearly equalled those of the new churchwide mission program.

On paper, race relations occupied a small space in the tiniest department. During 1940, the Woman's Division organized three departments: Foreign Missions, Home Missions, and Christian Social Relations and Local Church Activities. The Departments of Foreign Missions and Home Missions accounted for 97 percent of the budget and work of the Woman's Division. Yet the Department of Christian Social Relations prepared to help lead both church and society into a new era in race relations.

Southern Methodist women emerged from the 1930s poised to give leadership to a new national church. Diligent study of the Bible and social injustices led them to recognize the importance of putting their faith in God's calling when it conflicted with injustices practiced in their beloved church. With greater frequency, they found in scripture a call to live in equality with people of all races.

The women's choice to align themselves with the black caucus during discussions preceding the merger raised their awareness of institutional racial discrimination in the new church. Sensitized by the merger to experiences of discrimination based on gender, especially those impeding women in ministry, they cultivated new political sophistication, getting more delegates of their choice elected to General Conference.

Three significant changes occured when the WMC prepared Thelma Stevens to lead the new Methodist women's organization in race relations work. They established that:

91

(1) Southern Methodist women, knowledgeable about southern culture, would guide the process of change;

(2) from 1939 on, African American Methodist women would participate in decision-making and leadership of the Methodist women's campaign for civil rights; and

(3) Methodist women would be forward-thinking and use their semi-autonomous position to exert pressure on the denomination to end racial discrimination.

Just who were these bold women who dared to call upon their church to change?

Women have blazed the way so that doors of opportunity and fellowship might be opened to all . . . In our hearts there is something of gratitude—a spiritual thing we cannot express. . . . I am here because many women wanted me here. I am here because my Church wanted it. I am here in His strength to say to you that the God of yesterday is the God of today. . . .

—Mary McLeod Bethune
Address to the Central Jurisdiction
Annual Meeting (1944)

As Christian women you want to stand with your feet pointing the way to a better world. These are your moments now, your vision extends—your creative ability is getting into action. . . . May we go on trusting, loving, serving, understanding, putting arms around those who need us; reaching down into the alleys, the valleys, for there are millions out there waiting for you. Go out—way out where there's no electric light, no telephone, no beautiful choir, no wonderful surroundings. They are waiting for you—for me. You have been filled here to go out in His name to minister unto those who need you. God gave unto you the knowledge of your responsibility that you may go out to make this beautiful world all He would have it be.

—Jackie Darr
A Light in the Wind, 124

CHAPTER 6

These Are the Women:
Profiles of Woman's Division Leaders

The Methodist women's campaign for civil rights grew out of several generations of race relations work. Christian teachings, distinctive Methodist emphases, hymns, the social gospel, and friendship networks passed through Methodist families. Race relations work that began as acts of charity by a privileged, educated class of white women in the 1880s gradually evolved into a call to higher Christian living for women of all classes and races. Women took increasingly greater risks as they challenged segregation and worked for integration. This chapter explores factors that brought Methodist women to their positions of leadership in the Woman's Division of The Methodist Church and its campaign for civil rights.

Beyond charity.

Five women's biographical sketches offer insight into the formative development of women who led Christian Social Relations work of the Woman's Division of The Methodist Church, either as staff members or as elected officers. Their work spanned the twenty-eight-year life of The Methodist Church, two races, two generations, and huge changes in interracial experiences. Cora Ratliff's call to interracial work led her to believe in the intrinsic value of every person. Susie Jones cultivated the art of hospitality. What she learned from listening to the heart and soul of America's African American leaders, she used to guide the Methodist women's civil rights campaign. Thelma Stevens' life was changed when she witnessed a lynching and vowed to spend her life eradicating racial barriers. Motivated to do something worthwhile with her life, Theressa Hoover devoted her entire professional career to service in the church, even when that meant riding in the back of the bus between church meetings. Hoover became the first high-ranking African American staff member in The Methodist Church. Experiences with poverty in rural Mississippi, vivid post-war observations in Japan, and missionary life in Korea helped Peggy Billings bring a comprehensive analysis of the complex dynamics of institutional racism to her 1960s civil rights work.

One by one, Methodist women who led the campaign for civil rights came to believe that they must take responsibility for the social fabric of church and nation. Their imperative came from God and always invited them to take risks. They, in turn, invited other women to join them in living as if all people are equally loved by God. This they understood to be holy living, life under God's influence, where all persons are respected.

Wesleyan

A Group Profile

Methodist women leaders who extended civil rights between 1940 and 1968 represented the fourth generation of organized Methodist women's work in race relations. After the Civil War, the first generation organized women's home missionary societies. These societies and women valued acts of charity such as giving baskets of food to families in their own community. The second generation, dating from the 1902 founding of Paine College Annex by the women of the Methodist Episcopal Church, South, (MECS) expanded institutional development of schools, homes, and Bethlehem Centers, and in 1913 first publicly opposed lynching. Between 1920 and 1939, the third generation organized interracial work and built networks of communication across African American/white racial lines. In the period 1940–68, the fourth generation carried on extensive programs that changed attitudes in church and society. Dissatisfaction with segregation and support of integration based on biblical foundations and practical experiences helped Methodist women take responsibility to work for civil rights.

The church denied first-generation women (1880–1901) all other opportunities for service and leadership in the church. These women created missionary societies and used new channels of service because their vision of Christian service included reaching out to their community, the nation, and the world. They were married women with children or single women who cared for relatives. Unlike their mothers, they had attended school but they also educated themselves on a wide range of subjects.

Some of the second generation of Methodist women leaders went to college or attended the Scarritt Bible and Training School in Kansas City founded by Belle Harris Bennett in 1892. A few daughters of Methodist women leaders of the first generation led the second generation. The second generation read social gospel authors. On the average they had fewer children than their mothers and more time and money to devote to women's work. They developed acute business and management skills in women's missionary societies that owned and operated schools, hospitals, and homes. These institutions hired single women as professional administrators. Missionary societies employed editors and authors.

Between 1920 and 1939, third generation women's missionary society members whose husbands could support them often served as full-time volunteers for the missionary societies. In addition to depending on volunteers, the Woman's Missionary Council hired staff to coordinate race relations work. Some of these staff women had graduate degrees.

MECS women lived close enough to segregation to know how a woman's sphere could be used to their advantage in controversial work. In various ways, they expanded the meanings of household, family, and hospitality. "I'm going to a church meeting," or "I'm going to Mrs. Smith's for a missionary society meeting," covered a lot of situations. Some women influenced their husbands' decisions regarding racial issues in business, law, medical practice, and farming.

Women executives either had the support of their husbands or appreciated being single because they could exercise independent judgment. Employed staff of the Woman's Missionary Council, usually single women, had freedom to engage in controversial interracial activities without jeopardizing the jobs of husbands. *Single women*

During the fourth period of organized Methodist women's work in race relations, 1940–68, leaders continued to come from middle and upper middle classes. Most professional staff had a college education and some had graduate degrees as well. Mainstay volunteer officers of the organization usually were married women without college education but with children. Differences between single professional women and married volunteers gradually diminished as more married women sought college education or jobs during and after the 1940s.

In the early 1900s the daughters of slave-owners took leadership in race relations. They had the financial means to give time and money, recognized that they were beneficiaries of the slave system, and acknowledged that those to whom more has been given have a greater obligation to assist others who are less fortunate.

By the 1920s southern Methodist women were two generations removed from slavery and much more middle class. They engaged in racial work because they believed that people of all races are God's children and Christians should be charitable to all.

MECS women leading race relations work between 1920 and 1939 had fresh awareness of issues of gender and racial inequality stemming from World War I and the depression. In scripture they found that Jesus taught about and acted on God's equal love for all people.

Southern women grew up amidst a confusing array of racial messages. They learned to curtail affection toward mammies and household servants, and to break off friendships with black children between the ages of six and eight. They knew that black servants lived in two different communities with two communication networks. White women also knew that lynchings terrorized communities in part to cover for the promiscuity of white men and to maintain a sexual double standard based on race. They saw their society convict black men of having sexual urges of legendary proportions. They watched southern society idolize the purity and virtue of white women in a hollow way related to stereotypical role rather than individual character.

Always some white southerners doubted or questioned the denial and double-talk they heard. Those influenced by the social gospel and those who traveled and witnessed other social arrangements were more willing than most to raise questions and doubts. The few who dared to cross racial barriers found a new world opening before them. The Woman's Missionary Societies provided a passport to new understandings and experiences. The women who came into civil rights leadership in the Woman's Division did not come from especially privileged backgrounds. Instead they came through the door of life-transforming experiences.

Selected Leaders for Civil Rights, 1940–1968

In these pages you will read about five women who provided leadership to the Department of Christian Social Relations of the Woman's Division of Christian Service of The Methodist Church: Cora Rodman Ratliff, Susie Jones, Thelma Stevens, Theressa Hoover, and Peggy Billings.

Cora Rodman Ratliff

Cora Rodman Ratliff (1891–1958), who served as chair of the Department of Christian Social Relations and Local Church Activities (CSR/LCA) from 1944 to 1948, was born in Oletha, Kansas, in 1891, the daughter of James Alfred Rodman, a blacksmith, and Mamie Lee

Steele Rodman, who died when Cora was eight years old.[1] The Rod-mans moved to Arkansas, where Cora graduated from Earle High School at the top of her class. She did not dream of attending college, nor could she have afforded it. She went to New Orleans where she found employment in a department store and became personnel supervisor. In 1913 she married William Hardy Ratliff, who managed a store in Sherard, Mississippi, the town where her father was living. The newlyweds settled in Sherard.

Cora Ratliff raised three children, gardened, sewed, cooked, and read. Together the Ratliffs managed to buy a plantation from Will's employer and send all three children to college. Cora belonged to the Woman's Missionary Society of the MECS which became the Woman's Society of Christian Service of the MEC. She constantly expanded her understanding and perspective by reading "excellent and unusual books."[2] Ratliff served as president of the Woman's Club of Clarksdale as well as president of the PTA. The Ratliffs often hosted weddings, dinners, and luncheon parties for the community; for visiting Method-ist ministers, superintendents, and bishops; as well as hosting meetings of the Woman's Missionary Society.

Her background and contacts with the Woman's Missionary Society led Cora Ratliff to become involved in justice issues. Her daughter Mamie Finger wrote about her, "Cora Ratliff's abiding and basic prin-ciple was always to help those who were deprived by society, either racially, economically or personally. This was her response to having to achieve on her own at uneven odds against her."[3] For Ratliff, this translated into building contacts between the Sherard MECS and families of workers in the local stave mill.

The Delta Farm Cooperative was founded by Sherwood Eddy as a social experiment in cooperative interracial life and farming located nearby. It brought prestigious board members such as Reinhold Niebuhr, Harry Emerson Fosdick, and Arthur Raper to the area. Ratliff wel-comed the socially isolated members of the cooperative, using hospital-ity in her home as a vehicle to introduce people from Sherard to cooperative members.

Ratliff held successive offices as president of the Sherard Missionary Society, president of the North Mississippi Conference Woman's Soci-ety of Christian Service (WSCS), and president of the Southeastern Jurisdiction of the WSCS. She served as a delegate from the North Mississippi Conference of the MECS to the 1939 Uniting Conference that formed The Methodist Church. She was chair of the Department of CSR/LCA of the Woman's Division from 1944 to 1948. Through these channels she introduced innovative ideas and progressive pro-

99

grams. She challenged complacency about racism when she addressed Methodist women:

> What is our message? Shall we teach the intrinsic value of every person? Every day we embarrass our missionaries by our patterns of discrimination here at home. We can no longer send a message through mission which we are unwilling to make real in our own homes, churches, communities and nation. It is the responsibility of women to set the moral patterns in homes and communities.

In 1939, as the first president of the North Mississippi WSCS, Ratliff said in her inaugural message:

> We have a department called Christian Social Relations. This is really just Christian Living based on the teachings of Jesus. . . . Because of our Bi-racial population in Mississippi, our inter-racial work is probably our largest field for personal and group service. . . . We are growing in our understanding and appreciation of the fact that what affects one race bears a direct or indirect effect on the other.[5]

Ratliff used meetings as opportunities to transcend cultural racial taboos. She selected race relations themes for jurisdictional meetings and led a 1947 School of Missions at Lake Junaluska that broke color barriers at that facility. When Ratliff and three others who had carpooled to Lake Junaluska arrived, the gatekeeper sent Mrs. Harvey to the rear gate. Mrs. Tilly insisted that the four had arrived together and were staying together. And so they did. "Women like Mrs. Tilly, Mrs. Ratliff and Miss Stevens opened vistas for black and white, rich and poor. They knew the meaning of Civil Rights and fought for civil rights."[6] Stories of the breaking of racial barriers often were not told at the time in order to allow surreptitious interracial activities to continue to occur. This helps explain why several Lake Junaluska integration stories all claim to have set precedent by breaking racial barriers.

Cora Ratliff wrote to staunch segregationist Methodist Governor Fielding Wright about her concern over Mississippi's unequal funding for Jackson College and Alcorn College, state colleges for African American students. Her letter prompted a personal visit to these campuses from Governor Wright and subsequent changes.[7]

Will Ratliff supported Cora's activities in race relations. His store in Sherard, Mississippi, was the local gathering place where people picked up their mail and the Memphis *Commercial Appeal*. Some local members of the community who gathered at the store said that the Delta Farm Cooperative was communist, implying that Cora's work was communist-related. Concerned for her safety, Will provided a car and a driver to accompany her.

In 1945, Ratliff actively worked with other leaders of the Woman's Division to extend voting rights regardless of race.[8] In 1946, Dr. P. W. Hill, from the Southern Regional Council, wrote a supportive letter praying "that God will crown the efforts of such God-sent women like yourself and others in Mississippi in the coming Primary in August."

In the 1950s, Ratliff went to the rescue of white physician Dr. David Minter and his wife, Sue, who were literally in the hands of members of the White Citizens' Council, being attacked because he treated African American patients. "Mrs. Ratliff drove over that muddy road and got out of her car parked among the patrol cars, a perfectly groomed lady, as if she'd just driven around the corner to see a friend."[9] She held the patrol officers accountable to their civic duty.

Ratliff's life was cut short by a car accident in 1958. Thelma Stevens wrote that her memory "will keep on *pushing us forward*."[10] Dorothy Tilly eulogized:

> How the Negroes in Mississippi will miss her! She has been their spokesman many a time.[11] We will miss the support she gave us as we took stands against the mores of our section. We need her so. She never waivered in her conviction of right. No Bishop could shake her. . . . Her Mississippi needs her.[12]

Susie P. Williams Jones

Susie P. Williams Jones (1892–1984) served as a mentor to the Woman's Division in matters of race relations through a close friendship she developed with Thelma Stevens. With Mrs. Paul Arrington, Susie Jones co-chaired the Committee on Minority Group Relations of the Department of CSR/LCA of the Woman's Division.

Susie Williams was born to Professor and Mrs. Frank L. Williams, in 1892 in St. Louis, Missouri. In 1915 she married David Dallas Jones, a 1911 graduate of Wesleyan University in Middletown, Connecticut, a Greensboro native and son of Sidney Dallas and Mary Jane (Holley) Jones.[13]

Susie Jones' personal story is intertwined with the history of Bennett College and with the career of her husband, who became president of Bennett in 1927. She lived on campus from 1927 until her death in 1984. Bennett College was founded for the education of African Americans in 1873, under the auspices of the Freedman's Aid Society, by Methodists gathered at St. Matthew's Methodist Episcopal Church.

In 1890, Dr. Dudley, then president of Greensboro Agricultural and Technical College (A & T), wrote to Mrs. Booker T. Washington, "asking her what Methodist women could be doing" for African American women.[14] The result was the founding of a program for women students at Bennett College in the early 1900s and development of a long-term relationship between Bennett College and the Woman's Home Missionary Society (WHMS) of the Methodist Episcopal Church. In 1926 Bennett reorganized as one of two senior colleges for African American women. WHMS provided funds for the construction of dormitories in 1937 and in 1948 the Woman's Division helped build a dormitory and a student union.[15]

As wife of the president of Bennett College, Susie Jones provided hospitality to guest speakers, entertainers, educators, and church leaders who visited Bennett College. Charlotte Hawkins Brown, president of Palmer Memorial Institute in Sedalia, North Carolina, and Mary McLeod Bethune, president of Bethune-Cookman College, were frequent speakers at Bennett College and guests in the Jones' home. Dorothy Height, executive director of the YWCA, often stayed with the Jones family. Other visitors who enjoyed their hospitality included Howard Thurman, Mordecai Johnson, Eleanor Roosevelt, Mathew Davage, Samuel Huston, A. J. Muste, Ira De A. Reid, Benjamin Mays, Paul Robeson, Rolland Hayes, Charles C. Webber, Dorothy Mayner, Channing H. Tobias, Leontyne Price, and Martin Luther King, Jr.[16] The Jones family intentionally cultivated a sense of family among faculty, students, administration, their own four children, and guests at Bennett College.

Susie Jones had the privilege of being freed for volunteer work by being assisted with domestic duties. Starting in 1927, when Jones went through a period of illness, and continuing for many years, Alsie Trammell lived with the family and helped run the busy household. Various students cooked for the Jones family.

David and Susie Jones worked as a team, although she had fewer official or public roles and did not share the platform with him on public occasions. Dr. David Jones, from 1940 to 1944 a national officer in the Methodist Federation for Social Action, discussed the interracial work of that organization with Susie, who brought many of their suggestions into the work of the Woman's Division. He, in turn, learned from her about the programs she was leading in the Woman's Division, and shared information with the Methodist Federation. The more honored of the two, David's motto was "Don't let anybody turn you 'round."[17] She was equally determined and very deliberate, firm in her own ideas. She stood up to her strong husband. Ellease Colston, a co-worker at Bennett College for many years, commented, "David Jones was more a follower of DuBois than Booker T. Washington, and Mrs. Jones was right with him on the issues."[18]

When David Jones died in 1956, Dr. Thelma Adair, a 1938 Bennett graduate, paid tribute to Susie Jones as well. "He had respect for others and their ideals. . . . But no tribute to him would be complete without a tribute to his wife—Mrs. Susie Jones—who was not only his 'balance wheel' but the model to which he hoped the Bennett girls would aspire."[19]

Susie Jones participated in civil rights marches during the 1960s.[20] She counselled young women from Bennett College who struggled with questions about civil disobedience and ethical behavior during sit-ins and marches. Bennett College students arrived at downtown demonstrations wearing dresses and hats. At Bennett, labeled by *Ebony* the "Vassar of the South," Susie Jones provided a model for students who were meticulously trained in the social graces of dress, grooming, and manners.[21] Nevertheless, students and faculty routinely were arrested, and when jails filled, they were incarcerated at the local polio hospital. Extending hospitality to her student "family," Susie Jones provided food from campus for those in jail.[22]

Jones' gifts for listening and communicating helped change the course of history both in Greensboro and in the Woman's Division. She attended court hearings in Greensboro, by her presence insisting on the need for fairness in decisions. Because she listened to their troubles in an understanding way, people often went to her for advice and counsel.[23] Although not a writer, scholar, public speaker, or activist, Jones naturally gathered people around her and frequently spoke to local Methodist women's groups. Her charisma drew together a group of civic-minded women who met regularly as a ladies' club in Greensboro over many years. Club meetings ended when she died, but this communication network helped changes in race relations come about more smoothly in Greensboro. Friends described her as level-headed, as a person who worked through problems rather than engage in situations in a conflictual way, and as a person with a broad outlook on life.

Susie Jones pioneered the way for African American leaders in the Woman's Division of The Methodist Church. Starting in 1940 she co-chaired the Committee on Interracial Relations and Minority Affairs of the Department of Christian Social Relations. She remained in leadership on related committees until 1952. She graciously endured the unusual requirement of having a co-chairperson serve with her because she was African American and the task was race relations, while no other committee had more than one chairperson.[24] She helped implement the first inventory of racist practices among Methodist missionaries and institutions. She and Thelma Stevens together dreamed of and brought into being the first compilation of U.S. state laws on race and color. She was instrumental in making arrangements for the Woman's Division's World Understanding Team program. She was among the first women from the Women's Division to march in civil rights demonstrations in the 1960s.

Susie Jones and Thelma Stevens became close friends at the New Year's Fellowship Conference at the end of 1938 and thereafter Stevens relied on Jones' directness and honesty in advising Stevens on how to handle racial issues. Susie Jones and Thelma Stevens had a deep sense of respect and trust for each other. Their relationship was such that Jones would tell Stevens, who took great pride in her independence of judgment, what to do to lead Methodist women in race relations. Jones knew how to lead because she constantly took the pulse of racial issues, nationally and internationally. In addition to books and newspapers, the Bible and her church, her tutors were the national and international visitors who came to her home. When Stevens pondered how to respond to a racial crisis or when she sensed that the Woman's Division needed to take a new direction or stronger stand on racial issues, she talked with Jones.[25] Jones gave her encouragement when bitter attacks left Stevens feeling discouraged.

Jones remained active in civic, church, and college-related activities in Greensboro until her death in 1984.

Thelma Stevens

At age six, Thelma Stevens (1902–1990) joined a local Mississippi congregation of the MECS[26] about the same time that her perceptions of racial inequality were forming. She could not fathom why her African American playmates did not have a school to attend, as she did, and became determined to extend educational privileges to other African American children. Bereaved of her mother and raised by an older sister, a teacher who also pastored a small church when her husband was ill, Thelma learned that women can do almost anything. When teaching high school at age nineteen, her students took her to witness a lynching.[27] Devastated by the barbarity that she witnessed, she committed her life to eradicating the barriers of race.

Stevens graduated from State Teachers' College at Hattisburg (now the University of Southern Mississippi), but not before she had oriented her classmates, other prospective school teachers, through banned contacts with African American teachers, to the blighted condition of public education for African American students in Mississippi. While Stevens attended State Teachers' College, a recruiter for the Methodist deaconess program tried in vain to enlist Stevens. Stevens thought that the church was too bigoted to be a place where she could work, so she took a teaching position in Perkinson, Mississippi.

As a college graduate and teacher of pedagogy at a junior college in Perkinson, she launched an experimental teaching project among herself, ten white college students, and local African American school teachers, to provide supplementary instruction in teaching methods to teachers with a fifth-grade education. Within five years, Stevens had made a vocational turnaround and a different commitment to the church.

One day the mail brought an opportunity for graduate study at Scarritt College in Nashville. The mysterious arrival of that letter seemed to be an act of God, for as much as the hypocrisy of the church repelled Stevens, the opportunity for graduate education appealed. In 1926 Thelma Stevens entered Scarritt College for Christian Workers in Nashville, Tennessee, completing a master's degree in 1928 and a thesis entitled "Jesus and the Pharisees."

From her New Testament studies, Stevens learned that Jesus handled criticism from religious leaders by finding a deeper authority coming directly from God. Jesus experienced God's guidance as an inner voice which helped him know right from wrong when other voices of tradition, religious authority, or society demanded conformity.[28] This conclusion strengthened her resolve to act from inner integrity rather than social conformity or the pressure of criticism on the issue of segregation. She wrote:

> Jesus never quotes a text as having authority simply because it was found in the Scriptures. He set aside all that contradicted his own inward experience. Jesus recognized the validity of the Law and emphasized its binding character.[29]

Stevens' vocational commitment changed as she discovered some Christians who were open to new ideas and whose social vision she shared. At Scarritt, Stevens entered an academic climate influenced by the social gospel and by forward-thinking southerners. She met professors who shared her theological understanding that people should be treated with justice regardless of race. Stevens' professor of World Mission and Sociology, Mabel Howell, nurtured Stevens' understanding of Christian mission as action and engagement with issues of peace and justice in a global context.

Another one of Stevens' mentors was Louise Young, professor of Sociology, who guided her through field work experience at the Bethlehem Center in Nashville and eventually to her position as director of the Bethlehem Center in Augusta. Young had come to Scarritt from Paine College, in Augusta, where she had been the only white faculty member.

Stevens reconsidered becoming a deaconess. She had decided to remain single so that she would not be limited by husband or family in pursuit of her professional aims. Now she applied to be a deaconess and was refused! Her doctor would not recommend her to the Deaconess Bureau because he didn't expect her to live more than three years as a result of a bad ulcer.[30] Surgery led to a remarkable recovery.

From 1928 to 1940, Stevens served as director of the Bethlehem Center in Augusta, Georgia. With her friend and co-worker, Dorothy Weber (Carter), Stevens managed a bustling community center, oversaw the construction of a new building, purchased a forty-acre camp site, and developed some of the earliest interracial camping programs in the nation.[31] Through the depression years people often were hungry and unemployed. The Bethlehem Center helped people in the community care for one another. One summer six hundred children attended the Vacation Bible School. Stevens met weekly with a group of African American pastors, teaching them Bible study skills, examining with them the sermon text for the following week, interpreting it for troubled lives in troubled times, and hearing their sermons.

Stevens, from 1940 to 1968 the executive secretary for the Department CSR/LCA, took bold new steps to address social issues in general and race relations in particular. She believed that Christians ought to implement the ethical principles of the teachings of Jesus in all aspects of their relationships.

Stevens had numerous leadership gifts and abilities: (1) to understand and articulate a social vision based on religious teachings; (2) to define the goals to be reached, the steps to be taken, and the committee work and programs needed to meet objectives; and (3) to attract, educate, and direct skilled and dedicated volunteers willing to be leaders in church and society. Stevens creatively integrated ideas of other thinkers and leaders, providing much of the original thinking that guided Methodist women in their campaign for civil rights between 1940 and 1968. She built strong team leadership and volunteer support by down-playing her own role and giving credit to group efforts. Without specifying roles, historical records of the Woman's Division of the Board of Missions document what women in the Division felt that women ought to do, what they set out to do, and what they accomplished. The testimony of Stevens' co-workers suggests that she was instrumental in conceiving of and guiding nearly every major Methodist women's forward-moving race program during her tenure.

An exceptionally articulate champion of human rights, Thelma Stevens was known by thousands of Methodists and other churchwomen and was in popular demand to address conferences and workshops. Stevens wrote a brief history of the Department of Christian Social Relations and in her later years was herself interviewed by historians.[32] Her distinctive writing style and characteristic point of view can be identified in reports of the Department of CSR/LCA and monthly columns of *The Methodist Woman* even where her name was not signed and the writing represented a group effort.

Stevens retired from her position in 1968 when The United Methodist Church was born. In retirement she worked against sexism and heterosexism, prejudices as deeply rooted as racism, which likewise created barriers to full human relations. She organized, spoke, wrote, lobbied, and called both church and society to account for attitudes and policies that perpetuated injustice. Stevens advised and contributed funds to the Ecumenical Women's Institute in Chicago, gave countless volunteer hours to Church Women United, and helped with the formation of the United Methodist General Commission on the Status and Role of Women. She continued to travel to meetings, to exhort audiences of church leaders to work for justice, and to serve as mentor to younger women as they moved into leadership positions. She spent her later retirement years at McKendree Towers in Hermitage, Tennessee, and Brooks-Howell Home in Asheville, North Carolina, and died on December 18, 1990, at age eighty-eight.

Theressa Hoover

Theressa Hoover (1925—) came to the Woman's Division in 1948 to take the post of field worker and stayed with the Division until her retirement in 1990. Hoover was born September 7, 1925, in Fayetteville, Arkansas, to James Cortez Hoover and Rissie Vaughn Hoover. Theressa, along with her sisters and brothers, became active in St. James Methodist Episcopal Church. Her grandfather, a Methodist preacher without a horse, had walked his circuit, covering up to two hundred miles to visit assigned churches. Hoover caught the spirit of his persistence and dedication.

Both Hoover and her family expected that she would do something worthwhile with her life and that she could achieve whatever she set out to do. "All of us went to college and that was in a system which provided only an eighth grade education for Blacks."[33] With no high school available to her or other African Americans in her home town,

Theressa went to live with a school teacher aunt in Atlanta, Texas, so she could attend a public high school. Her hardworking, thrifty parents used her father's income from City Hospital to assist all five children in obtaining both high school and college education. Theressa worked her way through Philander Smith College, first in the campus dining room, then part-time as an office secretary at nearby Wesley Chapel. Upon graduation she worked for the Little Rock Methodist Council, a group of twelve Methodist churches and two Christian Methodist Episcopal churches which engaged in joint programs of Christian education, leadership training, and social action.[34] One of the joint projects, funded in part with a grant from the Woman's Division, involved buying a turkey farm near Little Rock to create Camp Aldersgate, intended to serve church and non-church groups as a much-needed site for interracial meetings in the area.

After two years as associate director of the Little Rock Methodist Council, she was tapped by the Woman's Division to take a professional position as a field worker. From 1948 to 1958 she traveled among the Woman's Societies, attending and resourcing district, conference, and jurisdiction meetings, maintaining contact with leaders at different levels of the organization, and helping people know what was going on and what they were to do. She was on the road for eleven months of the year and her speaking engagements and teaching assignments took her across jurisdiction lines. She interpreted mission themes, taught in conference and jurisdiction schools of mission. Most of her early work was in the Central Jurisdiction, although it was never limited to that.

In her travels she found racial barriers. She was required to ride in the back seat of a bus, yet at her destination would be met by a white woman and entertained in an interracial setting until she traveled to her next engagement, again in the back seat of a bus.

Hoover moved to New York City in 1958 when she became a staff member of the Department of Christian Social Relations, working with Thelma Stevens. She took advantage of her new-found stability to earn a master's degree in 1962 at New York University's Center for Human Relations in the School of Education.

The whole staff of the Woman's Division, including Hoover, jointly planned race programs for Methodist women and designed and implemented National Seminars and other programs. Hoover drafted memorials to the General Conference, including petitions to end the Central Jurisdiction structure. She helped develop the Amendment IX plan for transferring and uniting conferences across racial lines. As a staff member, Hoover helped plan both the 1950 National Roll Call of Methodist Women that was designed to enlist Methodist women to register to vote, and the World Understanding Teams that brought women together to discuss issues with women from around the world. Hoover traveled with several of the teams. Although local groups of the WSCS and the Wesleyan Service Guild (WSG) were not racially integrated, interracial planning took place for special events such as Citizenship Brunches, Race Relations Day, Brotherhood Week, and United Church Women's World Day of Prayer and May Fellowship Day. "It occurred often enough that we were on the right track. People had lived in the same town and didn't know each other." But joint churchwomen's events brought the two races together.

The Woman's Division kept up a constant, unrelenting barrage of programs and activities designed to change women's attitudes about human relations and break down racial barriers. "My grandmother used to say, 'A constant drip will wear a hole in iron,'" Hoover shared.

"Nothing was true everywhere," Hoover reflected about the distance between the design of programs and their implementation in local communities. Yet she could see changes in the way things were done. "We rarely did any program without getting women together across racial lines."[35] The fact that women often held their meetings in homes was important because they had more freedom to invite guests of other races to homes than to meetings at the church.

Women were persuaded to try new things. "Local women will basically support what the Woman's Division does if we will let them know what and why," Hoover asserted. "Methodist women contributed greatly to the change in attitudes on race in the U.S." Women who had never exercised their franchise registered and voted because societies emphasized voting and responsible citizenship. The Woman's Division ran Rumor Clinics in the 1960s to help women and communities deal with racial tensions. Two staff members participated in the 1965 march from Selma to Montgomery. This was a sensitive issue, not so much for the staff time involved as for the complaint that society members did not want their pledge to mission to go for bail. When asked what generated the most criticism, Hoover replied, "Everything about race." Some Methodist women complained that money collected for UNICEF "went to children in communist countries." Others had problems with the Citizenship Brunches because they thought they pushed a particular presidential candidate.

Hoover took a position as assistant general secretary in the Woman's Division in 1965 with responsibility to lead the Section of Program and Education for Christian Mission. Three years later, when a merger formed The United Methodist Church and when Dorothy McConnell retired, Hoover was chosen to head the entire Women's Division.

Theressa Hoover's long view inspired her observation that "seeds planted in one generation may not bear fruit until another." Pauli Murray's research on states' segregation and race laws, conducted for the Woman's Division starting in 1948, "was a real eye opener," yet it built on programs of the women of the MECS ten years before.[36]

Quality programs of Methodist Women changed hearts, theology, attitudes, and behavior. "Women's minds were fertile fields," Hoover believed. Each year's mission study book reached thirty thousand to forty thousand women. "We are theologians because we do theology," Hoover asserted. The Division rooted its actions in scripture, in the teachings and history of the church, and in the world context. "If you look behind the scenes to ask what made women do these things you will find good leadership, respect for constituency, and the understanding that if people know, they act differently."

Since retiring at the end of 1990, Theressa Hoover continues to live in New York City.

Peggy Billings

Peggy Billings (1928—), who in 1968 succeeded Thelma Stevens as assistant general secretary of the Section on Christian Social Relations of the Woman's Division, was born in McComb, Mississippi, on September 10, 1928, to Eynes Melissa Dickerson and Clement David Billings.[37] She was the youngest of nine children, seven boys and two girls. David Billings, an engineer for Illinois Central Railroad, had steady work through the depression, but times were tight.

In 1931, when depression economics forced the Billings family to supplement their income with farming, they moved to a country home near Carter's Creek, Mississippi. During summers with the Billings family, Peggy's maternal grandmother told stories of her grandfather's life as a Methodist circuit rider in central Mississippi. These stimulated Peggy's earliest interests in religion.

Her father kept his job through the depression so the Billings family suffered less than many others did. Her mother usually managed to hire an African American woman to help with cleaning the house and cooking. In 1939 the Billings family benefitted from a rural housing development project of the Roosevelt administration that built houses with electricity and indoor plumbing. They were able to purchase a home closer to town. The combination of hard times prompted by the Great Depression and the existence of two societies in Mississippi that were separated by race provided grist for Peggy Billings' later grasp of social issues. With her family, Peggy became active in Pearl River Avenue MECS located in the working class part of McComb. She joined the church when she was twelve years old, along with her brother Bob. Their minister, Brother H. L. Daniels, prayed "that we would be used in the service of the church."[38]

In a town with Sunday blue laws, church provided the center of religious and social life and recreational opportunities. Both at church and in Fernwood Consolidated High School, Billings found dedicated teachers and leaders interested in young people. Billings joined the Methodist Youth Fellowship, which met on Sundays, and the Youth Society of Christian Service, sponsored by the WSCS, which met mid-week.

The 1940s brought hardships and uncertainties with five brothers in military service. At home alone with her mother, fifteen-year-old Billings shouldered major responsibilities while she tended her mother who was ill with cancer. During this time she wrote her first letter to the Board of Missions and made a decision to serve the church through its mission programs, a commitment that would remain constant. In 1945, her extended family, along with caring adults at church and school, helped her through the period of her mother's illness and untimely death. She went to live with her brother Clifford and his wife, Gladys, who saw her through high school.

In 1947 Billings entered Methodist-affiliated Millsaps College in Jackson. Her mother had encouraged her teenage dream to be a medical missionary, and at Millsaps she studied biology and chemistry. Women from her local church directed her toward a scholarship offered by the WSCS and the WSG. Without it, she could not have attended, but with it she entered the community of women whose commitments to mission stretched their vision beyond the social norms of the time. Determined to save money by shortening her time in college, Billings finished in three years, graduating in 1950. Despite her heavy study load, she attended interracial events, including an interracial seminar sponsored jointly by the YWCA and YMCA, and took an eye-opening sociology course in race relations. She served as assistant leader to a Girl Scout troop at the Bethlehem Center in Jackson.

Billings noted the courageous public stands in race relations that Mrs. Paul Arrington, co-chairperson (with Susie Jones) of the Committee on Minority Group Relations of the Department of Christian Social Relations, was taking at the same time her husband was lieutenant governor of Mississippi. The Arrington home was open to people of all races, and Mrs. Arrington's commitments were well known.

Billings' good grades admitted her to medical school, but did not win her a scholarship. In a hurry to advance her education, Billings followed the alternative suggestion of her Methodist women friends and in the fall of 1950 left for Nashville to study social work at Scarritt College.

After a year at Scarritt, influenced by Koreans there, Billings left to study Korean at Yale University Institute of Far Eastern Languages, and by 1952 the Woman's Division of The Methodist Church commissioned her as a missionary and sent her to Tei Wha Community Center in Seoul, Korea.

Billings arrived in Korea by way of Japan where two experiences jarred her thinking. Her first-hand view of Hiroshima seven years after atomic destruction left an indelible mark, as did her introduction to the Korean community in Japan, and observation of discrimination that Koreans encountered. Billings arrived in Korea before the Korean War had ended and witnessed the effects of war—refugees, hunger, physical injuries, death, and widespread destruction of social systems. In this crucible, new experiences challenged the social and political attitudes she had grown up with and the culturally dominant assumption that the military resolves international problems. She saw that war only created a new set of problems. It failed to deal with human despair, poverty, and hopelessness. No longer could she take things at face value. She noted that people on the bottom of the social structure suffered, while those at the top did not see the depth of the suffering and did not seem to care.

In the U.S., dramatic changes marked the decade that Billings spent in Korea. The Supreme Court's landmark 1954 school desegregation decision spawned efforts for compliance but also many forms of resistance as communities across the nation polarized with racial tension. The Montgomery bus boycott took place in 1955, followed in the 1960s by sit-ins, freedom rides, and boycotts of businesses. In early 1963, from her international perspective, Billings wrote to her supporters in Mississippi about the contradictions she saw between the gospel and what was happening in Mississippi. Her letter was published in the *Mississippi Advocate* edited by her friends Sam and Ann Ashmore under the heading, "An Open Letter to Mississippi Methodists." The letter achieved a broader circulation than Billings ever anticipated. Thelma Stevens, who on a visit to Korea had met Billings, saw the letter and distributed it to Methodist women.

Billings returned from Korea the summer of the 1963 March on Washington. Stevens invited Billings to the Woman's Division's 1963 National Seminar to describe her understanding of white racism. At the National Seminar Billings observed the broad extent of Methodist women's support for racial justice.

Impressed by what she found in Billings, Stevens responded to her interest in race relations by offering her a staff position within the Department of CSR. The fact that there was no such position did not deter Stevens, who went on to create the job. In the fall of 1964, Billings joined the staff of the CSR as Secretary for Racial Justice, working with Thelma Stevens, Margaret Bender, and Theressa Hoover.

Billings' assignment addressed two priorities: eliminating segregated structures in The Methodist Church and supporting civil rights. In 1965, Billings went to Selma, Alabama, along with Ruth Harris, a staff person from the Board of Missions program related to the Methodist Student Movement. They participated in the march from Selma to Montgomery.

Billings traveled throughout the U.S. during the next three years, working inside and outside the church on a variety of race-related assignments. Designated to serve on the Board of the Delta Ministry, a justice movement in Mississippi founded by the National Council of Churches, she attended meetings in Mississippi where she found that both she and her native state had changed immensely!

In 1968, without warning, the Board of Missions voted to change the staff retirement age from sixty-eight to sixty-five. Dorothy McConnell, then head of the Woman's Division, Thelma Stevens, and Margaret Bender suddenly retired. When Theressa Hoover was tapped to head the new Women's Division, Peggy Billings was appointed to serve as assistant general secretary of the Section on CSR, a position she held until 1984. Working with a well-qualified staff, Billings provided strong leadership for United Methodist Women over the entire range of social issues of the day, keeping faith with historic commitments of the Section to racial justice, international understanding, and justice for women and children.

Billings continued to prize the relationship she helped the Women's Division to forge between the international human rights movement and new understandings of ecological justice manifested in the Section's special project on the Law of the Sea as well as in the National Council of Churches' policy statement on Ethical Uses of Energy Resources. Billings wrote, "In this period we pushed forward the Women's Division's understanding of working on broad-based coalitions to achieve justice goals."[39]

In 1984, Billings applied for the top executive position with the World Division of the General Board of Global Ministries (formerly the Board of Missions), and took administrative oversight over its entire

FELLOWSHIP OF LOVE

program. Forward-thinking programs of the mission board had been under attack for decades. Conservative critics of Billings' outspoken and progressive analyses of social and mission issues raised protests against her election and against programs administered by the World Division under her leadership. Unsuccessful in blocking her election, the group culminated years of antagonism toward the Board by creating an alternative mission agency. Some key members remained as directors of the Board of Global Ministries. Their agenda for reform of the Board included removing Billings from office. A conservative coalition prevented the renewal of her contract at the end of 1988.

Since 1989, Billings has lived on a farm near Trumansburg, New York, where she is executive director of the Church, Ethics, and Society Project sponsored by the World Division and Women's Division of the General Board of Global Ministries.

Other Leaders in the Department of Christian Social Relations

Charlotte R. French joined the department staff in 1941 as full-time secretary and the first African American employee of the Woman's Division, managing the office while Thelma Stevens traveled. She left the Department in 1959 in order to care for her ailing parents. Dorothy Weber, a white woman from Louisiana who had lived with Stevens and worked at the Bethlehem Center in Augusta, Georgia, for ten years, joined Thelma Stevens on the executive staff of the Department in 1945. She lived with Stevens and worked for the Woman's Division until 1952 when she married.

Eleanor Neff joined the staff as assistant secretary of the Department of CSR/LCA from 1945 to 1950 in order to help with post-war planning. She arrived already informed about the work of the Woman's Division and committed to the perspective of the department. Stevens entrusted Neff to represent the department in Washington, D.C., where Neff gathered legislative information which was sent to societies and guilds for action, and made valuable contacts on Capitol Hill. Others who served on the CSR staff included Margaret R. Bender, 1950–68; Eunice Thompson, 1953–54; Ethel L. Watkins, 1953–57; Minnie Stein, 1965–69; and Mia Aurbakkan, 1967—.

Southern women led the Department of CSR and the Methodist women's campaign for civil rights. Prior to 1940 women of the Methodist Episcopal Church had few programs about race. Following the

114

merger, Methodist women from the South provided staff leadership for the Department of CSR of the Woman's Division. Southerners Thelma Stevens and Dorothy Weber were joined in later decades by Minnie Stein, Theressa Hoover, and Peggy Billings.

While previous chapters have been about southern women and the MECS the chapters that follow show how the Methodist women's societies incorporated women across the nation into a movement for civil rights. The five women whose stories have been highlighted, all southern women, provided some of the most dedicated and visionary leadership among Methodist women to the broadening movement.

Creating a Caring Attitude

Leaders of the Woman's Division believed in working together as a team of officers to change the racial practices and policies of the Woman's Division, The Methodist Church, and the nation. They attended many meetings, convened workshops and seminars, and wrote myriad reports because they were convinced that by working together they could make a difference. They subscribed to the motto, "All Action Is Local,"[40] because they were intent on putting their faith into practice. Each grew up in a family where she was expected to take responsibility for her choices. Holding high expectations for their daughter's future, the parents in each family left their daughter free to make her own choices about vocational directions. Those who married had supportive husbands who encouraged their wives to take leadership.

Women leaders of the fourth generation of Methodist work in race relations (Cora Ratliff, Susie Jones, Thelma Stevens, and Theressa Hoover) believed that by focusing their work through the church they could significantly influence the nation's moral fabric of attitudes, principles, and justice regarding race. Their goal was to engage the nation in the task of caring for its people. At the heart of this task was a powerful "Yes!" to God's call to live as faithful Christians.

Women who led the Woman's Division in civil rights work learned about discrimination early in life. Strengthened by their faith and by friends, they acted on their commitments. Often the actions they took were ordinary, yet required courage of conviction to break religious and social taboos. The many small steps they took for civil rights eventually added together to build a movement.

Yet a larger movement was already gaining momentum around them. International events and travel, the rising influence of Gandhi, and a growing network of voluntary organizations devoted to strengthening social responsibility in areas of racial injustice marked the 1940s. Many major organizations that helped shape the civil rights years were formed in that decade. These key Methodist women became part of this network that brought secular and religious groups together around civil rights.

As Christians, we are required to believe in the worth of every human being in the eyes of God, who alone is a competent judge of worth. Because of Christ, we are convinced that God cares for each human being. We who follow him must share his concern. Our proposal to Christianize the relations and institutions of men is as definitely religious as the proposal to purify the hearts and sanctify the wills of individuals. Both are halves of a single whole. Each must complement the other. Both stem from the convictions that God is Christlike, that he is active in history, that the moral order is real and inviolable.

—Journal
Woman's Division of Christian Service
Eighth Annual Meeting
(December 2–12, 1947), 14

CHAPTER 7

The Context of the 1940s: Social and Religious Forces Combine

An African American agenda formulated in 1942 provided the basis for a concerted effort by Americans to re-evaluate the social and religious underpinnings of segregation. In the 1940s, civil rights moved into the arena of national politics, where President Truman, Congress, and elected officials participated in highly charged public debate. The National Association for the Advancement of Colored People (NAACP) launched an intensive legal campaign for school desegregation. Adapting Gandhi's teachings, the Congress of Racial Equality (CORE) developed strategies for social change for the racial situation in the U.S. The Southern Regional Council (SRC) used research and education to demonstrate crucial links between economic development, racism, and education. The Methodist Federation for Social Action (MFSA) took its first radical public stands against segregation, partly in response to the formal segregation adopted by The Methodist Church. Thus, in the 1940s, Methodist women lived and worked within a network of partners in the struggle for civil rights who took their cues from African American leaders.

African American and White Liberal Voices

In 1940 even white liberals expected to benefit from racial deference, to advocate gradualism, and to serve as tutors to African Americans.[1] The Woman's Missionary Council (WMC), the Commission on Interracial Cooperation (CIC), and the Association of Southern Women for the Prevention of Lynching (ASWPL), which had worked closely together in the 1930s, all manifested white paternalism. White leaders feared losing control over the volatile southern racial situation.

119   *white paternalism*

In the 1940s, some white liberals began to relinquish their role as "tutors" to become students and learn from African Americans. This change was particularly profound in CIC, which experienced death and rebirth as the SRC. Will Alexander of CIC left regional work for national leadership to spend his time between the Rosenwald Fund offices in Chicago and Washington, D.C., the War Manpower Commission, and the Office of War Information. Alexander was instrumental in organizing and advising the American Council on Race Relations, a coalition for change, which had prominent members such as Mary McLeod Bethune, Charles Hamilton Houston, Ralph Bunche, author Pearl Buck, and Lester Granger of the National Urban League.[2]

Jessie Daniel Ames, leader of the ASWPL, lacked the ability to share interracial leadership equitably with African Americans, but facilitated a crucial change. Ames told Virginius Dabney, "In the Commission . . . we have never treated Negroes as equals. . . . [We] have comforted them as we would children."[3] Ames observed that "doing for" African Americans gave whites the impression that they were helping people inherently inferior and incapable. Yet it was Ames who communicated with Gordon Blaine Hancock, professor of economics and sociology at Virginia Union University in Richmond, and Virginius Dabney, editor of Richmond's *Times-Dispatch*, to set in motion two preparatory conferences which signaled the demise of CIC and ASWPL and the rise of the SRC in 1945.

The Durham Declaration defined the new race relations agenda of the 1940s. At the Durham Conference, held October 20, 1942, a group of African American men prepared the Durham Declaration.[4] Leaders declared their fundamental opposition to the "principle and practice of compulsory segregation" and their intent to work for a southern way of life "consistent with the principles for which we as a Nation are fighting throughout the world."[5] Organized into seven sections, the report addressed political and civil rights, industry and labor, service occupations, education, agriculture, military service, and social welfare and health.

The declaration called for guarantees of political and civil rights for all citizens: the right to vote, freedom from discrimination and intimidation, and protection from abuses of power by law enforcement officers. The declaration urged immediate abolition of the poll tax and the white primary. Both excluded people of color from elections. The declaration called for inclusion of African Americans for jury service.

The declaration challenged industry and labor to practice racial fairness in job training, hiring, and pay. It spoke of the right of service workers to organize and bargain, and it stated that all workers deserved old age insurance, unemployment compensation, worker's compensation, and minimum wages.

The key to equal opportunity for all citizens, these leaders believed, was equal access to quality public education. African American leaders called for better schools, longer school terms, improvement in school buildings, quality graduate and professional training, and federal subsidies for education.

The new platform urged farm tenancy reforms: longer leases, higher farm wages, and written contracts; equitable federal assistance to African American farmers and land grant colleges; and appointment of blacks to government policy-making bodies. The declaration pointed to the demoralizing effect of discrimination and inequality in the military.

Finally, the leaders called for social welfare and health services represented by access to public hospitals; employment of African American doctors, nurses, and social workers; and extension of federal low-cost housing programs. The Durham Declaration concluded that the world would never know lasting peace until people protected the rights of minorities everywhere in the world.

The Durham Declaration pointed the way for significant developments in the 1940s. A similarity between the Durham Declaration and the 1947 report of the President's Committee on Civil Rights (PCCR) points to the astute leadership of the African Americans who assembled in Durham and their success in persuading President Truman and the PCCR to respect NAACP and SRC leadership.

A group of white social and religious leaders met in Atlanta, Georgia, on April 8, 1943, to respond to the Durham Declaration. Ralph McGill, editor of the *Atlanta Constitution*, chaired this conference. The white leaders proposed to cooperate with the African American leaders and humbly confirmed the conclusion that laws and law enforcement discriminated by race. "This is a violation of the spirit of democracy. No Southerner can logically dispute the fact that the Negro, as an American citizen, is entitled to his civil rights and economic opportunities."[6] The tempered language of their statement contrasted sharply with the crisp, clear platform to which they responded. With passive voice they advanced the front lines of organized liberals: "It is recognized that there is often practical discrimination by some peace officers and in some courts in the treatment of Negro prisoners and in the abrogation of their civil rights."

White liberal leaders were not yet ready to make commitments to end segregation or write into law the provisions of the Durham Declaration. Yet these liberal leaders of the 1940s determined to leave paternalism behind and open doors so that all persons, regardless of race, color, religion, or national origin could enter more fully into the political and democratic processes of national life.

The Durham and Atlanta conferences, the Southern Conference on Human Welfare, and the decision to replace CIC all contributed to the formation of the SRC in 1945. Using research, education, and advocacy as its means, the SRC emphasized economic development and extension of political rights in the South. The SRC documented by race such factors as *per capita* income, school expenditures per pupil, and voter registration in southern states. Pressure from the SRC changed policies of newspapers. White-owned papers began to cover news of African American subjects, tempered story captions to be less racist, and added courtesy titles of "Mr." and "Mrs." when referring to African Americans, corresponding to the practice that was common for white persons. Inner circle leaders of SRC opposed segregation, but four years passed before the organization took that position as its public stance. While the SRC, which attracted southern liberals and became increasingly outspoken, stood in opposition to segregation in 1949, Methodist women spoke out against segregation in 1944. Politicians preferred less visible and vulnerable positions.

National Political Conflicts Over Race

Roosevelt's election created an uneasy coalition of mainstream Democrats, southern Democrats, and African American supporters. Some African Americans switched from the Republican to the Democratic ticket to elect Franklin D. Roosevelt as president and support the New Deal. Even so, Roosevelt had no platform for civil rights legislation. Holding a carefully drawn middle line, he did not attack segregation or discrimination. New Deal programs provided federal agricultural assistance to the South, yet did little to help African Americans struggle against discrimination in business and industrial employment.

Although African American voters had cast decisive presidential election ballots, it was not until A. Philip Randolph, president of the Brotherhood of Sleeping Car Porters, organized the March on Washington movement in 1941 and promised to bring forty thousand people to the capital that Roosevelt lent an ear to their concerns. In exchange for Randolph cancelling an internationally embarrassing protest of grievances against the U.S. for failure to act democratically during a war against Germany's racist policies, President Roosevelt issued Executive Order 8802.

This far-reaching order created the Fair Employment Practices Committee (FEPC) with the power to enforce federal anti-discrimination policies in the awarding of military contracts, government training programs, and government industries. President Roosevelt funded the FEPC until 1945 when Congress disallowed executive branch funding and axed the committee. After the war, Congress debated whether or not to establish a permanent FEPC. The Woman's Division recommended that Methodist women work for the passage of Senate and House bills which would establish a permanent FEPC.[7]

Upon FDR's death, President Harry Truman inherited a precariously balanced Democratic political coalition and received tremendous pressure from African Americans to establish civil rights programs where none existed. Truman's core belief in fairness and democratic principles led him to speak for human rights as had no president before him. As Missouri's senior senator, he outlined his beliefs in 1940:

Truman

> I believe in the brotherhood of man; not merely the brotherhood of white men; but the brotherhood of all men before the law. I believe in the Constitution and the Declaration of Independence. In giving to the Negroes the rights that are theirs, we are only acting in accord with ideas of a true democracy. If any class or race can be permanently set apart from, or pushed down below the rest in political and civil rights, so may any class or race when it shall incur the displeasure of its more powerful associates, and we may say farewell to the principles on which we commit our safety.[8]

Truman did not enjoy the same popularity as Roosevelt, nor was he as skilled in the art of persuasion. Consequently, when southern senators held up federal anti-poll tax and anti-lynching measures with filibusters and committee trickery, Truman kept his hands off Congress and civil rights measures died. Racial violence erupted in 1946, spurring a proposal from Attorney General Tom Clark that the president create a President's Committee on Civil Rights (PCCR). He deemed that a committee's work would "be of utmost value in the task of preserving and implementing our civil rights."[9] To counter the effect of African Americans who were leaving the Democratic party over its inaction on creating a permanent FEPC, Truman seized the opportunity to cut his losses and created the PCCR.

The committee's report, issued in 1947, challenged Truman's fence-sitting. Truman stood to lose southern support if he followed the committee's recommendations, and African American votes if he didn't. In either case he might not win the 1948 election. Miraculously, due to a third-party split, the following November Truman retained office.

123

In February 1948 based on the committee report, President Truman introduced the first comprehensive civil rights program ever presented to Congress. Truman proposed: to establish a Commission on Civil Rights, a Civil Rights Division in the Department of Justice, to adopt federal anti-lynching legislation, to protect the right to vote, to establish a Fair Employment Commission, to prohibit discrimination in interstate transportation, to grant statehood to Alaska and Hawaii (states with ethnic minority populations), to settle claims of Japanese Americans, to grant home rule and the right to vote in presidential elections in Washington, D.C., and to set up a joint Congressional Committee on Civil Rights.[10] Hopes of civil rights supporters were dashed by filibustering southern senators who stalled all congressional action on these civil rights issues, without any protest from Truman, until Truman left office. Methodist women, in an unprecedented move, published a list of Senate members and their positions on the compromise to change Senate rules to permit motions calling for an end to discussion and an immediate vote on motions as well as bills, and urged women to write to their senators.[11] Henry Wallace criticized Truman: "He talks glibly of 'equal opportunity' and 'equal treatment,' dodges always used to avoid action, but fails utterly to attack the heart of the matter—segregation."[12]

Ironically, Wallace's comments came two days after Truman authorized one of his most far-reaching civil rights provisions. Truman issued Executive Order 9981 which decreed that there should be no discrimination in the armed forces based on race, color, religion, or national origin. The order also created a President's Committee on Equality of Treatment and Opportunity in the Armed Forces to study and resolve problems of discrimination and segregation in the military. Moreover, racial inequality had not survived constitutional challenge.

The NAACP Legal Challenge to Segregation

Although the Fourteenth and Fifteenth Amendments to the U.S. Constitution protected the civil rights of American citizens regardless of race, the lack of enforcement of these provisions by lawmakers and government executives left the refinement and definition of civil rights to courts. This permitted state and private discrimination and segregation.

In 1935, starting with a grant of $10,000 from the Garland Fund, the NAACP began a legal campaign to overturn segregation. Charles Hamilton Houston, hired as legal counsel, viewed the monumental task before him as one of social engineering, the same term used by social gospel leaders who believed in using their skills to shape society. Houston counseled his law students to be "prepared to anticipate, guide and interpret group advancement; . . . [to be the] mouthpiece of the weak and a sentinel guarding against wrong; . . . [and to ensure that] the course of change is . . . orderly with a minimum of human loss and suffering. . . ."[13]

Houston advised the NAACP to focus its efforts on changes in education "[s]ince education is a preparation for the competition of life. . . ."[14] He argued that a racial group holds an inferior position in society if it is not educated.[15] For the next five years, Houston designed and led the legal program of the NAACP, deliberately choosing to use litigation as a means for educating and involving local people in cases of segregation and discrimination. Although a few cases might have established sufficient legal precedents for change, he worked with many local school desegregation cases as a way of turning the eyes of the nation toward racial problems and the debilitating effects of racism in this country.[16] Not surprisingly, with so many African Americans afraid of taking action, legal struggles and successes rallied courage and began to wear through layers of apathy. The choice of a patient, deliberate campaign gave time for poor whites, who possibly were most threatened by desegregation, to begin to discern "the logic and justice of the NAACP position" and reduce their resistance.[17]

The NAACP legal campaign for desegregation began with cases concerning specific instances of inequalities in teacher salaries, transportation of students to school, and opportunities for graduate and professional students. Local people joined the review of discriminatory practices, just as did the WMC, YMCA, and YWCA in the 1930s. The NAACP publication *Crisis* sponsored a photo contest for pictures illustrating discrimination in education. The NAACP, CIC, YWCA, and WMC sought to document inequalities in education and to press for equality of opportunity. Each discovery had potential for litigation over length of school year, pay for teachers, transportation, quality of building and equipment, or *per capita* expenditures. The legal campaign took years to build and process through the courts; but by the late 1940s the Supreme Court began to erode *Plessy v. Ferguson*, the "separate but equal" decision of 1896. For several decades, Charles Hamilton Houston or his former student and protegé, Thurgood Marshall, participated in or contributed arguments to most of the legal cases reaching the U.S. Supreme Court.

A number of African American challenges to racial laws originated outside of the NAACP. Labor unions sought redress for grievances, as did individuals. In some instances, local black communities chose persons to represent them as plaintiffs. As the legal challenges passed through state and federal court appeal systems, the NAACP's Legal Defense and Educational Fund provided recourse for advice and monetary support. Legal victories, however, did not assure nonviolence.

Leadership for Nonviolent Mobilization

In the U.S., a fascinating network developed and was composed of people who cultivated Gandhian teachings in youth, women's, and African American organizations. Methodists played a substantial role in expanding this network.

Founded in 1914 in England, the Fellowship of Reconciliation (FOR), an organization devoted to pacifism, began its work in the U.S. in 1915. It attracted ministers, students, teachers, YMCA and YWCA members, social workers, and people of many faiths "who recognize the essential unity of all humanity and who have joined together to explore the power of love and truth for resolving human conflict."[18] Between 1938 and 1945, membership tripled from five thousand to fifteen thousand. A. J. Muste, who held the post of executive secretary of FOR from 1940 to 1943, was succeeded by George Houser. Future CORE leaders Bayard Rustin and James Farmer, who connected potential for resolving the American racial struggle with Gandhian methods of nonviolence, joined FOR in the early 1940s.

As early as 1917, a series of African American leaders began to follow the actions and writings of Mohandas Gandhi in his South African campaign for an end to racial pass laws and apartheid laws, particularly those applied to people from India. By the 1930s, Gandhi's nonviolent freedom movement in India received regular attention in the American press. The African American press helped people of color identify with the struggle for racial quality both in South Africa and in India. Some African Americans likened their situation to that of the Untouchables. Mordecai Johnson, president of Howard University; W. E. B. DuBois, editor of NAACP's *The Crisis*; and Gordon B. Hancock held Gandhi in high esteem. Juliette Dericotte, Frank T. Wilson, Howard and Sue Thurman, and Edward and Phenola Carroll were among those who went to India to visit with Gandhi and discuss the application of *satyagraha*, direct action, noncooperation, and strategies of nonviolence to the specific African American situation in the U.S.[19]

Americans began comparing Gandhi's life and work to their understanding of the teachings and life of Jesus. Drusilla Dunjee Houston wrote, " . . . Gandhi may seem to have failed, but ultimately he has in his life and present power proved the mightiness that comes from following the teachings of Christ."[20] She and others linked the way of Gandhi with the way of Jesus.

Starting in the 1920s, Methodist women studied Gandhi's nonviolent movement and methods in South Africa and India in George Hayne's book, *The Trend of the Races*. The white American press of the 1940s provided enough information about India's campaign for independence that Methodist women related Gandhi's teachings, nonviolence, and their mission studies about race.

James Farmer, who led CORE for many years and applied Gandhi's methods in the U.S., grew up in Texas participating in youth camps and programs of the Methodist Episcopal Church (MEC). He first took interracial national leadership as a member of the National Council of Methodist Youth. After graduating from Wiley College in Texas in 1938, Farmer studied theology at Howard University. Dismayed by the segregated jurisdictional system of his church, newly merged as The Methodist Church, he decided not to become a minister.

Under Howard Thurman, who introduced him to Gandhian teachings on nonviolence, Farmer wrote his graduate thesis on the role of religion in preserving theories of racial dominance, discrimination, and segregation. He argued that certain Protestant teachings—especially the Calvinist distinctions between the elect and unelect transformed into superior and inferior races—became American perversions of theological thought that undergirded rationalizations for slavery. James Farmer resolved to destroy segregation.[21]

As a recent Howard University graduate who was steeped in the social gospel, Farmer was assigned in 1941 to the post of race relations secretary in the Chicago FOR regional office. When the interracial staff wanted housing or to eat out or to go roller skating, they faced discrimination and created experiments that tested the limits of segregation practices.

At a 1942 FOR meeting, Farmer proposed that FOR mount an organized and direct attack on "the evil practice of apartheid in America" because it tore apart both church and community along racial lines.[22] A. J. Muste moved that Farmer start a new organization whose purpose would be to apply pressure on segregated policies such as restrictive housing covenants, and FOR gave its assent.[23] A few weeks later, twenty-eight people began what may have been the first civil rights sit-in in the U.S. at a local Jack Spratt restaurant in Chicago.

The next few years proved to be times of trying and testing various nonviolent strategies for integration. Using carefully planned demonstrations, between 1943 and 1948 CORE successfully integrated several amusement parks, theaters, restaurants, and swimming pools in New Jersey, Denver, Detroit, Cleveland, and Los Angeles.

The 1946 Supreme Court decision prohibiting segregation on public interstate travel led to a FOR and CORE co-sponsored event to test its application, a 1947 freedom ride through the South. The freedom ride on Greyhound and Trailways buses prompted some arrests and gave national publicity to the use of nonviolent direct action in opposing racial discrimination.

Word of CORE's experiments and successes spread among law students at Howard University where Pauli Murray was the only woman in her class of '44. Murray belonged to FOR, had studied its literature on direct action, and was "eager to adapt Gandhian techniques to our own struggle. . . ."[24] In 1939, she had read about Gandhi in Krishnalal Shridharami's book *War Without Violence*.

Murray knew first-hand about discrimination. In 1938 the University of North Carolina, based on her race, rejected her for admission. Richmond police arrested her with a friend for sitting slightly forward of the rear of a bus in 1940. In the 1943–44 school year at Howard Law School, Murray was at the top of her class and met the requirements for receiving the title of chief justice of student government. However, because of her gender, Howard Law School refused to designate any student to receive the title, rather than award it to a woman. When she applied to Harvard Law School for advanced graduate study, the school denied her admission because she was a woman.[25] By 1945, Murray was nominated as one of the twelve outstanding women in American life by the National Council of Negro Women. Just two years later, while living in New York City and working for the American Civil Liberties Union (ACLU), Murray accepted an assignment from the Woman's Division to compile states' laws on race and color. While her legal research boosted the legal attack on segregation, economic and sociological research strengthened the work of organizations dedicated to changing race relations in the U.S.

The Southern Regional Council

Continuing with a focus on research and education similar to that of CIC, the SRC gave more power and voice to its African American members. A broad cross-section of African American and white educators, editors, and business leaders served on the Board of Directors. Dr.

Guy B. Johnson, the new executive director, represented the board's new commitments to economic and political issues in race relations. Two years later, Johnson was succeeded by George S. Mitchell. The seventy-eight-member board included Gordon B. Hancock, Charlotte Hawkins Brown, Jessie Daniel Ames, Will W. Alexander, Hodding Carter, Virginius Dabney, Charles S. Johnson, David D. Jones, Benjamin E. Mayes, Howard W. Odum, Ira De A. Reid, F. D. Patterson (president, Tuskegee Institute), Arthur J. Moore (bishop, The Methodist Church), Aubrey Williams (publisher, *Southern Farmer*), P. B. Young, Sr. (editor and publisher, *Norfolk Journal and Guide*), Rufus E. Clement (president of Atlanta University), and Grace Towns Hamilton (director of the Atlanta Urban League). Cora Ratliff was elected to the Board of Directors in 1948. In 1946 the board resolved to focus on "the enforcement of all laws designed to thwart or punish mob violence," and called on southern citizens and their religious, social, and civic institutions to create "a sound public opinion deeply antagonistic to organized bigotry and mob violence."[26]

In 1946, Dorothy Tilly, noted Methodist civic leader and tireless worker for cvil rights, was a field secretary for the SRC. She also was serving as North Georgia Conference Secretary for Christian Social Relations (CSR) of the Woman's Society of Christian Service (WSCS) and had just been appointed to serve on the President's Commmittee on Civil Rights (PCCR). Over two hundred people from sixty-five organizations and thirteen states gathered for SRC's Conference on Human Rights and World Order planned by Tilly. The meeting undergirded the anticipated PCCR report and "prepare[d] the leaders of women's organizations of the South to face clearly and understandingly that the 'denial of human rights to any group anywhere affects the peace and safety of all people everywhere.'"[27] Tilly's travels took her to Mississippi and Alabama in 1947, but she focused on Georgia where she worked with political factions torn by racial hatred, investigated lynchings, raised money, organized local committees, and led Atlanta's efforts to secure African American police officers. After a ten-day tour of Georgia that revealed the "heartaches and heart throbs of a State in trouble" she wrote, "I challenge the SRC to find the technique of making the fellowship so strong in the human heart of the South that no exploiter of hatred can invade it."

SRC gathered four hundred southern leaders in February 1948 to interpret and implement the provisions of the report of the PCCR. Thelma Stevens of the Woman's Division of The Methodist Church shared the platform with Turner Smith from the Department of Justice, James B. Carey of the CIO, Boris Shiskin of the AFL, Frances Williams who assisted Tom Clark of PCCR, and Ira De A. Reid, sociologist from Atlanta University. Stevens led a workshop on equality of opportunity.[28] The Southwide Meeting on Human and Civil Rights, whose sponsors were educational or religious in character, heard Paul Williams, the president of SRC say:

> [Our job is to bring] about in our home communities a habit of day to day operation of our community life in such a manner that men and women will have sure confidence in their rights to safety and citizenship and opportunity, and beyond that, even, in their rights to live without fear, in honorable and responsible relationships to their fellows.[29]

The meeting drafted a civil rights platform calling for training in civil rights for law enforcement officers, an end to the poll taxes and other barriers to voting, full citizenship for American Indians, equal opportunity for employment and advancement, a federal minimum wage law, and the end of segregation in all graduate and professional schools.[30]

The SRC, following up on investigations by members, staff, and sociologists such as Ralph Bunche, Gunnar Myrdal, Arthur Raper, Howard Odum, Ira De A. Reid, and Charles S. Johnson, began to publish data about African American voter registration in twelve southern states. Hard-core Alabama and Mississippi qualified only .9 and 1.2 percent, respectively, of African Americans of voting age. Georgia and Texas led the way in new African American voters registered. Between 1940 and 1947, Texas' rolls expanded from 30,000 to 100,000 and Georgia's increased from 20,000 to 125,000, or nearly 19 percent of eligible African American voters.[31]

Many factors colored the campaign for African American voting rights. The poll tax amount varied, as well as requirements for paying poll taxes for years prior to voter registration. Education, literacy, and property requirements varied from state to state. The level of fear created by intimidation and violence around registration varied from one community to another. Official abolition of the white primary in 1944 encouraged voter registration, although states found ways to circumvent the federal courts.[32] In the 1940s, SRC efforts to increase African American power at the polls focused on making changes in state and federal laws.

SRC used sociological research to document needs in the South, to educate leaders, to provide evidence for litigation before the Supreme Court, and to guide plans for change and development. Through the late 1940s SRC also tracked inequities by race in education, patterns of violent racial crimes, and the entrance of African American men and women into law enforcement.[33]

The SRC took advantage of the fact that women still faced doors closed to many opportunities. Much of the day-to-day work of meetings and local organizing for change was accomplished by women. The Council gave wide press coverage to the work of churchwomen, especially Methodist women, who were the largest and best organized group among predominantly white liberal churches.

A letter provides one example of the relationship between Methodist women and the SRC. Inez S. White of Petersburg, secretary of Christian Social Relations and Local Church Activities of the Florida Conference WSCS wrote to Margaret Price of SRC:

> Attached you will find clippings which tell their own story. We thought we had things going nicely for a Negro beach, the papers got hold of it, property owners protested and now it looks as though we might have to start over again.
>
> Add to your list of towns using Negro police—Punta Gorda. They have one man—not in uniform. I just recently learned this. This makes the total of Florida towns thirteen according to my records —without St. Petersburg or Jacksonville. . . . Jacksonville undoubtedly will have them soon according to the women working on it up there.
>
> I am making a check now of Negro beaches. It is pitiful with our one thousand miles of coast and countless lakes that there are so very, very few places a Negro can swim. I have given Negro police and bathing beaches to my Methodist women as a project this quarter. [I] [t]hink they will get things started.
>
> I shall probably meet you next month. I expect to attend your Civil Rights Conference. Am looking forward to both very, very much.
>
> Am still boosting for SRC. Everywhere I spoke in February at our W.S.C.S. Seminars I boosted SRC and gave out membership cards. Hope a few of them get mailed in.[34]

In the 1940s organized churchwomen provided substantial leadership that effected change in the attitudes and climate of local communities. They were aided by an unofficial Methodist organization.

The Methodist Federation for Social Service

While bishops of The Methodist Church turned their attention to issues of world peace during this decade dominated by World War II, the Methodist Federation for Social Service (MFSS) gave prominent

131

attention to racial issues. Founded in 1907 by pastors, educators, and social workers affiliated with the MEC, the Methodist Federation for Social Service aimed to make the principles and teachings of Jesus real and effective in the life of a church and society that had grown numb to cries of social pain. Harry F. Ward, as executive secretary, led the Federation from 1911 to 1943.

The Federation had a long history of representing the reconstructionist wing of the social gospel movement. It believed that many social problems could be addressed if institutions would make substantive changes. In 1919 members of the MFSS investigated Pittsburgh Steel Company. Striking steel workers objected to a sixty-eight hour work week. They demanded a shorter work week and better working conditions.

During the 1930s depression, MFSS studied economic conditions and theories. The MFSS publication, *Social Service Bulletin*, viewed strikes by southern textile workers (usually female, mostly African Americans) as representative of a class struggle in which "the churches of the South were the captives of the mill owners."[35]

The Federation had opposed provisions for racial segregation in the 1939 merger that created The Methodist Church. With segregation in the church an accomplished fact, MFSS set out to desegregate its own organization and work for the extension of human rights beyond racial barriers.[36] David D. Jones, president of Bennett College and husband of Susie Jones, was elected to the governing Executive Committee in 1939. Within the next eight years, MFSS took increasingly forthright actions on racial issues. Promptly, MFSS went on record demanding passage of the anti-lynching bill that was then before Congress and expressing concern for educational and religious needs of tenant farmers.[37]

Mary McLeod Bethune, who had headed the Division of Negro Affairs of the National Youth Administration, joined the Executive Committee in 1940, bringing tremendous knowledge and influence to the Federation, as well as African American presence. Thus Bethune held office in MFSS and in the Department of Christian Social Relations of the Woman's Division, while the Jones family divided the leadership between husband and wife and between MFSS and the Woman's Division. David and Susie Jones probably discussed their work on racial and civil rights issues, comparing notes between the two organizations and sharing good ideas with one another.

There were differences between the two organizations. On the whole, MFSS dealt more with economic issues while the Woman's Division paid closer attention to the particular needs of women. The

Federation made bolder public pronouncements while the women held more meetings with interracial contacts.

The MFSA publication, *Social Questions Bulletin* (*SQB*) presented a feature article on "Negro Methodists and Their Problems" in April 1940 based on information provided by David D. Jones. Jones discussed the suspicion and fear bred by segregation in the church. He protested against the emotional and psychological damage done by segregation which established two classes of citizenship. The *SQB* informed Federation members about current federal legislation, including the Civil Rights Act (H.R. 8896) that proposed to desegregate all public transportation and places of public accommodation in the District of Columbia. MFSS opposed segregation in the military and urged members to endorse the Wagner-Steagall Housing Act that provided low-income housing benefits for people regardless of race.[38]

The *SQB* gave coverage to prominent African American civil rights leaders. Roy Wilkins, assistant secretary of the NAACP, in 1941 wrote a guest article for the *SQB* describing segregation and discrimination in the armed services, industry, labor, and national defense industries, as well as the barriers to voting. A year later, Wilkins provided an extensive report of the federal investigations into discriminatory practices in defense industries made in compliance with Executive Order 8802.[39] The NAACP received more coverage in the *SQB* than any other group working for civil rights.

Methodist women reported to the Federation about their social action work in a guest article written by Thelma Stevens in 1942. The curt list of their projects in race relations and civil rights dwarfed reports of Federation activities on racial issues in proportion to the difference between a few thousand members of MFSS and 1,200,000 members of the Women's Societies.[40]

MFSS took more radical positions and actions than did the Department of CSR/LCA of the Woman's Division. In 1943, MFSS sent staff member Charles C. Webber to Virginia to help the Amalgamated Clothing Workers of America organize white and African American workers into one union. Clothing factories, required by law to pay 32.5 cents per hour, were getting around the rule by paying 25 cents as a learner's wage for three weeks, then laying off workers. Those re-hired had to start over again at 25 cents. Webber found that the industry misled workers by claiming that wages were frozen and that collective bargaining was useless. Webber had obtained reports from the Office of War Information, which provided the accurate information that "Wages are stabilized, not *frozen*. To freeze wages would be to freeze injustices. . . ." This proved useful in publicizing the industry's disregard for the living standards of its workers. Threatened by the Ku Klux Klan, Webber persisted in organizing. Resistance centered in churches when the City Council refused to allow workers to meet on city property.[41]

A group of five Alabama pastors who belonged to MFSS joined together to write a series of essays intended to persuade Methodists that to be faithful to the gospel and ethical principles of Christianity, the church needed to be "more representative of the common man in agriculture and industry." Given their southern setting, their discussion had implications across racial lines for applied economic theory and churches. They declared:

> The Social Creed of our church does not hedge on our responsi-
> bility to the worker. The share-cropper in the country has his
> companion in the industrial town or city, for a clock-puncher is
> strangely related to a sharecropper and very likely moved in from
> the country.[42]

In different ways, the SRC, MFSS, and the WSCS all made commitments to work to meet human economic needs, being well aware that discrimination contributed to poverty, lack of education, and lynching.

The resignation of Harry F. Ward presented an identity crisis to the Methodist Federation. Members discussed the purpose, viability, and direction of the organization. MFSS represented an unpopular radical voice within Methodism. Reorganizing as the Methodist Federation for Social Action (MFSA) and taking a membership loss, the organization continued and pressed on with its commitment to racial inclusiveness in issue analysis and membership.[43] As terms of office expired, new leaders joined the executive committee. Mary McLeod Bethune and David D. Jones retained office for another four years and were joined by Thelma Stevens, who was elected secretary. The addition of Stevens strengthened the connection between Methodist women and MFSA. A few months later Stevens wrote about these links:

> The history of the Methodist Federation for Social Service reveals
> conclusively that the organization has always launched out ahead
> and dared to present needs and facts that were sometimes "taboo"
> and usually not very popular with the general church constitu-
> ency.[44]

Stevens, who admired courageous, forward-thinking leadership, appreciated the work of the Federation even when, a few years later, she resigned her public position under pressures of the McCarthy era in order to retain the coalition of public support needed for her own work. Stevens believed that the Federation could engage in federal legislative research and research in areas of social tension, "gleaning facts" and "interpreting them in terms of *church responsibility*." She added, "*These should be used extensively by Methodist women and other groups as basic study and action material.*"[45]

The Federation boldly took a new step in 1945 by electing Bishop Brooks as its first African American president. Jack McMichael, the new executive secretary chosen in 1944, maintained close contact with the SRC, exchanging information needed for anti-lynching work, educating the PCCR, and lobbying for the passage of civil rights legislation in Congress.[46]

A growing band of organizations supported each other in working for justice. The new 1940s network of organizations working closely together now included the Woman's Division of The Methodist Church, the MFSS, and the SRC. In turn, these relied on leadership from the NAACP, FOR, and CORE, and all put pressure on the Truman administration and Congress for federal action in critical areas of civil rights. Methodists were also dealing with their own organizational segregation and discrimination.

Segregation in The Methodist Church

At the 1938 General Conference of the MEC, 250 African American leaders met to protest the provisions for segregation and creation of a Central Jurisdiction that were part of the 1939 merger. Thirty-three of the forty-four official African American delegates decided to protest the Plan of Unification. David D. Jones spoke for them. The piety that couched the plan made it one of the ugliest forms of segregation. Segregation, he said, "sets them [some people] aside, it labels them, it says that they are not fit to be treated as other people are treated." Jones expected white church leaders to be able to understand and agree when African American church leaders objected to segregation.[47] Bishop Robert E. Jones, who was the brother of David Jones; Bishop Matthew W. Clair; and Mary McLeod Bethune voiced opposition to the plan for segregation. Among liberal white opponents to the merger plan, the WMC was most vocal. They believed that the whole church must cross racial boundaries in performing the common tasks of Christian mission:

> We believe that such a Methodist connectionalism transcending
> race and nation and economic class will be better able to create in
> us the mind which was in Christ Jesus who taught us of one God

135

who is the Father of all and in whom we are all brothers one of another.[48]

African Americans confronted a larger majority who had decided on northern/southern unity based on racial segregation, and overrode the negative votes of the African American annual conferences. Dr. Albert C. Knudson, a leading white ethicist from Boston University School of Theology, argued that God intentionally created different races. A vote against the merger was a vote of prejudice.

A study by Peter Carlisle Murray of The Methodist Church's efforts to become more racially inclusive indicated little action being taken in the 1940s by the denomination as a whole. Hospitality in Kansas City for the 1944 General Conference was segregated. Since restaurants refused to serve African American delegates, a room in the convention center was hastily converted into a dining hall and the bishops apologized to the delegates. Yet, overall, "attention to racial matters paid by the Methodist church as a whole" was "slight" except for the Central Jurisdiction, which was "very much involved in the struggle. . . ."[49]

In the late 1940s, Dwight Culver engaged in research for his doctoral dissertation, published in 1953 as *Negro Segregation in The Methodist Church*.[50] Culver found in 1946 that only four of sixty-seven reporting Methodist-related homes for the elderly and children claimed to have any African American residents. Half of the sixty-seven had no established policies regarding employment of minorities. Five hospitals related to The Methodist Church refused services to African Americans, even in emergencies.[51] Only three of forty-eight nursing schools in white Methodist hospitals had African American students enrolled.[52]

Culver examined local churches that were predominantly white but attended by some African Americans, as well as white-only congregations, and studied white attitudes about race. He found that formerly African American neighborhoods in racial transition had inclusive churches, while white neighborhoods in racial transition held firm racial barriers in their congregations. Some predominantly white churches welcomed African Americans and voted to accept members regardless of race, but most white churches made no conscious effort to be racially inclusive.[53]

Churches that did welcome people regardless of race had two strengths to offer the movement for social change. They provided pockets of hope where people voluntarily mingled across racial lines, and they acted out of faith, two important unifying factors.

Church, State, and Social Change

Methodists actively participated in the life of the nation through a niche carved out by a network of voluntary organizations. They gave significant leadership to the emerging civil rights movement acting on the basis of commitments to broadly conceived religious arguments, belief in democracy, reliance on the legal system and the U.S. Constitution, affirmation of the goodness of human nature and the ability of people to learn and change, and the conviction that violence could be ended. African American leaders engineered and guided interracial organizations and federal programs in unprecedented challenges to segregation.

Using the power of volunteers and organizational networks, Methodist women claimed a high moral ground in the 1940s that helped shape national attitudes about segregation. This high moral ground undergirded Methodist women as they set out to create a new social order without racial barriers based on the teachings of Jesus.

The church should be the agency to set the pace in *interpreting* the revolution in the United States in terms of a Christian world order of changed attitudes and practical action—*where the traditional practice of segregation and discrimination against minorities either racial, religious, or cultural groups, will be superseded by equality of opportunity in all phases of life, and unhampered freedom of movement and communication of all peoples without fear of physical, mental, or spiritual intimidation.*

—*Journal*
Annual Report of the Woman's Division
(December 1944), 189

CHAPTER 8

The Early 1940s:
Toward a New Social Order

In 1940 the Department of Christian Social Relations and Local Church Activities (CSR/LCA) of the Woman's Division established its purpose: to "seek to make real and effective the teachings of Jesus as applied to individual, class, racial, and national relationships."[1] This purpose gave Thelma Stevens the position and portfolio she needed to help Methodist women organize and lead their organization, church, and nation in a campaign for civil rights. Spurred to action by the teachings of Jesus, the social gospel, and by moral principles of human dignity and equality, Methodist women took responsibility for the reform of social institutions that failed to live up to the principles Jesus taught and lived.

Using the Bible and the Declaration of Independence as guides, Methodist women gradually developed an understanding of human rights that encompassed far more than civil rights. Once committed to protecting and working for human rights, decisions to support racial equality followed. They engaged in mission studies on the theme of race, made social pronouncements, trained leaders to deal with racial issues, and began to find ways that biblical teachings called them to change their attitudes. Ideologically and politically, they laid a religious foundation for the civil rights movement.

Following the Teachings and Example of Jesus

The Woman's Division of Christian Service of the Board of Missions of The Methodist Church was nothing short of ambitious as it set as its objective in the 1940s to create a new social order, a world in which people would be treated fairly, where there would be no artificial barriers of race, and where people could live in peace. Quoting Walter

139

Rauschenbusch, a pioneer in the social gospel movement whose writings had led Methodist women into fields of social action, the Woman's Division adopted a resolution in 1943 calling for Christians to work toward the formation of a new world order as a way of eliminating many of the world's evils: "We do not want to blow our existing institutions to atoms, but we do want to remold every one of them."[2]

With a budget of $15,000 to pay one executive staff member and two secretaries, cover rent and travel expenses, and run its program, the tiny New York office of the Department of CSR/LCA seemed an unlikely place for an important part of the civil rights movement to emerge. The Woman's Division gave uninformed approval to the department's first program. Division members, still meeting in an extended session at about 2:40 a.m. at its first annual meeting on November 28, 1940, were so exhausted with hearing reports that Mrs. W. Raymond Brown, one of the most conservative of the members of the Woman's Division, moved that the report of the Department of CSR/LCA be adopted without being read." The next morning when the women reconvened and found out what they had approved, some members were appalled to find that they did not agree with the report's declaration: "There is a clarion call to Christians in the United States to combat all forms of intolerance against minorities. . . ." Other controversial items filled the report. Nevertheless, with the report officially approved, the Department of CSR/LCA set out to work for the rights of minorities.[4]

To undertake the task of interpreting the teachings of Jesus to their mid-twentieth-century generation the Woman's Division used the authority of their community of faith and the principles of democratic society. Women invoked the authority of the community of faith to appeal to religious institutions at the same time they summoned language about democracy to shape the attitudes and actions of the broader society. Unlike efforts of the radical religious right in the 1990s, the Woman's Division interpreted the teachings of Jesus in terms of social principles which could guide the actions of Christians, rather than prescribe moral behavior.

One of the greatest gifts that Methodist women brought to the network and coalition of national organizations working on civil rights in the 1940s was their grounding in biblical, theological, and ethical thinking. The same gift had its drawbacks, for often, out of respect for religious diversity, Methodist women never named in secular settings the religious motivations behind their thousands of hours of volunteer work.

From the outset, the Department of CSR/LCA based its work on ethical foundations. The department presumed that its perspective was

Christian and that in seeking to express Christian opinion, its judgments were guided by the "teachings of Jesus" and its goal was to make these teachings "real and effective." Since members of The Methodist Church took vows promising to "receive and profess the Christian faith as contained in the New Testament of our Lord Jesus Christ," the broad guideline appealed to all who had taken this church membership vow. Thelma Stevens, executive secretary of the Department of CSR/LCA, believed that everything Jesus said and did demonstrated God's impartial justice for all people. Peace accompanied justice. Jesus instructed his followers to carry on his work. The task of Christians was to translate Jesus' message into actions. Stevens claimed that three devastating evils stood in the way of building a new world. These evils were "powers that oppress," "walls that divide," and "wars that destroy."[5]

Mission study books used by Methodist women, written by church leaders and scholars at the invitation of the Woman's Division, noted that Jesus treated all people with respect and love because they were persons loved by God. Every person deserved to be well fed and to have "a just share of the necessities and comforts of daily living."[6] Jesus, who moved freely across social lines and classes, associated with disciples and followers and ate meals with common people, bartenders, Samaritans, tax collectors, sinners, rich persons, and religious leaders. Members of privileged religious and social groups of Jesus' day were infuriated by this behavior. Yet Methodist women held up Jesus as an example for contemporary living.

Finding Moral Principles

The "teachings of Jesus" remained general and not specific for Methodist women because leaders assumed that Jesus provided moral guidelines and principles rather than a code of laws prescribing Christian behavior. Albert Knudson, a former professor and dean of Boston University School of Theology and leading Christian social ethicist of the 1940s, noted that since scripture casts the teachings of Jesus in specific times and places, Jesus' moral principles needed to be reinterpreted by and for each generation.[7] For Knudson, Jesus' motives in dealing with other people set a universal example because of the "quality or spirit of [Jesus'] life as a whole." Methodist women did not aspire to follow only one specific teaching of Jesus, but rather found in Jesus' life and teachings the love of God interpreted as a life they desired

141

to emulate. Methodist women assumed that part of the church's mission was to serve as moral critic and teacher of contemporary culture using the teachings of Jesus as a guide.

Use of an ethical methodology which appealed to a higher moral law helped Methodist women choose their path between conflicting moral principles. Moral presumptions establish a basic commitment to principles which are given priority until strong evidence indicates that another principle has greater weight. For example, Methodist women presumed not only that democracy was a superior form of government but also that the Woman's Division should use democratic methods, hear the opinions of minorities expressed, and find ways to include minority women in committee work and leadership. For Methodist women the right of all Americans to vote took precedence over state laws which restricted the ballot by use of discriminatory laws and poll taxes.

When discrepancies arose, the Woman's Division urged Methodist women to assess the customs of culture or the teachings of their own church in the light of the teachings of Jesus which they presumed had greater authority. When either the church or the nation failed to live up to the principles it espoused, Methodist women assumed that it was their responsibility and that of every member or citizen to reform the practices of the institution. Principles of love, justice, human dignity, and equality had priority over racial supremacy, racial purity, and segregation because God loved all people and all were "God's children." For Thelma Stevens, the identity of persons as human beings created by God, who as individuals and members of community find wholeness and fulfillment in relation to God and to each other, inherently qualifies them to be treated with care, fairness, and respect.

Scripture provided the source for the ethical principles of Methodist women as well as for Jesus who often quoted the Hebrew Bible. The prophets Isaiah (55:12; 65:25) and Micah (4:1-4) claimed that when God's rule of justice was established on earth people would live in peace. Widows and orphans would have adequate provisions and no one would go hungry (Jer. 31:12-14; Is. 65:17-23). People would not deceive one another, cheat, rob, or kill, but instead would worship God by doing what was righteous (Amos 5:21-24). The heart of Jesus' understanding of his mission, cited by Thelma Stevens as "Isaiah's call for peace and justice," came from the prophet Isaiah:

> The Spirit of the Lord is upon me,
> because he has anointed me
>   to preach good news to the poor.

He has sent me to proclaim release
    to the captives
and recovering of sight to the blind,
to set at liberty those who are
    oppressed,
to proclaim the acceptable year of
    the Lord.

—Luke 4:18-19. See Isaiah 61:1-2.[8]

The Woman's Division relied on the Social Creed,[9] a statement adopted by the General Conference of the Methodist Episcopal Church in 1908 (and modified over the years) to guide Methodists in relating to social issues. The Social Creed established the teachings of the New Testament, the spirit of Christ, and "law of love" of God and neighbor as principles central to resolving problems of the social order. Asserting that human rights transcend racial barriers, in 1940 Methodists officially claimed: "We stand for the rights of racial groups, and insist that the above social, economic, and spiritual principles apply to all races alike."[10] The 1908 creed affirmed the responsibility of the whole Christian church for the "great moral concerns of humanity."

The Department of Christian Social Relations also extracted authority for combatting racism from statements issued by the Federal Council of Churches and from the World Council of Churches (WCC).[11] The Federal Council of Churches (FCC), a council of major Protestant denominations in the United States, and the WCC, composed of Protestant and Orthodox Christian groups, issued statements representing the cumulative reflections of these religious traditions and the consensus of religious leaders. In 1946, before most churches acknowledged their own participation in segregation or called for an end to its practice, the FCC vowed to work for "a non-segregated Church and a non-segregated society."[12]

The Woman's Division shaped denominational policies on race. They submitted memorials to General Conferences for consideration and addition to the *Discipline* of The Methodist Church. A statement of the Woman's Division on "The Christian Church and Race," added to the *Discipline* in 1948, proclaimed that racial discrimination violated "the Christian belief in the fatherhood of God, the brotherhood of man, and the Kingdom of God" and identified it as "unchristian" and "evil."[13] Once the General Conference had spoken for the denomination, the Woman's Division cited these interpretations of moral principles.

143

Guidance from the Social Sciences

Methodist women relied on developments in psychology and sociology to aid their interpretations of human rights and race relations. Psychological studies of prejudice provided academic credentials to support the struggle against racial bigotry and segregation. Psychological studies also were beginning to report the damage done by segregation to children's attitudes of self-worth.[14] Leaders of the Woman's Division kept abreast of studies of prejudice in children in the 1930s and added to their own mission study books and publications information about racial prejudice. In 1944 Gunnar Myrdal's book, *An American Dilemma*, gave credence to the voices of African American leaders and educators as well as ordinary African American people who objected to the prejudices and inequities they experienced daily. As a Swedish sociologist, economist, and guest in the United States, Myrdal received reliable information from African American scholars about the broad scope of racial problems.

Myrdal posed a conflict between the country's aspirations to be a moral nation governed by law and order and the harsh realities present in the subordinate position of African Americans. Myrdal dismissed the popular explanation Americans often gave that they did not adhere to the ideals of the Constitution, and proposed that Americans actually take seriously the "American Creed," a dynamic corpus of national values, and debate earnestly the moral problems of the nation.[15] Myrdal proceeded to report on migration, the economy, southern agriculture, industrial employment, housing segregation, aspects of African American culture, the African American church, and social trends in such detail that he undercut the racial doctrine of "separate but equal."[16]

Concern for Democratic Principles and Human Rights

Since foundational American documents such as the Declaration of Independence espoused ethical principles also derived from biblical sources, for Methodist women the difference in interpretation between Christian principles and democratic principles centered on the expression of qualities of love and mercy applied to the administration of justice and equality. Methodist women's 1952–53 study of Fred Brownlee's book, *These Rights We Hold*, powerfully shaped their claim to religious grounding in democratic principles. Love meant concern and genuine caring for all people, even one's enemies. Biblical language anchored the value of human life in relation to God and espoused universal ethical principles. Democratic language, the language of discourse about the rights and obligations of persons, discussed ethical principles in terms of rights.[17] Equal rights implied both equitable treatment and participation in decision-making. Stevens embraced empowerment but feared power "unless its direction and use are oriented toward achieving and protecting rights and freedoms of humankind. . . ."[18]

Human Rights

Americans widely discussed democracy in the context of World War II and post-war years, and differences in emphasis emerged. Leaders concerned with race relations and discrimination capitalized on the nation's concerns for the preservation of political democracy and peace. In 1940, when The Methodist Church affirmed that "the United States should remain in a position to preserve democracy within its own borders . . . ,"[19] the Department of CSR/LCA challenged Methodist women to extend these same values and concerns to the area of human rights at home and abroad.[20] By definition, democracy is participatory, yet within the United States African American citizens were denied equal participation in many arenas, including the armed services. African American combatants in segregated military regiments returned from France, only to be denied the freedoms for which they had risked their lives, such as the right to vote, to buy a home of their choice, or to work where they desired.

Many church leaders, having watched World War II erupt so soon after World War I, now believed that a lasting peace was not possible wherever injustice prevailed. In the post-war period, organized Methodist women appealed for the kind of human relationships needed in a peaceful new world order calling for a generous and caring spirit in each local community.

The time had come to construct a new social order for the nations of the world, an order in which racial equality helped make peace possible. Widespread concern for a lasting peace contributed to the dream of an international organization where leaders of nations could sit down together, discuss their problems, and resolve conflicts with the assistance of a world court. The principle of racial equality constituted a basic component of this dream, central to the notion that leaders of nations might negotiate as equals.

In 1944, the Woman's Division supported the formation of the United Nations founded on racial equality. They adopted a resolution urging "That in the final draft of the charter for collaboration of the United Nations the principle of racial equality be recognized. . . ."[21] The United Nations, formed in 1945, adopted in 1947 the Universal Declaration of Human Rights which became a master charter for race relations work among Methodist women.

The Woman's Division's history illustrates how African American women and white women took vital concepts of democracy and Christian tradition, which in powerful ways excluded them, and broadened the use of these terms in the American experience to make them more inclusive. As soon as they could articulate new developments in their understandings of human rights, they began to voice them in the public arena.

Position Statements on Race in the Early 1940s

A Methodist women's conference held in 1942 and three documents shaped new commitments to work for civil rights. The conference and documents built on the 1938 New Year's weekend interracial conference, held at Paine College, which had set the tone for an interracial agenda for the Department of CSR/LCA. Susie Jones, from Bennett College in Greensboro, had brought ideas from the 1938 conference into the work of the Department's Committee on Minority Groups and Interracial Co-operation.

Once again, Susie Jones was the moving force behind the call in 1942 for a conference on "The Status of Minority Groups in a Christian Democracy." Mary McLeod Bethune, Louise Young, and other prominent members of the Woman's Division gave active support.[22] The conference, which piggy-backed on the annual meeting of the Woman's Division held in Cleveland, for a full day engaged women in discussion of race, "the most pressing issue on the national scene."[23] The conference, which stimulated Methodist women's commitments around racial issues for the rest of the decade, affirmed that Methodist women would "accept our responsibility for the making of public opinion as it relates to members of minority groups."[24]

The conference generated many positive responses. White women present committed themselves to work toward the redress of minority problems and vowed to eliminate inequities. Methodist women who had not attended the conference studied the outcomes. For many years afterwards, Methodist women held training sessions on human relations at annual meetings.[25] The Woman's Division sent a recommendation to the directors of the Rosenwald Fund, (which was then directing millions of dollars into public education for southern African Americans), encouraging them to prepare school instructional materials which were inclusive of the life and customs of diverse cultural groups.

146

Methodist women saw that racial issues were the same, whether people were Japanese Americans or African Americans. Discriminatory social policies treated persons as members of a racial group rather than dealing with people according to individual character or behavior. The round-up of Japanese Americans which began in 1942 spurred the Woman's Division of Christian Service to become one of the first groups in the nation to oppose this new national policy. The women offered humanitarian aid and opposed discrimination:

> Recognizing the complexity of the issues involved, we affirm our conviction that the Japanese living in the United States should be given the same treatment as that accorded to Germans and Italians, namely, the taking into custody of politically dangerous individuals rather than general internment on a racial basis. We are led to this judgment by our concern for both political and Christian democracy.[26]

By 1943 the Department of CSR/LCA connected peacemaking with working for justice in the local community. Thelma Stevens wrote, "Methodist women face grave situations in this time of global warfare. The nature of peacemaking is clarified if we see that it begins at home, that it involves 'the presence of justice' in one's local community." In underscoring the responsibility of Christians to work for a new world order Stevens placed an emphasis on local action and empowerment of local women through the local church. She wrote, "THE LOCAL CHURCH WOMAN HAS THE KEY TO THE LARGER COMMUNITY when she remembers that her neighbors are not determined by geographical location, social status, race, religion, or cultural patterns, but by common interests and needs."[27]

Because the United States stood for a democratic way of life, the treatment of minorities was a source of constant embarrassment. The same inconsistency and embarrassment appeared in The Methodist Church's policies. Previously criticism of segregation and racial inequality had come from African American Methodists, but now it began to come from within the church, from the Woman's Division.

On many occasions in annual reports or monthly columns of *The Methodist Woman*, Thelma Stevens pointed to conflicts between what people did and what they said they believed.[28] Methodist women agreed that they could not recommend major social changes to other institutions when their own house was not in order.[29] They recognized that Methodism's jurisdictional system accepted and did not challenge the principle of segregation.[30] By 1943 the Woman's Division pointed to segregated jurisdictions as a concrete example of church life contradictory to Jesus' teachings.

Thelma Stevens, a voracious reader of books, newspapers, and articles concerning the church, theology, and social issues, helped Methodist women understand the relationship of justice, rights for minorities, and a peaceful social order. She shared timely resolutions and declarations by other organizations which had a bearing on the work of the Woman's Division. In three successive years she reprinted significant public documents in *The Methodist Woman.*

The 1943 "Interfaith Declaration on World Peace" linked world peace, world order, the rights of the oppressed and of minorities. The document itemized points critical to maintaining world peace, including securing the rights of minorities, and concluded that moral law must govern and be justly administered.[31]

The next year, Stevens reprinted "Nine Freedoms," a call for social commitments to fair pay; to adequate food, clothing, shelter and medical care; to economic security; and to "equality before the law, with equal access to justice in fact."[32] The United States was unwilling or reluctant to make these commitments.

In 1945, Stevens explored the dynamics of lasting social change. She drew from a statement of the 1938 Madras Conference, a worldwide ecumenical Christian gathering. Because attitudes and assumptions pass from generation to generation through social institutions, customs, and laws, the Madras Conference claimed lasting change would not be brought about *"unless you organize those changed individuals into collective action in a wide-scale frontal attack upon those corporate evils."*[33] Changes in American understandings of civil rights required not only new ideas, but also new ways of living out these values in community.

Leadership Training

Thelma Stevens believed that the first step toward building a peaceful, racially inclusive new social order is to reform the present order to reflect the new values. To this end she helped the Department launch a series of leadership training events called District Institutes, planned and led by committees whose membership overlapped conference and racial boundaries. Stevens suggested that interracial planning would generate more wisdom about what would serve the needs of all the Methodist women in the geographical area. Stevens instructed her white officers to issue invitations to Methodist women of non-white groups so that they could <u>participate fully on the same basis</u> as everyone else.

To encourage reflection and action on cutting-edge issues the Department of CSR/LCA initiated national seminars, first held every summer in the 1940s, and later held every two, then every four years. Several weeks in length, a national seminar provided approximately forty persons with an in-depth look at one major social issue. National seminars developed recommendations for action which were directed to the Woman's Division and The Methodist Church. Jurisdictional leadership training, shorter in duration and regionally located, provided training for conference and jurisdictional leaders who then held conference leadership training events for district and local officers.

Under the leadership of Thelma Stevens, <u>national seminars</u> became places where creative leaders of Methodist women studied social policies, identified problems, and set directions in which they wanted to lead both Methodist women and The Methodist Church as a whole. <u>In racially mixed settings the process of open discussion enabled prejudiced assumptions to be re-examined</u> and challenged while women <u>lived and ate together.</u>

In 1946 at DePauw University the national seminar participants agreed that segregation which existed within the denomination provided a <u>central conflict with the church's own teachings.</u> They believed that the creedal statement which had been adopted by the General Conference had greater claim than the church's own discriminatory laws. <u>Methodist women faced heavy opposition</u> from people who counted on upholding segregation laws and traditions.

Rising Pressure for Local Change

Bastions of <u>segregation proved resistant.</u> Lillian Smith, the editor of *South Today*, and a Methodist, published statements which illustrate the entrenched resistance to desegregation that the Woman's Division faced from noted southern leaders. During the 1946 filibuster over the formation of the Fair Employment Practices Commission, Senator Richard Russell said, " . . . <u>But we will resist to the bitter end</u>, whatever the consequences, any measure or any movement which would have a tendency to bring about social equality and intermingling and amalgamation of the races in our states."[34] Hodding Carter, liberal editor of the Greenville, Mississippi, *Delta Democrat-Times*, wrote in 1948, "I cannot emphasize one point too strongly. The white South is as united

149

as 30,000,000 people can be in its insistence upon segregation."[35] Reflecting on these statements Lillian Smith asked, "Why will not Christian ministers in the South—with the exception of a valiant handfull—preach against [segregation]?"[36]

Top leaders of Methodist women read and were influenced by the work of Lillian Smith, noted author of a 1944 novel, *Strange Fruit*, which was banned in the South. Lillian Smith articulated for her generation, born at the turn of the twentieth century, the childhood awareness that motivated rare individuals to work for change:

> Even its children knew that the South was in trouble. . . . Some learned to screen out all except the soft and the soothing; others denied even as they saw plainly, and heard. . . . The children knew this "trouble" was bigger than they, bigger than their family, bigger than their church, so big that people turned away from its size. They had seen it flash out and shatter a town's peace, and had felt it tear up all they believed in. . . .

> This haunted childhood belongs to every southerner of my age. We ran away from it but we came back like a hurt animal to its wound or a murderer to the scene of his sin. The human heart does not stay away too long from that which hurt it most. . . .

> I learned to cheapen with tears and sentimental talk of "my old mammy" one of the profound relationships of my life. I learned the bitterest thing a child can learn: that the human relations I valued most were held cheap by the world I lived in."[37]

In 1942 African American women of the Central Jurisdiction gathered at the school of missions held at Gulfside, Mississippi, and offered guidance and counsel to show the Woman's Division how to work to end discrimination in public facilities. Although the Woman's Division asked Methodist women to work for an end to discrimination, most Methodist women did not intend to desegregate public facilities.[38] Instead they heard the appeal to end discrimination as an invitation to make facilities equal. Nevertheless, the Department of CSR/LCA asked women of the Central Jurisdiction to lead Methodist women in working for the elimination of discrimination.

In both public and private ways Methodist women took steps indicative of their commitments. One group persuaded their state legislature to appropriate $50,000 for scholarship aid for African American students. Another secured a Rosenwald library for a local school. Thelma Stevens challenged: "In all areas of life women should seek to integrate minority groups into the larger life of the community, beginning with our own church institutions for minority groups."[39]

Black
Leadership

150

Gradually the attitudes of Methodist women changed. To provide models for courageous witness the Committee on Interracial and Intercultural Relations of the Department of CSR/LCA gathered stories and published them in *The Methodist Woman*. A brief vignette shows the growing edge of white Methodist women's attitudes.

> A Negro was protesting the effort of a bus driver to make him move to the rear seat. He cited the recent decision of the Supreme Court, adding that he would bring suit against the bus company.

> A white lady who heard the altercation handed the colored man her calling card and in a quiet voice said, "I will be glad to serve as a witness." The driver took his seat and continued the trip.[40]

Methodist women were clear about their focus. They were helping to bring in a new social order based on the teachings and example of Jesus, on moral and democratic principles. They were learning from the social sciences and speaking their mind to church and society. They were taking leadership in church and community. The new social order was beginning locally.

In his book *Raising Up a Prophet, The African-American Encounter with Gandhi*, Sudarshan Kapur has followed Lerone Bennett and James Farmer in suggesting that one of the most significant aspects of Martin Luther King, Jr.'s, contribution to the civil rights movement was his ability to plant the movement in the religious community. Kapur wrote, "His real gifts lay where they were needed most—in rooting the nonviolent struggle in the religious heart of the community."[41] King, as a Boston School of Theology student of Dr. Harold DeWolf, a Methodist scholar and student of Borden Parker Bowne, was grounded in the social gospel tradition and rooted in an ethic of love and justice of the same school of thought that informed Methodist women.

The center of the civil rights movement, its very foundation, pillar and strength, was in its religious core and its commitment to spiritually rooted nonviolence. In the 1940s that core, although mostly segregated for worship and ecclesiastical polity, was nurtured and tended by Methodists present in every key organization in the U.S. working for civil rights. The religious heart of the community was fed by the social gospel. Religion and democracy converged on a single-minded imperative for equality and human rights.

These connections were already present in the Woman's Division of Christian Service in the 1940s. Using her ability to integrate scripture and daily life and to understand movements of her time, Thelma Stevens helped bring churchwomen to a solid understanding of the religious and moral imperatives of the civil rights movement. Women of the Central Jurisdiction remembered that annual meetings

> ... were at once rooted in biblical theology and in practical social reality. They unequivocally taught the universal love of God and the responsibility of all Christians to love neighbors as they love themselves.[42]

Members of the Central Jurisdiction paid tribute to the long-standing commitment of the Department of CSR in these words:

> It was CSR/LCA, headed for 28 years by Miss Thelma Stevens as executive (staff) secretary, which mobilized Methodist women of all ethnic identities into one of the most sustained campaigns against racism ever witnessed in America. . . .

> More than a dozen years before the national civil rights movement became front page news, the Woman's Division, through the Department of Christian Social Relations and Local Church Activity [sic], was educating its members on the meaning of equality and preparing them to cope with hostility without rancor.[43]

The Woman's Division provided opportunities for Methodist women to analyze, discuss, reflect, and bare themselves to study of scripture and self-examination of prejudices. The sharp contrast between general public opinion in the South and the decisions and actions of the Department of CSR/LCA of the Woman's Division points to the significance of what organized Methodist women were doing.

From the early 1940s on, the Department of CSR/LCA gradually laid groundwork essential to an attack on segregation. Women saw that many changes were needed if public policies were to embody principles of equal justice for all, regardless of race.

The directions for civil rights work became clear. Efforts would be guided by the teachings of Jesus and directed toward inconsistencies between principles and policies. They would be measured by progress in federal legislation, integration within The Methodist Church, and broad participation of all racial groups in the life of the local community. The Department of CSR/LCA challenged Methodist women to take responsibility for shaping public opinion and urged The Methodist Church to lead the nation toward becoming an integrated and just society while reforming itself by living out commitments to racial equality and justice.

The religious foundations for the civil rights movement were laid before the 1950s arrived. Martin Luther King, Jr., brought an ability to preach that message, an opportunity that had been denied to Methodist women. He reached deep into the heart of the African American Baptist church, tapping a reservoir of power not previously unleashed.

The new day calls for a new way of life where the Negro, the Mexican, the Jew, or the Japanese-American can secure and keep a job commensurate with his skill without fear or hurt. The Christian Church is in a position to lead the way in creating a conscience that means justice for all.

—Thelma Stevens
Journal of the Woman's Division
(November 27–December 3, 1945), 8

CHAPTER 9

The Later 1940s: Launching the Campaign to End Racial Discrimination

During the 1940s the Department of Christian Social Relations and Local Church Activities (CSR/LCA) unauspiciously launched a campaign to end racial discrimination. It began by leading the Woman's Division and local units of the Woman's Society of Christian Service (WSCS) and the Wesleyan Service Guild (WSG) in addressing public forms of discrimination.

Early in the 1940s the Department of CSR/LCA adopted the slogan "All action is local" to emphasize its goal of enabling Methodist women to translate their Christian understandings of race relations into concrete local actions. By the end of the decade Dorothy Tilly claimed that Methodist women had learned that racial justice was an elusive ideal unless practiced in every community.[1] Small contributions by hundreds of societies over many years created cumulative change in attitudes and behavior between the African American and white ethnic groups in the South.

The prevalence of discrimination inspired a wide array of responses. Central Jurisdiction women guided Methodist women to take action. They called for equal access to public utilities, buses, trains, and street cars; and for communities to hire African American police officers and to reduce police brutality toward civilians and military service personnel. They asked women to work in their towns to upgrade inadequate schools and educational opportunities.[2]

Although Methodist women took actions in these areas, the Department of CSR/LCA focused the attention of Methodist women on less interactive forms of desegregation such as voting rights, anti-lynching work, and federal legislation for civil rights. As never before or since, Methodist women established connections with the White House and interacted with the President's Commission on Civil Rights (PCCR).

Becoming More Involved in Public Issues

In the United States, changing public policies around segregation and racial discrimination required a huge outpouring of effort. Though there were sympathizers who would support change, apathy, inertia, and lack of awareness first had to be overcome. The Woman's Division's campaign for civil rights unfolded slowly in the 1940s, beginning with a focus on education, gradual changes of policies within the Woman's Division itself, and statements of public policy. All of this occurred before many local groups became actively involved.

Declarations of intent to work for change in public policies were organizing tools that helped change not only public opinion but also the attitudes of Methodist women. In this book, when a claim is made that either the Department of CSR/LCA or the Woman's Division took an action or called on The Methodist Church or Methodist women or the public to take a particular stance or action, this means that the item in question was reported as a decision or recommendation of an elected body of officers. Decisions came either from approximately ten to twelve women who, as chairpersons of committees or department staff were members of the executive committee of the Department of CSR/LCA and who met three times a year, or from the Woman's Division, approximately fifty to eighty women who also met three times a year and included members of the executive committee of the Department of CSR/LCA. All the actions of the Woman's Division on social issues came as recommendations that had first passed the executive committee of the Department of CSR/LCA.

In the 1940s when Thelma Stevens played a central role first as the only executive staff member, and then as one of two, her ideas and recommendations figured strongly in the reports. Stevens valued group process and decisions made by consensus. The strength of the early stands that the Woman's Division took on racial issues is a tribute to Stevens' ability to persuade others of the need for Christians to take social responsibility. Each arena of discrimination required particular attention. This chapter examines ways Methodist women took stands on or investigated discrimination related to conscription of labor, public education, domestic workers, rents, the Fair Employment Practices Commission (FEPC), public benefit programs, recruitment of African American women for the armed services, and racial integration of public facilities in Washington, D.C.

Methodist women resisted attempts to conscript labor for the war effort. In keeping with segregation customs, war industries declared labor shortages when they could not recruit enough local white laborers. Some industries went to extreme lengths to import white labor from other parts of the country while at the same time large numbers of unemployed African American men and women searched for jobs in that very vicinity. Other war industries accepted African American laborers and induced mass migrations, bringing a sudden influx of persons of color to formerly all-white communities.[3]

In 1945, Methodist women helped communities adjust to the relocation of Negro service personnel and related issues that created tension—housing policies, hiring and firing policies, and high rates of unemployment. The Department of CSR/LCA recommended that churches cooperate across faith and race lines in sponsoring community-wide workshops on demobilization. Dorothy Tilly, a staff member of the Atlanta-based Southern Regional Council (SRC), and chairperson of Christian Social Relations (CSR) for the Southeast Jurisdiction of the Women's Society of Christian Service, brought together twenty-six civic-minded leaders from the Atlanta environs. Georgia, North Carolina, South Carolina, and Tennessee sent their leaders of the Department of CSR/LCA to the first demobilization workshop.

As the 1940s progressed, Methodist women expressed deep concern for public education. Racial tensions ran high. Rampant discrimination characterized public education in the South.

The poorest region of the nation maintained not one, but two public school systems that were segregated by race. Both systems were less well funded than schools in other parts of the nation. In 1945 nine southern states spent on the average "$19 a year for the education of each Negro child, compared to an expenditure of $59 for each white child, and an average expenditure for the nation as a whole of $88 per pupil."[4]

The Department of CSR/LCA recommended that societies "work immediately for the equalization of educational opportunity in the United States for all people without regard to race, creed, or place of residence"[5] and supported federal aid to public education with the stipulation that federal funds be used without discrimination and the administration of schools remain under local supervision.

The department's 1947 report supported federal aid to education.[6] Methodist women endorsed a bill that proposed funding for all public schools rather than authorizing states to determine which schools could receive public money. One 1947 Senate bill for federal aid to education would have enabled states to use federal school funds to defy federal integration plans, if ever integration were mandated.

For ten years the Woman's Missionary Council (WMC) had studied and learned about economic problems related to the low wages of domestic workers, with little improvement to show for its efforts. Members of the WMC had worked with Arthur Raper, formerly a staff member of the Commission on Interracial Cooperation (CIC) and subsequently a co-worker of Gunnar Myrdal, in a survey of domestic workers conducted in 1938. The Woman's Division encouraged changes in both federal policies and local hiring practices.

The Woman's Division helped Methodist women examine their own practices regarding hired workers and ways they discriminated. The Central Jurisdiction recommended "the support of appropriate legislation so that the living standards of [farm workers and domestic servants] may be raised to the American standard of living."[7] The Central Jurisdiction women convinced the Woman's Division to support efforts to include domestic workers and agricultural workers in federal Social Security legislation designed to provide survivors' insurance and old age benefits.[8]

The Woman's Division sought to persuade government agencies to provide impartial services to all population groups. Women were encouraged to monitor government programs for agricultural adjustments, the National Youth Administration, agricultural extension, farm security, health and public welfare services, schools and colleges, and employment practices in defense areas with the intent to secure quality service for minorities. The Woman's Division asked Methodist women to make a special effort to inform low-income and minority groups about the services of the Consumer Division Office of Price Administration.[9]

Where discrimination and cheating in government were rampant, Methodist women set out to learn the practices of state departments of labor in the administration of unemployment compensation. Either intentionally or without knowledge of new federal laws and without scrutiny by these alert Methodist women, agencies were likely to apply discriminatory practices. Women's investigations uncovered and reduced the proportion of inequities based on race.[10]

Methodist women also kept a watchful eye when the federal government failed to enlist African American women into the armed services. The nation was considering a military draft in order to obtain needed personnel and, at the same time, was rejecting the possibility of enlisting any of approximately eight thousand qualified African American nurses.[11] So the Department of CSR/LCA led a drive to secure broader acceptance of qualified African American nurses into the military services and asked Methodist women to write or wire their senators and leading Army and Navy officials.

The first clear statement of the Woman's Division in opposition to

First clear statement

segregation outside The Methodist Church came in 1946 at the annual meeting when the Woman's Division decided to examine segregation practices in society and vowed to make a determined effort to work for their elimination.[12] The Woman's Division concurred with the Assembly of the United Council of Church Women in urging that churches, organizations, and communities make a united impact on segregation practices: by supporting the enforcement of civil rights laws in states having such laws; by interpreting and enforcing Supreme Court rulings on transportation, education, and the right to vote; and by ending segregation in Washington, D.C. Methodist women decided to integrate Methodist institutions in the capital, including the office of the Board of Temperance and its cafeteria.[13] During 1947, with additional pressure from the Congress of Racial Equality (CORE), "[t]esting and negotiations integrated the Methodist Building Cafeteria on Capitol Hill. . . ."[14]

So many forms of discrimination abounded that the Department of CSR/LCA decided to give particular attention to voting rights, anti-lynching efforts, and civil rights.

Voting Rights for All

A contorted form of democracy survived in the South, where deterrents obstructed potential black voters. In the early 1940s Methodist women began to work for voting rights and citizenship education for all. Twenty years before the voter-registration campaigns of the civil rights movement, some Methodist women's societies sponsored classes in citizenship for new voters.[15]

Voter registration affected far more than elections. Juries, selected from the list of persons registered to vote, did not represent the racial mix of the population. Since jury members were selected from the rolls of voters who had paid the poll tax for three preceding consecutive years this effectively excluded many African Americans from being selected for jury. The case of Odell Waller dramatized the injustice of this system. In 1940–41 an all-white jury found Waller, a young African American from Virginia, guilty of first degree murder without evidence of pre-meditated intent to kill his white landlord.

Even though Methodist women worked to secure broader participation in public elections, little changed. In Virginia and seven other states, three out of four adults, or approximately ten million citizens, were not listed on voter rolls.[16] The poll tax system denied poor people

159

a voice in their own government. To change the system, more voters who opposed it were needed. The department recommended that churchwomen support action to remove all restrictions to the right to vote.[17] Leaders of the WSCS from Georgia wrote to Governor Ellis Arnall and members of the state legislature in opposition to the poll tax and its "smoke screen of 'revenue for education.'" They said, "In fact, we wish to register our disapproval of acquiring revenue for schools through any measure that defeats democracy."[18]

In 1943, Methodist women found that passage of an anti-poll tax bill was being delayed by filibuster in the U.S. Senate. A two-thirds majority was required to vote for cloture. Southern legislators and enough of their friends to comprise a one-third minority could and did delay almost all civil rights legislation. Methodist women unsuccessfully attacked this problem by trying to convince their southern senators that "the folks back home" wanted to end debate and pass the legislation.[19]

Women Continue Anti-lynching Work

In the 1940s, when lynchings captured national attention and widespread condemnation, Methodist women applied pressure to change public opinion. The contrast between technological advancements in communication and transportation and barbaric acts of lynching in the United States, which sometimes were published in news reports around the world, placed Americans in an untenable position. Methodist women renewed efforts to end lynching by condemning failures to administer justice and lauding people who did uphold justice. They not only asked but also expected public officials to sign and uphold the anti-lynching pledge. Methodist women could and did gather enough votes to retain or remove elected officials from office.

Through the Association of Southern Women for the Prevention of Lynching (ASWPL), Methodist women flexed considerable anti-lynching political muscle. In 1941, Jessie Daniel Ames told Lillian Smith, editor of the *North Georgia Review*, that Methodist women had secured anti-lynching pledges from sheriffs they had interviewed. They had also written letters to governors and congressional representatives. Out of a total of forty-three thousand anti-lynching pledge signatures filed with the ASWPL, Ames identified at least forty thousand as those of Methodist women.[20]

Some of the anti-lynching work of Methodist women required courage. At times women entered towns where a lynching had been committed. Typically, less than two weeks after a lynching they began an investigation, and in the ensuing year they spoke out in a public forum against lynching. Ames reported, "Whatever has been needful to be done, they have done it."[21]

Ames told the following story:

Mrs. Mullino Prevents a Lynching

How do some 40,000 crusading southern women work? On Christmas Day, 1934, Mrs. Ames was preparing for holiday festivities. Her telephone rang. An Associated Press editor informed her that a Negro had killed an officer in Schley County, Georgia, and that a mob was forming. Mrs. Ames rushed to the office. She discovered that the Association [ASWPL] had no signatures in Schley County. But in adjoining Macon County lived a member of the Georgia Council of the Association, Mrs. F. M. Mullino of Montezuma. Mrs. Ames telephoned Mrs. Mullino, who stopped preparation of her Christmas dinner and started telephoning everyone she knew in Schley County, urging each to bring pressure on the sheriff to prevent a lynching.

A short time later, Mrs. Mullino was informed that the Negro was in a swamp in her own county. She called the sheriff and his deputies, and a number of ministers and other public-spirited citizens, urging them to aid in preventing mob action. Until mid-afternoon she stayed at her telephone. Finally the Negro was captured—by officers. That Christmas Day was not blackened by a lynching in Georgia. The law took its course. Had Mrs. Mullino gone to the mob and pleaded for restraint she would have been taunted. She knew that. She knew, too, that a sheriff, even though disposed to carelessness in such cases, couldn't afford to take any chances after dozens of influential voters had demanded that every possible precaution be taken to insure a constitutional trial for the accused Negro.[22]

Handing an African American man accused of murder over to law enforcement officials was tantamount to a death sentence because of corruption of the judicial system, yet Methodist women valued the use of legal rather than extra-legal measures. They identified problems in the judicial system and within a decade went to work on those as well.

The anti-lynching work of one outstanding Methodist woman gives the flavor of Methodist women's increasingly comprehensive understanding of racial issues. In 1941, The Southern Frontier, a publication of the CIC, celebrated ten years of anti-lynching work by Mrs. L. W. Alford of McComb, Mississippi. During that time 5,895 Mississippi women in

356 towns had pledged to work against lynching. They had secured signed pledges from 160 county officers in 82 counties and from an additional 551 men. During this time, the women held twenty-three forums for lawyers, editors, judges, sheriffs, college professors, members of the legislature, preachers, and public school teachers. In addition they led numerous discussion groups and trained anti-lynching speakers to cope with opposition and heckling.[23]

Each lynching increased racial tensions and raised the pressure for an effective solution. A 1942 lynching in Sikeston, Missouri, spurred Louise Oldshue to ask Methodist women to support federal legislation against lynching. The bill then before the Judiciary Committee of the House of Representatives stipulated that the federal government must investigate any government agency failing to protect victims from mob violence and must request any government agency found guilty of neglect to pay an amount ranging from $2000 to $5000 to the family of a victim.[24] In 1947 the Woman's Division also asked Methodist women to work for the passage of the bill that defined lynching as a federal crime punishable by prison terms up to twenty years and fines of $10,000. Public officers who were convicted of willfully failing to prevent mob violence could be punished and local communities could be sued for negligence.[25]

When lynchings were prevented, an unjust justice system presented a new set of challenges to an expanding network of organizations concerned about civil rights. In December 1945, on the basis of identification of kinky hair and a T-shirt, Willie McGee was charged with the rape of a white woman who said that her husband and children were sleeping in adjacent bedrooms and that she had a sick child in bed with her at the time of the rape. McGee was condemned to death in three trials and for a while escaped execution by a last-minute reprieve, but his appeals ran out.

In 1949 Cora Ratliff, chair of the Department of CSR/LCA, became involved in an effort to bring clemency to a warped judicial system in order to spare Willie McGee from execution. She learned about the case from the SRC. She wrote for additional information to Hodding Carter, editor of the *Delta Democrat-Times* and winner of the 1946 Pulitzer Prize, and to Jack McMichael, executive secretary of the Methodist Federation for Social Action.

Cora Ratliff thought the SRC could provide substantial pressure on Mississippi's Methodist governor, Fielding Wright. She advised McMichael, "do not plan any 'group' visit to the Governor for me" because she would be out of town (not in Sherard, Mississippi) for ten days. "I would have to pick my own group anyway."

162

Cora Ratliff's response influenced the multi-organization strategy. Immediately McMichael wrote to George Mitchell at the SRC, "Our mutual good friend, Mrs. Ratliff from Mississippi, has been talking to us about the Willie McGee case." McMichael enclosed a fact sheet on the case from the Civil Rights Congress and discussed the formation of a delegation of persuasive people to make a direct appeal to Governor Wright.[26]

The Woman's Division supported federal protections against racial hate crimes spurred by human rights violations and lynchings in Columbia, Tennessee, and Freeport, New York, in 1946. Dorothy Tilly initiated the Woman's Division's contact with Attorney General Tom Clark. In 1947 the Woman's Division asked individuals to join them in writing letters to the Attorney General requesting that the Department of Justice safeguard the civil rights of African American people.[27]

In June 1947, tensions surfaced again, fueled by the gruesome lynching of Willie Earle in South Carolina, and by a racially motivated attempted murder in North Carolina. A missionary from China sent a clipping from a Chinese newspaper that had responded to the lynching of Willie Earle. "If that country (the U.S.) is to set the rest of the world an example in brotherly love, then the place to start lecturing is right there in South Carolina, where a white man has never been convicted of killing a Negro for nearly a century."[28]

A 1947 CSR/LCA report cited statistics indicating that 3,523 Negroes and 1,459 white persons had been lynched in the United States, for a total of 4,982 lynchings since 1882.[29] Lynching violated the Fourteenth Amendment to the Constitution of the United States, which provided that no state "shall deprive any person of life, liberty, or property without due process of law, nor deny to any person within its jurisdiction the equal protection of law."[30] In 99.2 percent of the lynchings, no punishment had been administered to the perpetrators.

Since democracy and justice remained dreams and were not yet realities pervading the land, Methodist women wrote letters to officials. In June 1947, the Woman's Division sent a letter to the governors of North Carolina and Alabama commending them for their recent actions during a race-related abduction. A similar letter was sent to Circuit Judge J. Robert Martin, Jr., who tried the thirty-one lynchers of Willie Earle in Greenville, South Carolina, and who recognized that "their acquittal by the jury had done violence to the basic principle of human freedom under the American system."[31] The Woman's Division urged U.S. Attorney General Tom Clark to use the Department of Justice to return integrity to the system of justice which had acquitted confessed lynchers. The Woman's Division requested that the PCCR take immediate steps to secure federal anti-lynching legislation and sent a state-ment of its position and actions to Dr. Robert K. Carr, the executive secretary of the PCCR. Their concerns began to be heard in high places.

White House Connections

In the years from 1943 through 1948 the Woman's Division had closer contacts with, and influence in, the executive branch of American government than at any other point in its history. In part this was due to the friendship between Dorothy Tilly and Eleanor Roosevelt which dated back to 1939 and Tilly's work as director of the Emergency Committee for Food Production.[32] Since 1934, Tilly had also worked with southern programs of the Farm Security Administration. Dorothy Tilly had served the Woman's Division on its Committee on Rural Life since 1933 and was well known throughout the South for her leader-ship of the Woman's Division of the CIC and for her participation in the ASWPL.[33]

Eleanor Roosevelt, stateswoman and crusader, was a friend to many who sought to extend rights to minorities. She served as unofficial ambassador to national meetings of numerous organizations of women and minority groups working for justice issues and peace.[34]

She served as liaison to the president. In 1934 Walter White, executive secretary of National Association for the Advancement of Colored People (NAACP), in an attempt to secure a public statement from President Roosevelt denouncing lynchings, had communicated with Mrs. Roosevelt following the grotesque lynching of Claude Neal. Despite Mrs. Roosevelt's attempts to convince him otherwise, President Roosevelt did not speak out.[35] Yet, Mrs. Roosevelt, knowledgeable about the details of the Claude Neal case, favored federal anti-lynching legislation and continued to press for African American civil rights. Like the Woman's Division, she supported the Fair Employment Practices Committee and President Truman's Committee on Civil Rights in 1946. She may have advised President Truman in the selection of Dorothy Tilly to serve as a member of the PCCR.

In April 1944, Mrs. Roosevelt invited several Methodist women to the White House to discuss justice issues and spend the night. Her guests on that occasion were Dorothy Tilly, Bertha Newell, Dorothy Weber, and Thelma Stevens.[36] Particularly through Eleanor Roosevelt, Dorothy Tilly, and Thelma Stevens, the Woman's Division increased its role as a liaison between local and federal agencies. Correspondingly,

the influence of Methodist women declined as Mrs. Roosevelt's own
influence waned.

The President's Committee on Civil Rights

In 1946 the Woman's Division was proud to have Dorothy Tilly, the
Southeast Jurisdiction secretary of CSR, serve on the PCCR. President
Truman formed the PCCR to address racial problems after he noted
the unequal distribution of freedom from fear. Hate groups increased
intolerance and failed to discourage mob action against persons on
account of racial origin or religious beliefs. The federal government,
restricted by inadequate civil rights statutes, was hampered in its
attempts to protect democratic institutions. President Truman sought
"recommendations with respect to the adoption or establishment by
legislation or otherwise of more adequate and effective means and
procedures for the protection of the civil rights of the people of the
United States."[37]

Tilly took an active role in the committee, sharing background
information and advice. She wrote to Robert K. Carr, executive secretary of the committee, "Much of our interracial trouble has not only
the sympathetic backing of our corporations but [is] financially backed
by them."[38] Tilly and Frank Graham, the two southern liberals on the
committee, filed a minority report because they opposed the proposal
to make federal aid to education contingent upon desegregation. They
thought the South "would rather 'be ignorant' than have Washington
tell them how to handle such sensitive racial matters." Tilly and Graham
claimed that to make progress the South would need "to raise the
educational level of the people . . . and to inculcate the teachings of
religion regarding freedom and equality. . . ."[39] Tilly did, however,
agree with the expanded federal role recommended in other portions
of the PCCR report.

From January through September 1947, the PCCR met ten times,
heard twenty-four witnesses, and corresponded with nearly 250 private
organizations and individuals, including Thelma Stevens and the
Woman's Division.[40] The Woman's Division described itself as working
to remove forms of discrimination and to end "so called 'Jim Crow' laws
that violate the basic human rights as embodied in the Constitution of
the United States." The Woman's Division asked the committee for
assistance in public concerns:

Can your Committee do such practical things as the following:

(1) recommend the extension of some kind of Civil Service program that will mean a compulsory training requirement in basic human relations for all policemen and law enforcement officers, bus drivers and operators of public conveyances of all types?

(2) a similar requirement for teachers in all public schools, making clearly defined study of an entire intercultural and interracial relations in the context of human relations, a basis for employment?

(3) *a.* give us a clear and simple interpretation of "civil rights" as they relate to the State and the United States;
      b. by what possible measure can a "Jim Crow" bill be deemed *"constitutional"* under the Bill of Rights of the United States?

(4) . . . A Committee like yours can map out a program that *all* groups can unite on—Jews, Protestants, Catholics and other groups.[41]

Of 190 letters of inquiry sent by PCCR to interested organizations and 103 replies, the Woman's Division was among 53 groups who made recommendations concerning the scope of the work and agenda of the committee.[42] The committee gathered information about discrimination and violation of human rights among religious groups, Japanese Americans, Native Americans, Hispanic Americans, nationalized citizens, aliens in residence, indigenous people of U.S. territories, and in the nation's capital, as well as among African Americans.

Dorothy Tilly, who had personally conducted an on-site investigation of each lynching in the past decade, served as the committee's resident expert in the troublesome area of lynchings. She queried whether all murder should be made a federal crime on the grounds that the right to live might be considered a constitutional right. She was frustrated that some juries refused to issue convictions for clear crimes related to lynching.[43] Tilly believed that problems of racial discrimination could not be solved without tackling the interconnected problems of poverty, lack of education, inadequately trained and underpaid teachers, and absentee ministers.[44] She also believed that racial prejudice was based on ignorance and economic competition.

The PCCR organized the information it had gathered into four broad areas: (1) the right to safety and security of the person, (2) the right to citizenship and its privileges, (3) the right to freedom of conscience and expression, and (4) the right to equality of opportunity. The PCCR report claimed that Americans held to the ideals of civil

Dorothy
Tilly
(PCCR)

166

rights (the promises of freedom and equality) protected by government, but that they did not have a working knowledge of the Bill of Rights and did not have clear expectations about what citizens or government should do.

Documentation gathered from all portions of the nation showed that American citizens were not treated equally in access to voting rights; opportunities in the military; pay for work; the right to education or housing; or access to public services, accommodations, or federal services. The nation's attempt to segregate races and provide equality had failed. Statistics showed that in forty non-poll tax states, 69 percent of potential voters voted in the 1944 presidential election, compared with 18 percent of potential voters in eight poll tax states.

Because the federal government had clear responsibility and sole control of the military, information about discrimination in the military was particularly potent. In the Army, while there was one white officer for every seven white enlisted persons, that ratio was one to seventy for African Americans. Only 2 African Americans had been chosen as naval officers from 21,793 African American enlistees. The report also documented discrimination in employment, housing, and health.[45]

The PCCR report took significant strides in defining the government's responsibility to secure the rights of citizens. "[Many] of the most serious wrongs against individual rights are committed by private persons or by local public officers," the report noted.[46]

The committee found that the government had a powerful constitutional foundation for a civil rights program. Members of the committee enumerated eleven powers of the government which included the power to protect civil rights: to vote, to fair legal process, to free speech and assembly, and to equal protection of the laws. The government could regulate interstate commerce, taxing and spending programs (such as Social Security), and use of public mail (protecting against anonymous hate groups). Further, the government could "protect civil rights which acquire a treaty status." The government had power to carry out treaty obligations, such as those of the United Nations Charter which espoused human as well as civil rights.

Finally, the committee found, government derived power from a republican form of government that included "the power to protect essential civil rights against interference by public officers or private persons."[17] Much of the strength of the report hinged on this analysis of the powers of government to protect civil rights. On the whole, Methodist women agreed with the committee and supported the argument that federal powers to protect civil rights took priority over the rights of states to enforce state or local laws.

The PCCR explored the potential for use of civil sanctions to shape public behavior. Cease and desist orders against discriminatory practices could be enforced in federal courts. Further, the people of the country, the committee declared, were entitled to have lower courts "apply courageously the established doctrines of law announced by the Supreme Court."[48] Equally important, the committee found that federal action would not be truly effective without a positive climate of opinion. Bigotry might be based on personal insecurities, but could not be sustained without group support of opinions based on ignorance. The committee concluded:

> The fewer the opportunities there are to use inequality in the law as a reinforcement of prejudice, the sooner prejudice will vanish. In addition, people must be taught about the evil effects of prejudice. They must be helped to understand why they have developed prejudices. It means trying to show them that it is unfair and stupid to condemn whole groups . . . that each man must be judged by himself, on his own merits and faults.[49]

Education for the eradication of racial prejudice had been one of the strengths of Methodist women's programs for many years. Here they were among good company with other organizations that shared their objectives, including the YMCA; YWCA; NAACP; SRC; Methodist Federation for Social Action; Fellowship of Reconciliation; CORE; Anti-Defamation League; National Council of Negro Women; and Baptist, Episcopalian, Presbyterian, Jewish, AME, and AME Zion women.

The report of the committee recommended: strengthening the Commission on Civil Rights; protecting the right to safety and security of persons with changes to the criminal code; strengthening citizenship privileges by federal action; protecting freedom of conscience; and expanding equality of opportunity. This last portion was the most controversial. The PCCR recommended eliminating segregation altogether from American life. A committee majority urged that federal grants to public agencies and schools be made contingent on providing nonsegregated services. A minority protested the requirement for the abolition of segregation. Subsequent recommendations for elimination of discrimination in areas of education, housing, and health services were consequently weakened by placing the burden of responsibility for enactment on states rather than on Congress. Finally, the report recommended a public education program "to inform the people of the civil rights to which they are entitled and which they owe to one another."[50]

168

A letter from Dorothy Tilly portrays the role of facilitator and bridge-builder that she played in the committee. Tilly helped the committee steer toward civil rights while bringing along a reluctant southern constituency. She and Frank Graham, the two southern liberals on the PCCR, recommended modifications to the first draft of the PCCR report. Tilly wrote to Charles Wilson and Robert Carr:

Now about my South and the report. The report is too beligerant [*sic*]. It is rather vicious as it raises a "whip-hand" against the South. It does not express an understanding of the problems of the South, but even drags in sentences to point up and at the sins of the section. I admit the accusations are just but we will have to use another method or else we undo the social progress the South has made in the last twenty-five years. . . .

The question of one school system [not two that are segregated] makes the groups always "see red". As I said before, the South will stay ignorant before it will be forced to having non-segregated schools. I believe every Southern newspaper will attack the report editorily on this score.

I am afraid, too, this will definitely kill the Federal Aid to Education Bill in Congress. . . .

We cannot avoid facing the segregation—but make it with a different approach. The report sounds like we are mad at somebody or some section of our nation. . . .

After all, do we not want to strengthen the civil rights of our people? Isn't this the real purpose of our committee? As the report is, it will be rejected by the South and the South knows how to *REBEL*.[51]

Tilly and Graham were highly criticized by segregationists for their role in the PCCR. One anonymous critic heralded, "Your recommendations are naught, but by your actions you have precipitated and agitated more assault, more rape and more bloodshed than the South has ever seen."[52]

Meeting just after the release of the report, the Woman's Division responded in a letter to Attorney General Tom Clark with concern over the pre-empting of constitutional guarantees in the recent dismissal of federal employees "without stated cause or trial." They wrote, "We recommend that you use every possible means of implementing the report of the President's Committee on Civil Rights."[53]

169

The women adopted an additional resolution expressing their caution about and support for legislative provisions that would release federal funds for public education contingent on policies prohibiting discrimination in admission or treatment of students based on race, color, creed, or national origin.

> We reaffirm our belief in the traditional American principle of separation of church and state. We likewise recognize the necessity of federal aid to education to safeguard this and other principles of democracy. We also support the principle of state distribution of federal funds for education. Although Bills S.472 and HR.2953 do not wholly agree with all of these principles, we urge the support of them as the nearest approach to our ultimate goal.[54]

The Woman's Division sent a letter to President Truman urging him to "rectify current discriminations in health, education, and employment within the federal services."[55]

The Woman's Division used PCCR's report, published as a book, *To Secure These Rights*, to help educate Americans about human and civil rights. Newspapers distributed 600,000 copies, giving the report wide circulation.[56] Approximately 350,000 copies were sold by publishers. SRC distributed 20,000 copies of a condensed version of the report. Even so, the Division spent $50 to purchase 6,000 copies of *To Secure These Rights* which they distributed to prominent leaders, friends of Dorothy Tilly, and officers of the WSCS and the WSG.[57]

The Woman's Division prepared a sixty-six-page book, *Here's the Way to Secure These Rights*, to guide Methodist women in the study of human rights.[58] While designed as a practical guide for leaders who wanted to do something about problems of racial and religious discrimination, the underlying and unwritten assumptions of the authors chosen to represent the Woman's Division are valuable. These assumptions helped make the role of Methodist women in the civil rights movement important.

The authors of *Here's the Way to Secure These Rights* believed that people cared about the moral attitudes and quality of life in their country and were willing to talk with each other about the problems of nation and community. They assumed that democracy and equality are foundational principles of society. The authors confidently anticipated that, for the good of all, communities and their citizens wanted to end discrimination. *Here's the Way to Secure These Rights* counseled that people would meet resistance: "But remember this: there is no moral justification for inequality in this country—and that's the crux of the matter."[59]

Methodist women were among the largest groups putting these beliefs into action. *Here's the Way* served as a manual, coaching leaders in how to plan what to do. They were to call a meeting that included people representative of all groups present in the population profile of their community. The local committee would plan and conduct a community survey. Based on the survey, they would decide which problems to tackle and obtain leaders and funding to do this. The Methodist women's program for ending racial and religious prejudice was designed to be a locally controlled, grassroots effort, ecumenically and community based, inclusive of people of all races and religions. In the process, though it was Methodists who were instrumental in forming numerous local Human Rights Councils, the Methodist origin of such activism was removed from consciousness and history.

Dorothy Tilly attempted to correct some of the popular misconceptions that generated huge amounts of criticism of the PCCR and its work. In a pamphlet, "The Story of the President's Committee on Civil Rights," also collected by the FBI, she assured readers that the committee originated out of the emerging new understandings of civil rights in this country, not as a weapon of political factions. "The appointing of the Committee was an answer to the ground swell of the anguish of the oppressed and the voices of others whose sense of justice was affronted."[60] The committee heard witnesses from "all the minority groups of the nation," she explained, even including persons from U.S. territories. Two principles guided the work: belief in the supreme value of the individual, and an interpretation of "'life, liberty, and pursuit of happiness' to mean all that it implies—security, health, housing, education, the right to work, etc. . . ."[61]

Tilly emphasized that the report was neither sectional, for discrimination occurred in all parts of the country, nor was it a race report. Rather the report underscored the point that the violation of the rights of any group of citizens is destructive and a threat to the security and freedom of all. The committee ultimately rested its trust in the people of the country and in the democratic processes that appeal to fairness, justice, and mercy. Tilly urged readers to eliminate prejudice in their minds. "'Tis not consistent in a democracy or fitting in a Christian to hold to any idea of superiority. Put the same value on human personality that Jesus did."[62] Citizens needed to influence government and bigots, working to create a "climate" that would not support prejudice, corruption, injustice, or intimidation. It was time for the church, for citizens to go to work.

The Department of CSR/LCA secured the support of the Woman's Division which sent its commendations to President Truman, applauding his appointment of a Committee on Civil Rights, and to the chair of that committee, Charles E. Wilson, "for the scope of the report and for its recognition of the importance of safeguarding the rights of all minority groups." The Woman's Division urged the president, as head of the federal administrative services, "to rectify current discriminations in health, education, and employment within the federal services."

Dorothy Tilly met Attorney General Tom Clark at hearings of the PCCR.[63] Tilly entered into correspondence with Tom Clark, as well as with state governors, sheriffs, and judges, in order to advocate improvements in the court system, broader interpretations of human rights, and specific cases related to lynchings.[64]

Methodist women called on the president to use his 1948 State of the Nation address to express to Congress and the nation his official recommendations proceeding from his study of the report of the PCCR.[65] Unfortunately, President Truman was under attack by southern democrats for his work on civil rights and did not push forward. Leaders of the Woman's Division expressed disappointment that Truman did not present to Congress his own conclusions from the report of the PCCR or make any legislative requests.

To Secure These Rights and the United Nations' *Universal Declaration of Human Rights* became two foundational documents for study by Methodist women in every WSCS and WSG across the nation. Women placed these documents in libraries of local high schools and colleges and held discussions and meetings to decide what they could do to work for human rights in their local communities.

Unresolved Civil Rights Agenda

After eight years of hard work directed toward broadening the attitudes of Methodist women and The Methodist Church on race relations, important changes were occurring: A growing segment of society was concluding that segregation was wrong.

Thelma Stevens, Eleanor Neff, and Dorothy Weber, the CSR/LCA staff, recommended actions which charted a course for the Woman's Division's work to overcome segregation, prejudice, and racial barriers. They hoped to help families develop tolerant and inclusive attitudes toward people of other races and faiths. They called for adoption of the *Universal Declaration of Human Rights* by the United Nations and its

members. They urged every local Methodist women's group to participate in a mission study on "The Bible and Human Rights," discuss the
PCCR report, and review court decisions about Jim Crow laws.

In 1948 Eleanor Neff, the official Woman's Division observer in
Washington, D.C., reported on the progress of civil rights legislation.
She anticipated that anti-lynching and anti-poll tax measures, one or
both, might pass, but that the fair employment practices bill would be
defeated. She was wrong. All civil rights legislation failed. Not until
1966 was the poll tax found to be unconstitutional. Public lynchings
continued into the 1950s and were gradually replaced by private
racially motivated murders.

In 1949 civil rights legislation languished. Congress failed to act on
FEPC measures, anti-poll tax and anti-lynching bills. Once Truman had
delivered a special message to Congress on civil rights, the executive
branch rested its case, thus failing to deal with integration of state or
local transportation systems, public facilities, or schools.

Booo Congress

Leaders of the Woman's Division had supported President Truman
and were disappointed that he did not take a stronger stand on civil
rights. Dorothy Tilly, in particular, was let down, for she had helped
President Truman carry the State of Georgia and win re-election in
spite of Dixiecrats who opposed Truman's position on civil rights.[66]

Methodist women were concerned that U.S. ratification of the
United Nations' human rights documents was stalled in the U.S.
Senate. They knew that if the U.S. ratified an International Covenant
on Human Rights the nation would be placed in an uncomfortable
position if it failed to grant civil rights to minorities and women. The
United States was not willing to grant to its own citizens the human
rights which became standards of the United Nations. The U.S. was
one of forty-eight nations that agreed in 1948 to accept the Declaration
and live up to its standards as nearly as possible, but Congress refused
to ratify the Declaration. Methodist women did not know that a nefari-
ous political bargain had been struck which doomed ratification.[67]

Booo U.S.

Concerned by the failure of the executive and legislative branches
of government to take bold forward strides in implementing the new
civil rights legislation, Dorothy Tilly convened 165 leaders of
churchwomen's groups in Atlanta on September 8–9, 1949. Together
the women founded the Fellowship of the Concerned (FOC), a coalition
of churchwomen dedicated to work for positive race relations and civil
rights for all citizens.[68] Methodist women expected federal legislation
to be an integral part of social change, yet many agreed with Dorothy
Tilly that progress related less to exercise of federal power than "to
rais[ing] the educational level of the people . . . and to inculcat[ing] the

173

teachings of religion regarding freedom and equality."[69] The FOC was an interracial group which actively worked for justice in the courts, voter registration, and desegregation of schools. The FOC held annual meetings until its termination with the death of Dorothy Tilly in 1970.[70]

In the late 1940s, momentum gathered for civil rights. The United Nations with its *Universal Declaration of Human Rights* and the President's Committee on Human Rights with its report, *To Secure These Rights*, broadened the concern of Methodist women. Attitudes that tolerated segregation in the 1940s would have to change before the nation could make commitments to voting rights, school integration, and desegregation of public facilities.

Lack of congressional support for civil rights discouraged Methodist women who, as never before, had rallied moral indignation and political action to work for the end of segregation. Thelma Stevens urged Methodist women to take heart. Gradually concerted efforts chipped away at entrenched segregation and discrimination, but changes in legislation were not fast enough for changing conditions. Pressure continued to mount as the 1950s arrived.

Peace . . . will come only when Christian men, women, and children of *every* local community work hard enough and sacrifice enough to uproot *fear* from the hearts of mankind everywhere! It will come when neighbors are friends without fear of artificial barriers—of separation! It will come when Christ's followers choose *His way*—even the Cross if need be!

—Thelma Stevens, Eleanor Neff Curry, Dorothy Weber
The Methodist Woman (September 1950), 25

CHAPTER 10

The Context of the 1950s:
Changing Attitudes

No one who lived through the 1950s in the U.S. escaped unscathed by the issue of race relations. Experiences, stories, and feelings lie seared in memory. From colleges to jails, from seats of government to isolated homes, and from mansions to ghetto apartments, Americans felt social upheaval and conflict as social conventions changed. Segregationists tried to dig in deeper as the ground shifted around them. Resistance to desegregation mounted. Positions polarized. Just as earthquakes reduce solid ground to quicksand, pervasive social upheaval shook the foundations of social institutions. African Americans sought refuge in black churches. A determined African American grassroots leadership began to consolidate, even as white liberal leadership fell into confusion and disarray.

White liberals, caught between ideals of racial justice and realities of a reluctant South, searched in vain for a comfortable middle ground. Southern white liberal strength wilted under pressure from segregationists.

Racism found hundreds of ways to resist change. Methodist women faced entrenched customs, stubborn prejudice, frightening harassment, and chilling pockets where racial discrimination froze and would not thaw. Methodist women could not be certain that, even if given enough time, people's attitudes about race could be changed. Without change, time perpetuated injustice. Attacks from the Right led many on the Left to retreat.

Behind the scenes, a core group of Methodist women continued to dismantle segregation. Dorothy Tilly gathered a group of women religious leaders committed to taking action in troubled times. The Fellowship of the Concerned (FOC), an interracial, multifaith group of women, predominantly Methodist, set out to hold legal and penal systems accountable for racial fairness and to expand voting rights to people regardless of gender, race, or class.

Methodist women's activities illustrated their new understanding of mission. They participated in dialogues and activities needed to make life more fulfilling for all. The Department of Christian Social Relations and Local Church Activities (CSR/LCA) staff members Thelma Stevens, Dorothy Weber, and Eleanor Neff, stressed "the practical recognition of our responsibility to share to the fullest in providing those resources that make possible a good life for the earth's people."[1] They invited Methodist women to engage in attitude-changing conversations, accept responsibility for improving living conditions in their local community, and recognize that their actions had an impact on the world community.

Human Rights, Freedom Movements, and Opposition to Racism

Methodist women believed that God called them to change their attitudes about race and to risk working for justice even when it was unpopular. Gradually Methodist women came to affirm that people of all races, entitled to inherent human rights, needed to have these rights ensured in practice.

By 1953 the Woman's Division was educating women about important global changes in attitudes about human rights. The Department of CSR/LCA asserted that by using moral leadership Christians could work to remedy the world's interrelated problems, enabling civil liberties and peace to replace racial and religious bigotry and oppression.[2]

Before World War II nearly 750 million people, mostly persons of color, lived under colonial rule. By 1956 four-fifths of these people had gained political freedom.[3] Following India's independence from Great Britain in 1947, the stirring for independence in Africa raised the issue of human rights both internationally and in the United States in a new way. African nations held by British, French, Portuguese, Belgian, German, and Italian governments pressed toward freedom. Nearly forty independent African nations were born in the 1950s and 1960s.

In January, 1956, the Woman's Division adopted a statement on "United States Policy in Relation to the World Issue of Dependent Peoples." The Division declared that the policy of the United States government should demonstrate "our belief that there is no substitute for eventual self-determination and self-government of all people."[4] Leaders of Methodist women agreed with United Church Women that foreign policy was inseparable from social policies in the United States.[5]

178

By linking human rights policies in the United States with governmental policies concerning human rights in other nations, churchwomen called for international opinion to help form a basis for measuring human rights. International consensus on human rights took priority over state or national laws which failed to administer justice. Where conflict existed between a minority group and those in power, questions about human rights were appropriate and ethical claims could be made on the basis of broad-based consensus involving the opinion of peoples not directly involved in the conflict. Members of the Woman's Society of Christian Service (WSCS) and the Wesleyan Service Guild (WSG), by virtue of their organizations' membership in United Church Women, heard recommendations for witness among Christian women as an appeal to each of them to become involved in their local communities to promote human rights and the integration of minority groups into the life of the church and community.

Methodist women drew strength for their task from strong anti-racism statements of the 1954 Assembly of the World Council of Churches (WCC), United Church Women, and statements prepared by the Department of CSR/LCA. At the annual meeting on January 8, 1955, the Woman's Division lifted up selected portions of the WCC statement as a model.[6] The WCC described racial discrimination as "an unutterable offense against God, to be endured no longer" and the corresponding task of the churches as being "to challenge the conscience of society. . . ."[7] The WCC declared, "The Church of Christ cannot approve of any law which discriminates on grounds of race...."[8]

Leaders of Methodist women were accepting their responsibility to guide in this direction. Yet such fine public statements could not mask a powerful segregationist backlash unleashed in the 1950s.

Under Attack from the Right

Suspicion and criticism clouded efforts for social change, including attempts by Methodist women to work against segregation in the early 1950s. A group of the nation's wealthiest industrialists and bankers began a campaign against change which equated "all economic or social legislation that impinges on the holdings, privileges and power of the extremely rich" with Communism.[9] Senator Joseph McCarthy's trumped-up investigation of leaders who worked for social change, and his use of innuendo, false charges, and defamation of character pitted government against people on the Left and worker against co-worker.

179

The House Un-American Activities Committee (HUAC) investigated prominent citizens about alleged conspiracy with Communist-related organizations in the United States, encouraged witch-hunting in government and private life, and accused people of vaguely defined offenses such as association with Communist sympathizers.[10] Right-wing extremists succeeded in adopting mandatory loyalty oaths for government employees and teachers in public and private schools and universities.

The Woman's Division spoke strongly for freedom of opinion and objected to use of innuendo and trial by committee or by the press in the face of attempts by HUAC to brand left-wing Americans as Communist and require loyalty oaths for government employees and teachers.[11] The Division itself faced a rising tide of opposition generated by McCarthy-era spokespersons for anti-Communism and racial bigotry.

In this period, as in the early twentieth century, the most potent way to rile up the public against white or black leaders who united across racial lines to work to change the social order was to label them Communist.[12] Interracial meetings and civil rights legislation sponsored by the Woman's Division provided "evidence" for critics that Methodist women were Communist.

Reader's Digest published an article entitled "Methodism's Pink Fringe,"[13] which alleged that Methodist leaders were Communist sympathizers. Among Methodist leaders, the Department of CSR/LCA stood like a lightning rod because of its outspoken position on race relations.

Organized propaganda campaigns were being conducted within The Methodist Church. Carloads of unsigned, undocumented, and out-of-context materials were distributed through the mails. Reprints of race-baiting and anti-Semitic articles stirred up hatred. Informed about the techniques of the hate campaign, the staff and officers of the Woman's Division determined to press on with their work.[14] The National Association for the Advancement of Colored People (NAACP) and the Southern Regional Council (SRC) cooperated in rebutting phony reports.[15]

Responses to Racial Hatred and Bigotry

Methodist women were among many groups that responded to criticism from the radical right. Thelma Stevens, Eleanor Neff, and Dorothy Weber asked local Methodist women's groups to assess the

180

program of the Woman's Division by inquiring, "*Is any part of this program recommended in Activities for 1950 contrary to the basic teachings of the New Testament?*"[16] The staff of CSR/LCA suggested that when women had answered this question to their own satisfaction they would be able to respond to people who were confused by the misrepresentation of basic principles in the recent *Reader's Digest* article.

The Department diffused criticism by pointing to the Woman's Division's board, which had representatives of Methodist women elected from every jurisdiction. These directors, elected by Methodist women, examined and adopted the program which the Department then implemented. The action of the Woman's Division did not bind any society or guild "to support a legislative program or any other program of action believed by the individual or group to be contrary to Christian principles and democratic procedures."[17]

Conservative threats to democracy prompted the Woman's Division to urge women to exercise their civic right to vote. One of the highlights of the 1950 Assembly of Methodist Women was the launching of the National Citizens Roll Call of Methodist Women. Methodist women, committed to support democratic principles as one manifestation of their Christian beliefs, were not all able to enter politics and campaign for human rights. Race stood as an obstacle to some and gender to all. The Woman's Division, however, agreed that every woman of voting age should register and vote, influence the nomination of political candidates, and express her opinion about legislative proposals. The Roll Call aimed to make "every Methodist woman an informed, registered, voting Christian citizen." Each WSCS and WSG was asked to work on at least one issue requiring political action and to study the issues involved in the upcoming November election. Women were encouraged to offer their services to their political party, rather than wait to be asked.[18]

The Woman's Division urged women to get out and vote in the 1952 presidential election. In "A Call to Methodist Women," the Department of CSR/LCA reminded women of their responsibilities as citizens to elect public officials who would "seek to enact laws and protect rights of all persons regardless of race, creed, or nationality."[19]

The tasks of citizens were the tasks of Christians as well. Thelma Stevens, Margaret Bender, and Ethel Watkins wrote, "We must work to enact legislation that will protect the rights of children and youth to health, education, decent housing, and protection from exploitation." They asked Methodist women to encourage the nation to improve the standard of living for "all the peoples of the world" by sharing its resources, and to work for peace by supporting the United Nations in its peace efforts.[20] Peace would come if people believed it was possible and would "work constructively toward its achievement." They concluded, "Toward this end Methodist women are committed to accept their full share of responsibility."[21]

The shared faith which contributed to Methodist women's understandings of race and what it meant to accept responsibility ran even deeper in the black church where people also experienced discrimination. God's call to Moses to lead the Hebrew people from slavery in Egypt into the promised land dominated the African American understanding of Christian faith.

In the 1950s the African American church (usually Baptist, AME, or AME Zion) grew rapidly with the migration of people from rural to urban areas. It provided a setting which nurtured the civil rights movement. Long a haven from white control, the urban black church offered comfort, safety, community, and vitality. Here one could feel the pulse of the people.

Financially independent congregations headed by pastors who took their cues from God, not from the state, provided pockets of resistance to segregation. Here pastors named oppression, invoked divine power to bear the burdens of people who resisted evil racism, and offered ultimate hope in the face of demoralizing and embittering experiences. College-trained ministers had studied under teachers such as Benjamin Mays (president of Morehouse College and a member of SRC's Board of Directors), C. D. Hubert, and S. A. Archer, leaders who perpetuated hope and aspiration to the new generation. Teachers exposed pastors-in-training to the power of the gospel and teachings of nonviolence.

In church, a person could *be somebody*. Pent-up emotions, of necessity controlled under scrutinizing eyes of whites, could be released in prayer, spirituals, hymns, and "Amens" to the lyrical sermons based on biblical verses that would "tell it like it is." The truth-telling power of the African American church was augmented by the community-building strength of the Bible, the church's location as a nerve center of the community, growing economic strength, and educated leadership. Thus the African American church became an essential resource to the civil rights movement in the 1950s. As civil rights scholar Aldon D. Morris has said, "The black church functioned as the institutional center of the modern civil rights movement."[22] It provided support, direction, and an organized mass base which aided developments on the legal front.

Leading the African American thrust for civil rights, the NAACP legal struggle began to reverse decades of Supreme Court decisions based on the 1896 *Plessy v. Ferguson* principle of "separate but equal." The U.S. Supreme Court decided in *Sipuel v. Oklahoma State Board of Regents* (1948) that the state must permit African American students the opportunity to "commence the study of law at a state institution at the same time as [other] citizens." In *Shelly v. Kraemer* the court ruled that restrictive covenants could not be legally enforced if they prohibited persons, because of race, from owning or occupying homes. The court refused to enforce private forms of discrimination.

In 1950, three landmark higher education cases undermined the legal foundations of segregation: *Sweatt v. Painter*, *McLaurin v. Oklahoma State Regents*, and *Henderson v. United States*. African American plaintiffs sought the right to pursue professional graduate training offered to other students by their state or the U.S. government. States could not afford segregation at the graduate school level. At this point of economic vulnerability, "separate but equal" was effectively challenged at a time when young black Americans, as never before, expected equality.

Desegregation of the armed forces cultivated a crop of African Americans who completed their tour of duty and entered the labor force as skilled laborers and white-collar workers. By 1953, in a whopping increase over the previous decade, African Americans owned about one-third of the residences they occupied. Nearly seventy-five thousand African Americans were in college. An economic shift of power was in process, of a magnitude dreamed of by the SRC.[23]

By 1950, the inner core of SRC leaders clearly opposed all forms of segregation. SRC was moving beyond the position that attitudes set the boundaries for race progress.[24] George S. Mitchell continued at the helm of SRC, assisted by Harold C. Fleming and Dorothy Tilly. Executive officers included Rufus E. Clement, Marion A. Write, Carter Wesley, Gordon B. Hancock, Alfred D. Mynders, and A. W. Dent.[25] The SRC closely tracked its top priority issues: voter registration, school integration, and public school lawsuits; and regularly monitored municipal hiring of African American police officers, training of police officers in human relations, and red-lining of maps to segregate housing through control of home mortgages.

A few predominantly white liberal groups also resisting attacks from the Right defined a position to the Left of SRC. These included the Southern Conference Education Fund (represented by Aubrey Williams, Will Alexander, Carl and Anne Braden), Highlander Folk School (Myles Horton and James Dombrowski), and the Fellowship for Southern Churchmen (a group of outspoken white clergy and laity, including the young educator and fledgling theologian, Nelle Morton). Still relying on education for leadership development and change of attitudes, these groups spent little energy trying to hold the South together and cater to those who needed more time for change. Instead, they gave attention and leadership to defining the positions and rationale essential to overcoming racial barriers. They relied on publications and meetings, workshops and polemic.

The politically radical Right also targeted Lillian Smith and Paula Snelling. In a unique way, Smith and Snelling, editors of the *North Georgia Review*, which became *South Today*, mounted a sustained thrust for integration based on their resources, a mountain top property, and writing skills. The quarterly journal reviewed new books and featured some of the South's most mature and literary reflections on southern racial attitudes.[26] Lillian Smith began her career as a teacher and Methodist missionary in China, but was called home to care for her family's property when her father took ill. She found racial prejudice both in China and in Georgia.

Lillian Smith and Paula Snelling directed a camping program that helped white teenagers understand discrimination. Old Screamer Mountain, the home of Smith and Snelling located near Clayton, Georgia, developed its reputation from a summer camp program for upper-class white teens from southern towns and cities. For twenty-four years the summer camp setting provided opportunities for Smith to plant questions about southern customs and culture, racial expectations and attitudes, in the minds of her youthful charges. Now and then parents would raise questions about the camp, which Smith personally answered, but the daughters usually remained enamored with the experience and begged to return.

As one of America's most noted women authors, Smith achieved national recognition with the publication of her 1944 novel, *Strange Fruit*. About interracial love, it immediately became popular and was banned from sale in the South, which, of course, added to its lure. Smith's 1949 book, *Killers of the Dream*, used biography and essays to describe the stolen dreams, inner poverty of spirit, and social conundrums of racial prejudice.

Everybody who was eminent among white liberals in the South read Smith. She was considered too radical by a majority and was deliberately excluded from the SRC. Since she spoke forthrightly, even calling for immediate school desegregation in 1954, Smith epitomized for white liberals the need to ask the question of what path liberalism should take toward racial reform in the South. Some thought that immediate change was risky and dangerous.

Southern White Liberalism

Southern white liberals found themselves enmeshed in a tangle of expectations. Anthony Lake Newberry has described three dilemmas that liberals faced: influence, extremes, and loyalties. Liberals who wanted to maintain influence and not be written off in the white community had to yield on some aspects of their personal commitment to racial justice, or, as they phrased it, "not get too far ahead of the people."[27] Lillian Smith noted with disdain that to protect their standing in the community, many liberals did nothing at all to speak or work for racial justice. Some liberal-minded ministers spoke for the broad principles of human rights but took no actions that threatened their position in relation to the church hierarchy or their local church budget and membership roster.

White liberals also found themselves situated between extremes, criticized from both Left and Right. Desiring to appear reasonable and finding that impossible, some concluded that they could not please everyone, and felt liberated by this discovery. Others remained trapped. Bouncing between walls, they tried to create a place for themselves by criticizing others. Some fired volleys of attack on the congressman from Harlem, Adam Clayton Powell, and on Walter White and the NAACP. Liberals who criticized northern African American leaders as dangerous radicals frequently also attacked southern whites who wanted to dismantle prejudicial and discriminatory southern racial mores. Such persons viewed Lillian Smith as a "shrill moral perfectionist" and Carl and Anne Braden, who in 1954 bought a home in a white neighborhood and sold it to an African American family, as "misguided" and "forcing" the issue.[28]

Leaders of the Woman's Division knew that Methodist women were often caught between voices from Left and Right. They carefully avoided labeling positions, a technique which facilitated processes of growth and change of position. *The Methodist Woman* encouraged women to study, discuss, think, and grow in their understanding of human relations. Only three approaches to racial issues were described as pernicious: those of the Ku Klux Klan, the White Citizen's Councils, and apathy!

Southern white liberals also often felt torn between their loyalties: love for the South and rejection of bigotry, inequity, intolerance, and injustice. Persons more to the Left found that they could separate these forces, while gradualists argued for a balance to be found in letting the South move at its own pace, set its own agenda, and use its own leadership.[29] The debate in the South over whether federal initiative

185

should be used to protect civil rights also contained a layer of judgment, perhaps felt especially by the SRC, that federal action represented a failure to achieve substantive local effort.

Newberry's summary of white liberal activities at mid-century aptly describes the work of the Woman's Division and the leaders of Methodist women. When tensions were low they "produced biting social commentary." They opposed violence against African Americans, worked for the "principle of equal treatment in public accommodations, hiring practices, the administration of justice, public spending, and exercise of the ballot." They also deflated racial rumors and stereotypes and "maintained contacts with middle-class blacks that were occasionally helpful in defusing racial tensions." Methodist women, in common with white liberals, courted federal legislation to bring full civil rights to all citizens. When changes approached, Methodist women helped southerners adjust. Local leaders appealed to conscience, but also made change palatable by softening controversial aspects, declaring that the fundamentals of racial patterns would remain in place, or surrendering to community plans for resistance to change.[30]

A case study from Tuskegee, Alabama, shows how the political Left and Right struggled for control of one community. In this instance, Methodist women remained curiously silent.

Liberals and Resistance, Southern Style

Alabama's Black Belt, an area in which African Americans outnumber whites, was also known as a bastion of segregation. Yet here anomalies are found. Free-thinking liberals also inhabit the area, descendants of people influenced by the French enlightenment, Jeffersonian democracy, an abolitionist spirit, Populists, the Social Gospel, and Methodism. In 1913 Mary DeBardeleben founded Augusta's Bethlehem Center which was sponsored by the Woman's Missionary Council. DeBardeleben came from the old established Bardeleben family in Tuskegee which had such roots. DeBardeleben, a graduate of East Alabama Female Institute, returned to Tuskegee to teach at her *alma mater*, now Huntington College. One of her prize students from DeBardeleben's Paine College teaching days in Augusta, Charles G. Gomillion, achieved prominence for his work in civil rights.

Prior to the Civil War, Methodists with a penchant for education founded in the Black Belt three white institutions of higher education that graduated numerous pastors and professionals who often remained in the area to live and work as lawyers, judges, doctors, and legislators. Graduates of Birmingham Southern College in Greensboro, East Alabama Male Institute in Auburn, and East Alabama Female Institute in Tuskegee who entered ministry valued their exposure to different points of view. In the 1950s, as many as seventy-five of these seminary-trained ministers served in the North Alabama Conference of The Methodist Church where they were consistently out-voted.

Gomillion, a sociologist at Tuskegee Institute, from 1934 on led a persistent campaign to expand African American voter registration in Tuskegee.[31] The Tuskegee County Board of Registrars, bolstered by devious state laws and generous amounts of personal discretion, severely limited the registration of African American voters in one of the nation's most flagrant cases of defiance of political rights.[32]

Yet in Tuskegee, torn by racial prejudice in the 1950s and 1960s, there were a few white people, men and women, Presbyterian and Methodist, who spoke and worked for civil rights regardless of race. Those who led forthrightly included Tuskegee Methodist Church's parsonage family, the Reverend Ennis and Julie Sellers, and their daughter, who helped integrate the public school. The Reverend Robert D. Miller of the Presbyterian Church and white Methodist liberals, such as school superintendent C. A. (Hardboy) Pruitt, Principal E. W. Wadsworth, and school board member Frances Hodnett Rush, put their reputation on the line.[33]

School desegregation was difficult in Tuskegee. Governor George C. Wallace decreed and enforced with troops the closure of Tuskegee High School to prevent its integration in the fall of 1963. When Wallace turned students away, the Justice Department intervened with a restraining order against Wallace. Wallace then called out the National Guard, but President Kennedy federalized the Guard and ordered them to return to their barracks. On the following day, schools in Birmingham, Mobile, and Tuskegee were integrated.[34]

Nearly thirty years after the 1963–64 racial crisis climax in Tuskegee over public school integration, the community had only a few stores and was 97 percent African American. Its economic base was concentrated in Tuskegee Institute and the VA Hospital. Many whites sold everything for pennies on the dollar and moved to Auburn. Leaving behind home, income, church and community, they took the ultimate step needed to maintain segregation. Liberal white church members who had risked their reputations on school desegregation were shunned and drummed out of their church and community.

It is impossible to claim with any certainty that 1950s programs of Methodist women changed minds and helped create the slim number of allies who stood publicly for school integration and at great cost in Tuskegee in the 1960s.

In Tuskegee, evidence of Methodist women's influence is tangential at best. Perhaps the long-time family connections and close friendships between Mary DeBardeleben and other white women in Tuskegee had an influence. Maybe the studies and programs of Methodist women slowly made small inroads among a few women. Possibly untraced historic ties linked rare female faculty of the Black Belt colleges with the Woman's Missionary Societies. Mothers of the seminary-trained Black Belt Methodist ministers in the social gospel tradition may have belonged to the missionary societies. Where white southerners determined to resist segregation, as they did very thoroughly in Tuskegee, there is little evidence of influence made by Methodist women.

Yet the work of Methodist women on racial matters made a cumulative difference, particularly in the South. Sometimes it did not bear the name "Methodist." Although no firm evidence shows direct links between Methodist women's programs and changed minds in communities less recalcitrant than Tuskegee, so much was happening that Methodist women and other churchwomen clearly had grassroots influence all over the South, enough that they were harassed.

The Fellowship of the Concerned

In 1951, *New South* paid tribute to the work being done by women of the Fellowship of the Concerned (FOC), a southwide organization of churchwomen founded by Dorothy Tilly in conjunction with her post as director of Women's Work of the SRC.

> It is one of the most important and effective continuing programs of the Southern Regional Council. . . .[T]he devotion and energy of Mrs. Tilly and the voluntary assistance of her fellow church women have brought remarkable results, against tremendous odds.[35]

From cities and county seat towns, three thousand women had pledged to "make their influence felt for equal justice" by attending court hearings so that judges, juries, attorneys, sheriffs, plaintiffs, defendants, and witnesses would know that they must be truthful and fair.[36] Some middle-aged white women voted for the first time and others accompanied African American women to election polls.[37] Women gathered samples of voter registration applications filled with cumbersome de-

188

Accountability

tailed requirements designed to screen out African Americans.[38] They worked with the SRC for simplified, expedited, and nondiscriminatory voter registration.

FOC women took particular interest in working on school desegregation, spending two days together in early 1955 workshops on the subject. The women promised to take immediate action by working with Human Relations Councils and applying what they had learned from court visits. They planned to attend school board meetings. If school boards had "nothing to hide, they will welcome [us]."[39] The boards would realize they were being held accountable to national policy and to those who favored desegregation. If the presence of women created a fuss then the women would gather large audiences for board meetings.

Members of FOC also agreed to educate themselves by reading Robert Speer's book, *Of One Blood*; Lillian Smith's, *Now Is the Time*; and Sarah Patton Boyle's *Saturday Evening Post* article, "Southerners Will Like Integration." In response to attacks on the NAACP, the women agreed to learn more about that organization and become familiar with the legal steps in desegregation. Thelma Stevens noted that churches needed to support litigation:

> Our generation was brought up to think that the churches could educate toward change, but we must not touch the law or get involved with litigation. Churches must now recognize the fact that lawsuits and court action are an effective way of instituting social change.[40]

Two thousand women participated in southwide and state meetings of the FOC. Methodist women served actively as leaders and members.[41]

Discussions of first steps to be taken in the home, community, and through United Church Women's groups reminded women how they could "cultivate right attitudes" toward desegregation. They faced frustrations and fears, but intended to effect change among children, families, social groups, and businesses. Some women noted with disappointment the hesitancy of the church to risk involvement. "[The] Church is taking second place in influence. Church is not as fearless as it should be. Sometimes it's the laymen, sometimes the minister who is frustrated in seeking progress." They added, "Perhaps our greatest [obstacle] is our own fear."[42]

Not all fears were unfounded. Four FOC women in Montgomery received threatening and harassing letters. They requested help from Dorothy Tilly who appealed to the federal Civil Rights Division for protection, and were assured that their complaint "is receiving our very careful attention." Even if harassment was not prevented, it was not kept secret.[43]

Harassment of Tilly, in addition to threatening phone calls, letters, and threats on her life which led to around-the-clock police protection of her home, included claims that she was a Communist. M. G. Lowman, from the conservative Methodist group Circuit Riders, Inc., wrote to one of the country's best-known preachers, Dow Kirkpatrick, stating as fact that she was:

> a person whose name is carried among the list of those 141 individuals identified by the Special Committee on Un-American Activities of the House of Representatives as comprising the Communist Party's supreme bid for power throughout its first 25 years of existence in this country.[44]

Kirkpatrick refuted Lowman's accusation, adding, "She has suffered a great deal of unkind and unchristian attack from many sources, but I've found her always to be one who received such attack in the same spirit as our Lord."[45]

Community leaders, working in coalition with a variety of community organizations, helped bring about some changes. Thelma Mills, a Methodist, reported on signs of progress in Houston:

> So many things have been happening in Houston. A Negro woman elected to the School Board; the United Church Women have combined with the Negro Church Women; a new liberal mayor is making changes possible.[46]

Mills' comments came in the context of her invitation to Tilly to attend Houston's first interracial event being sponsored by churchwomen. The community coalitions created success stories and their leaders provided a network of speakers for annual and regional meetings who carried the movement forward.[47]

Making Civil Rights Palatable: Compromise and Resistance

In the 1950s, integration of minority groups usually was interpreted as the act of bringing minority groups into the organizations and structures of white groups. The melting-pot motif pervaded assumptions about integration and, in the minds of most white Methodist women, implied that white groups should allow black persons equal opportunities to attend public meetings. It did not mean that the leadership of groups should change, or that the agenda of integrated groups would be altered to include concerns of the new members, or that power would be shared. Often white Methodist women were not aware enough of their own assumptions, agendas, and use of power to be able to raise such questions.

Some Methodist women were content to omit the controversial activities recommended by the Department and serve The Methodist Church in traditional ways. Thelma Stevens reported that more than eight thousand questionnaires returned in 1950 indicated that among local secretaries of CSR/LCA the predominant emphasis was on local church activities such as providing church dinners, caring for the parsonage, and catering wedding receptions. Even so, some Methodist women chose to work with justice issues.

Communication in the South has achieved both fame and notoriety for being indirect. Although taught that it was not polite to discuss the subject of race, white Methodist women broke that taboo. They would read, study, discuss, and pray about racial issues. As long as they were not required to actually do anything, they could appear to be going along with the program when, in some instances, they were incredibly resistant. A contemporary women's society in Ramer, Alabama, has expressed its opposition to the policies of the Women's Division of The Board of Global Ministries by functioning as an independent group not affiliated with the national organization of United Methodist Women.[48] In the 1950s, events pressed people to take action, but choices were polarized. Even liberals hunkered down, reined in their activities, and tried to weather the storm.

Women who were frustrated by resistance to racial justice and exasperated by the complacency of others in their local church usually joined a network of other like-minded women. They linked across denominational lines through United Church Women and with other Methodist women by serving on the committee for CSR/LCA.

This network provided emotional support for the concerned women who formed a grassroots movement for racial justice. Women in the network depended on and were accountable to each other. They empathized with and inspired one another. They often added a personal note to the business letters they exchanged. They frequently felt isolated and longed for each other's company. They worked hard to cultivate support from others in their church and community. They were convinced that racial prejudice was an artificial barrier to God's intent for people to live in community and love one another and they pursued living this faith with passion.

Where the big faith dream became too specific and too controversial to make headway along one path, Methodist women would find another avenue for action. Their persistence paid off, especially as they focused on two major tasks: educating Americans about segregation laws, and desegregating schools.

(education)

We are caught in the stream of change—whether we like it or not. If we resist it, we may find ourselves staying in one spot, but whirling round and round like a top. If we are willing to move we can add the weight of our lives to help in determining the direction the change will take. Are we moving toward freedom and light, or toward tyranny and darkness, or are we standing still, caught between the two streams of change, whirling aimlessly, like a top?

—Noreen D. Tatum
Report of Chairman of Christian Social Relations
United Church Women of Alabama [c. 1959]

Chapter 11

The 1950s: Methodist Women Covenant to End Segregation

Christians live as a covenant people, inheritors of promises made and kept between God and people. These promises are taught from generation to generation: that God's love is steadfast, and that God is present in all aspects of life, calling people to be faithfully working toward the perfection, fulfillment, and completion of all things in God. To this end, Jesus represented God's way, ministering to people from all walks of life and describing God's unexpected, undeserved love and mercy in parables and stories. In the 1950s, when Methodist women focused their racial program on education and bound themselves to the work of racial justice by signing a charter, they were living out their faith.

States' Laws on Race and Color

Two programs of the Woman's Division launched in the late 1940s made a major new impact on ways organized Methodist women proceeded with local efforts to overcome racial barriers: Methodist women published a book of segregation laws and adopted a Charter of Racial Policies.

In 1948, Thelma Stevens, Susie Jones, and members of the Committee on Racial Practices decided to compile segregation laws for those states in which the Woman's Division operated mission projects such as schools and hospitals. They hired Pauli Murray to research and locate the laws with the intention of publishing a pamphlet they could use to guide desegregation of their own institutions. By the end of 1949 they had completed a survey of government regulations and racial practices in institutions owned by the Woman's Division, including those institutions owned in other countries.

More segregation laws were found than anyone ever imagined existed. The project expanded to include laws in all states. In 1950, when it was finally published, *States' Laws on Race and Color*, edited by Pauli Murray, had become a book of 746 pages, a legal document of record, the first ever compilation of American laws on race and color.[1] "This book should be in every college library, every church institution and Woman's Society and in every public library in this nation," wrote the staff of CSR/LCA, who believed that knowledge of laws which bind or bring freedom could influence the "emancipation of some 25 million people in the United States. . . ."[2]

The new book was touted as the answer to many questions about racial practices in communities all over the nation. If women wanted to know whether it was legal to hold interracial meetings, host black women in local hotels or restaurants, ride together on buses, eat together on trains, admit black students to local high schools or universities, to amusement parks or playgrounds, or sell their homes to black families, they now had authoritative answers.

Methodist women recognized that problems of discrimination and segregation were not sectional. "They are the responsibility of the entire nation," wrote Thelma Stevens, Eleanor Neff Curry, and Dorothy Weber, the executive staff of CSR/LCA.[3] Every state had laws on race and color. Some attempted to provide civil rights, while others provided for segregation. At least one state did both! Women's societies were invited to buy copies of the new book and place them in local public libraries, high school and college libraries, and in nearby Methodist hospitals, homes, and schools. Oregon's Wesleyan Service Guilds (WSG) donated the book to every college in the state.[4]

Women began to end segregation within institutions owned by the Woman's Division. Occasionally schools owned by the Woman's Division quietly accepted a few students of color. Muriel Day claimed that Scarritt College in Nashville and the National College for Christian Workers in Kansas City had found ways to have interracial student bodies, even under segregation. International students faced fewer racial hurdles than American students.[5]

Methodist women who now had access to state laws followed closely the cases before the Supreme Court. The Supreme Court had decided that the University of Texas and the University of Oklahoma were required to admit Negroes, and that railroad dining car service was to be integrated even in states practicing segregation. "This ruling marked a great stride forward in the nation's effort to rid itself of discrimination and segregation in all forms," proclaimed *The Methodist Woman*.[6] Thurgood Marshall, who prepared and argued numerous civil rights cases before the Supreme Court, referred to *States' Laws on Race and Color* as the bible of desegregation.[7]

In 1952 the Committee on Racial Practices of the Department of CSR/LCA reported that the Marshall Field Foundation had contributed $3,360 which was used to distribute 712 copies of the book to a wide audience:

45 U.N. officials
20 state public agencies
121 law libraries
67 local public agencies
94 legal periodicals
86 national private organizations
63 bar associations
86 Negro colleges
18 special New York libraries
30 social science periodicals
82 colleges and universities.[8]

Laws changed so rapidly that within two years the Woman's Division authorized a supplement to be prepared to inform women of changes in race laws enacted since 1950.

The Charter of Racial Policies—1952

The second major effort of the early 1950s, the writing of the Charter of Racial Policies and its adoption by the Woman's Division in 1952, provided a landmark for new efforts in race relations.[9] The charter was to become a primary tool for the work of the Woman's Division in the area of race relations over the next decade and a model for future charters.[10]

The charter began with a preamble listing the beliefs rooted in tenets of the social gospel that were basic to the human rights policies of the Woman's Division.

CHARTER OF RACIAL POLICIES—1952

WE BELIEVE

1. We believe that God is the Father of all people of all races and we are His children in one family.

2. We believe that the personality of every human being is sacred.

3. We believe that opportunities for fellowship and service, for

197

personal growth, and for freedom in every aspect of life are inherent rights of every individual.

4. We believe that the visible church of Jesus Christ must demonstrate these principles within its own organization and program.[11]

The Woman's Division committed itself to build "a fellowship and social order without racial barriers."

The charter set ten policies for the Woman's Division. Progress in moving toward the enumerated ideals was to be assessed according to practical steps taken within structures of the Woman's Division, Woman's Societies, and Guilds. Hiring and nominations for office would be determined on the basis of qualifications, not race. All programs and facilities were to be open to all people regardless of race. Where law or custom was in conflict with this policy, local boards and staff were obligated to work to create a public opinion which would change such laws and customs. Local societies were charged with responsibility for integrating all groups into the life of the church. The Woman's Division committed itself to hold its meetings where people of all races could have access to the meeting facilities and to hospitality without discrimination.

The charter called on each jurisdiction and conference to ratify the charter. "Such a ratification will constitute a commitment to work for the speedy implementation of those principles and policies within the bounds of a respective jurisdiction or conference."[12]

 The significance of the charter lay in the requirement that women make a public commitment of their position on racial issues. Whether the charter was discussed in a local or a conference meeting, women could not simply listen and walk away. The charter was being presented for ratification. Women had to indicate their views on race in front of their friends. The Woman's Division itself would have to change hiring policies of missionaries and staff. Standards that could be monitored were being set. Officers would be expected to administer the new policies. Women were making a promise. They put their integrity on the line: they would want to keep their word.

The charter committed Methodist women to make substantial changes from time-honored traditions. Many women would not be supported in these endeavors by members of their community or members of their local church. Racism was being presented as an area of Christian growth for women in all sectors of the nation. While American society was still segregated, Methodist women were challenged by the charter to move toward complete desegregation of their organizations.

Thelma Stevens used the Charter of Racial Policies as a basis to call leaders of CSR/LCA to action. The charter was a guide that helped Methodist women examine their own racial practices, just as the Universal Declaration of Human Rights served to call all people and nations to account for human relations. For Methodist women this translated into the need to "make a consistent effort to create a public opinion in the local community that accepts all individuals as children of God, whose rights and personalities are equally sacred."[13]

At first the charter had little impact on local Methodist women's groups. Gradually conferences ratified the charter. At the 1954 assembly in Milwaukee, Wisconsin, a large copy of the Charter of Racial Policies, approximately six feet by six feet in size, lay on a large table in the exhibit hall. Sixty-five conference presidents signed the charter, signifying that their conferences had voted to ratify the charter. Twenty additional conferences reported that the charter had been presented for study.[14]

School Integration

Before the Supreme Court issued its May 17, 1954, decision on school desegregation in *Brown v. The Board of Education*, the Woman's Division started work on school integration. The Department of Christian Social Relations (CSR) challenged Methodist women with principles of faith.

> Regardless of what the [Supreme Court] decision [on school desegregation] may be, our job is clear. Time marches on! The ground swell of human equality under God is becoming unmistakably the ground swell of human equality under law! . . . [W]e must plant the right seeds.[15]

The charter provided the rationale for early efforts in school integration. Although the Charter of Racial Policies did not specifically name the Woman's Division to work toward the integration of public schools, it committed the Division to open its own schools and hospitals to all people without discrimination and to "build in every area it may touch, a fellowship and social order without racial barriers."[16]

In its January 1954 annual report, the Department of CSR recommended ways for women to begin the preparations necessary for smooth integration of schools. Women's primary role was that of bringing people together to hear facts and dispell rumors, to talk and work together. Women could influence public opinion and attitudes by

199

giving people opportunities to work cooperatively. By bringing together parents and teachers of both races they could deal with facts and fears and discuss problems. Methodist women could work consistently to secure necessary state and federal funds for making adequate opportunities through public schools available to all children without discrimination in any form. Methodist women launched neighborhood conversation groups to talk about public schools and segregation and thus influence local practices.

As the Supreme Court decision drew closer, Methodist women became increasingly specific about school desegregation. "Every Methodist woman in the nation has a responsibility directly or indirectly for the public schools of this land," heralded an article in the February 1954 issue of *The Methodist Woman*.[17] Equal opportunities needed to be interpreted in terms of teachers' salaries, length of the school term, teacher-student ratios, and even the number and age of school buses serving all the children of a community. Methodist women could not deny the inequities when they read that Arkansas spent $114 per white student and $75 per black student in 1951–52. Other states had similarly disproportionate ratios. Georgia spent $143 per white student and $80 per black student. In 1952, Florida spent $206 for each white student and $159 for each black student.[18] However, understanding the facts and overcoming racial barriers were two quite different matters.

Responses to Brown v. Board of Education

The 1954 quadrennial General Assembly of Methodist Women met in Milwaukee, Wisconsin, where the Charter on Racial Policies was presented for ratification by approximately one hundred conference units of the Woman's Society of Christian Service (WSCS). Meanwhile, the Supreme Court issued its long-awaited decision on school desegregation.

Immediately Thelma Stevens and Susie Jones met and drafted a resolution of support for the Supreme Court's decision. The resolution read:

"We affirm anew our determination to work with greater urgency to eliminate segregation from every part of our community and national life and from the organization and practice of our own church and its agencies and programs. We rejoice that the highest tribunal of justice in this land, the Supreme Court of the United States, proclaimed on May 17, 1954, that segregation in public education anywhere is an infringement of the Constitution and a violation of the Fourteenth Amendment.

"We accept our full Christian responsibility to work through church and community channels to speed the process of transition from segregated schools to a new pattern of justice and freedom."[19]

The resolution, adopted by the assembly, was the first public statement of Methodists that affirmed the Supreme Court decision.

A group of southern delegates to the assembly gathered to rescind their conferences' support of the charter. Stevens spoke with them. She said that although not every woman's society would be able to implement every part of the charter, the charter was needed to keep long-range goals before Methodist women.

In a special all-day session women gathered, intent on reversing their earlier decision. Sadie Tillman, chair of Christian Social Relations and Local Church Activities (CSR/LCA) who also chaired the session, allowed women to express anger over their dilemma, but encouraged them to understand that the charter upheld ideals.[20] Perhaps women in a local church were not ready to work for school integration, but it would be better not to scuttle the charter's vision of a future without racial barriers. Ultimately no conference rescinded the charter. Realizing that they had differing situations and understandings, Methodist women left the assembly officially committed to work for the integration of public schools.

The Woman's Division came under sharp criticism in 1955 for its stand on school desegregation. Sadie Tillman replied to the challenge, guiding the policy of the Division:

Sadie Tillman

> As a Woman's Division of the Board of Missions it is our responsibility to set the highest ultimate goals of Christian life and thought as objectives for all efforts. We recognize that there are varying stages of progress in different areas. . . .
>
> Because of the wide range of interests we represent, we must make our objectives so inclusive that they permit all groups to advance toward fuller realization of Christian ideals. . . . However, any deviation from an expression of the highest Christian concern in the rights and privileges of all men would be disastrous in its effect.
>
> . . . Each woman on the Division should be an interpreter in her own area, as well as an encourager of all efforts toward fulfillment of the ideal.
>
> . . . Leaders of several races and nationalities involved, whether white, Negro, Mexican, Indian, or others, must work out steps of progress in terms of local conditions.

... The glory of the enterprise is our united effort. We move in the same direction, recognizing the differences in backgrounds but realizing the joy of a common goal.[21]

After Tillman's presentation, Mrs. Roscoe M. White offered a countering proposal "That we commend those leaders in the several states and the national government who counsel that the time and manner of instituting integrated schools be left to the federal courts in the local communities."[22] The measure was defeated.

 CSR/LCA had agreed to work toward the Christian ideals they espoused, recognizing and accepting differences in interpretations and approaches.

Desegregating Methodist Institutions and Public Schools

Compared with the 1944–48 rise in expectations over the federal role in extending civil rights, the Supreme Court's school desegregation decision put the front lines of civil rights change right back into local communities. Change accelerated. Entrenchment and radicalization over school desegregation increased polarization. People had to make choices about whether they were going to resist or facilitate school desegregation. Some forward-thinking Methodist women founded, joined, or lobbied existing Human Relations Councils in numerous locations, including Greensboro and Nashville. These groups began to take a pivotal role in discussions with school boards.

The Supreme Court decision *Brown v. the Board of Education* freed the Woman's Division from legal constraints to move toward integrating its own institutions. The Woman's Division announced that Methodist women "welcome this opportunity to expand our program of racial integration in these institutions and expect our schools to stand by, ready to enroll students and to appoint faculty regardless of race or color."[23] Scarritt College for Christian Workers integrated in 1952 when Tennessee law changed. Other schools and colleges appointed members of various races to their faculties. Edith Carter, the superintendent of Boylan-Haven School, a Methodist school in Jacksonville, Florida, boldly declared, "The leaders among the members of the WSCS are ready for nonsegregation, I believe."[24] By 1957 Muriel Day, the executive secretary for the Bureau of Educational Institutions for the Woman's Division, reported interracial staff working relationships at Allen High School (Asheville, North Carolina), Browning Home and Mather Academy (Camden, South Carolina), Boylan-Haven School (Jacksonville, Florida), and Harwood Girls' School (Albuquerque, New Mexico).[25]

The Methodist Church lagged behind the Woman's Division in integrating its institutional ministries. In 1956, the Woman's Division petitioned the General Conference of The Methodist Church to take similar steps by requesting "that the institutions of the church, local churches, colleges, universities, theological schools, hospitals, and homes carefully study their policies and practices as they relate to race, making certain that these policies and practices are Christian."[26]

Public school integration proceeded slowly, plagued by tokenism. The National Association for the Advancement of Colored People (NAACP) reported that as of May 1955 "nearly 250,000 Negro and white children were attending classes peaceably together in 500 elementary and secondary schools which until last year had been for the exclusive use of boys and girls of one race or the other."[27] The Department of CSR indicated that the process needed to be speeded up. African American teachers were losing jobs. The Woman's Division expressed concern over this new manifestation of racism and urged women to engage community leaders in discussion of ways to prevent this loss.[28]

Rather than providing a master plan for school integration, the Department of CSR trained local leaders to run workshops so that specific local situations could be addressed appropriately.[29] In many communities church people played an inconspicuous but important role by attending committee meetings and community dialogues essential to successful school integration. Methodist women participated in community plans that successfully integrated public schools in Oak Ridge, Tennessee, "without undue disturbance."[30]

Clinton, Tennessee, experienced racial violence. The members of the WSCS of Clinton Memorial Methodist Church wrote to the black members of a neighboring Methodist church, expressing their regret over the racial incidents and requesting that both groups covenant to pray for the restoration of peace in the community. While the public schools were desegregating, the Clinton Memorial Woman's Society ratified the Charter of Racial Policies, publicly committing themselves to work for the removal of racial barriers in their own community.

In Nashville, Tennessee, the interracial Human Rights Council had been formed about four years earlier to study school integration. When tensions reached their peak over school integration, the United Church Women, of which Methodist women were a part, declared their support for the school board's plan for desegregation.

Mrs. J. S. VanWinkle of Danville, Kentucky, attributed the success of local community meetings of interracial groups to the guidance of the Lincoln Leadership School's interracial workshops, held every summer since 1951 at Lincoln University in Pennsylvania. The Woman's Division had provided finances, leaders, and students for these workshops. Integrated prayer groups in Danville had grown into small discussion groups relating to community problems. Interracial Bible study groups met in various churches during 1957. The first African American students entered Danville High School in 1956 and three of these graduated with the class of 1957. "The prayer groups, discussion periods, and the fellowship hours brought about understanding between the Negroes and the Whites. This helped to accomplish integration of the Danville High School without fears or misunderstandings."[31]

Similar stories could be recounted for numerous southern towns which never made the news because desegregation came about without racial violence. Shelbyville, Kentucky, integrated the first-grade classes without racial incidents. The Methodist woman who reported this success felt that the presence of Christian teachers and a Christian principal made the difference, and that they may have been influenced by the Civic Church Woman's Group which had met in Shelbyville for many years. A foundation of Christian understanding and attitudes had been laid by this interracial, ecumenical group who had taken it upon themselves to prepare Shelbyville's citizens for school integration. In hundreds of towns across the South, foundations for community interracial relations had been laid by African American community leaders, the NAACP, YMCAs, YWCAs, Human Relations Councils, Methodist women, and United Church Women in the three previous decades.[32]

In 1956 in Kentucky, before schools integrated in their community, the white youth of the Methodist Youth Fellowship from Flemingsburg Methodist Church invited African American youth from Strawberry Methodist Church to attend a regular Sunday evening meeting. The same white teens helped welcome their African American friends into the formerly all-white high school in ways that helped ease the adjustment of all students. Methodist women counseled the youth in these choices.[33]

Methodist women continued to support a strong federal role in school integration. Some women participated in letter-writing campaigns that lobbied congressional representatives to vote for federal aid to education to be distributed with the condition that funds be withheld from schools that refused to admit minority students. The Woman's Division continued to affirm both state control over public school systems and desegregation of these systems, and called on Methodist women across the nation to work toward these ends.[34]

fed.
vs.
Local

By 1959, school closures made mockery of the system of free public education. Entire city school systems closed and private schools for fee-paying students opened to circumvent forced school integration. The Woman's Division reminded Methodist women that parents who supported closure of school systems surrendered to others their voice in the free public education of their community's children. The Department of CSR appealed to parents and citizens to support the basic right of children to education so that the public school system could be saved.[35]

In this climate, Methodist Noreen Dunn Tatum presented to the United Church Women of Alabama her analysis of school desegregation and the church's response. She reminded her listeners that school desegregation applied to all parts of the nation and all races, and that the Supreme Court was protecting the "rights of all citizens to participate equally in the educational facilities provided by *public funds* for *public use*." Dire predictions had not come true in other instances: "abolition of the white primary, de-segregation in the armed forces, in public transportation across state lines, in Veterans Administration Hospitals, in Civil Service jobs (notably Postal employees)." Various groups such as labor and library associations were desegregating voluntarily, as had some state universities. "All of this has taken place without violence. . . ."

Tatum pointed out that African Americans who resorted to litigation had *not* wracked violence, and for that "Christian white people of the South should get down on their knees and thank God. . . ." She reminded her audience that they were part of the U.S., as was the Supreme Court, and therefore the school desegregation decision was not "something forced upon us by an outside agency." Yet the world was watching, especially Communists, who observed that democracy was for "whites only."

Among her points, Tatum appealed for women to move "toward freedom and light":

7. The Christian Church [h]as an unprecedented opportunity and an inescapable responsibility to help in the creation of an atmosphere in which growth in human understanding and goodwill can take place, and to lead out in the formation of plans which will make possible orderly and visible progress in human relations.

8. The importance of our stand as Christian women to the Christian missionary enterprise cannot be overestimated. . . . We are caught in the stream of change—whether we like it or not. If we resist it, we may find ourselves staying in one spot, but whirling round and round like a top. If we are willing to move we can add

the weight of our lives to help in determining the direction change will take.[36]

Growth, goodwill, and irresistible change: Tatum admired these characteristics of the lure of God toward justice.

Segregated Housing Impeded School Desegregation

Communities found a new way to avoid school integration. Housing areas could be marked so that African Americans would live in some areas and whites would live in other areas. Public schools would be open to all races, but if they were also neighborhood schools, only students from the neighboring area would attend that school, and school boundaries could be drawn to follow the color line. What had existed before in a general way as African American neighborhoods and white neighborhoods became more clearly defined and more rigidly entrenched with social threats attendant on anyone who dared to defy the new convention. Starting in 1957 Methodist women lobbied for an end to discrimination in federal housing policies, loan policies, urban renewal programs, and in restrictive housing covenants.[37] The Woman's Division set as its standard of attainment for the nation "a decent home and suitable living environment" for every family, regardless of color, race, national origin, or religion, to the end that segregation would exist "neither by law nor by custom."[38] CSR asserted the priority of housing, claiming that it was "the keystone on which the foundation of the future community pattern will be built."[39] Segregated housing perpetuated *de facto* segregation. Communities could not surmount racial barriers in churches, schools, businesses, recreational facilities, government, or work until people learned to live together.

Simultaneously, housing was a local issue, a human rights question, and a racial problem. Defined this way, Methodist women could tackle housing problems. In 1958 the Department of CSR suggested that citizenship brunches be scheduled to deal with housing problems. Citizenship brunches could be occasions when Methodists studied the housing needs of the nation and the pattern of increasing housing segregation, planned for open housing, gathered information, and took action on the housing situation at the local level.[40] For these workshops on housing, Methodist women could obtain maps from city planning agencies and locate racial areas, industrial and business areas, and deteriorating portions of the community. CSR directed leaders to

206

pick up copies of the town housing code, find out who enforced its provisions and how strictly they were enforced.[41]

Margaret Bender took the lead for CSR in advocating housing policies. She defined open housing as that which was open to anyone who could afford it, without barriers of race, nationality, or color. Segregated housing which was "open to minority groups" was not the same as "open occupancy housing."

In 1959 the Woman's Division urged Congress to meet the needs of all low income families living in substandard housing through federal programs for city planning, slum clearance, and urban renewal with "open occupancy features." The Woman's Division singled out the need for satisfactory accommodations for people moved out of redevelopment and slum clearance areas and also called for preventive measures to be taken, such as the regular rehabilitation of older housing, to prevent development of blighted areas. The Woman's Division favored the creation of a cabinet position on Urban Affairs and a President's Committee on Discrimination in Housing.[42] The Division wrote to President Kennedy in 1961, urging him to issue an executive order making discrimination in housing illegal for all housing covered by federal insurance, loans, grants, or any other forms of federal assistance. A year later, in November 1962, John F. Kennedy issued such an order.

School integration could not be fully completed or successful without a commitment to open and integrated housing. Methodist women found it easier to approach discrimination in housing by supporting changes in federal laws than by taking specific steps to integrate local neighborhoods. Although the Woman's Division sponsored integrated consultations to deal with tensions over school integration and housing[43] and recognized the inseparability of the two issues, large numbers of Methodist women at the local level were more willing to make a commitment to integrate local public schools than to integrate local housing. Their choice foreshadowed a divergence in national emphasis on these two significant steps in the advancement of human rights. The civil rights movement would avoid interfering with the sanctuary of home.

African American Leadership and Direct Action

At the end of 1955 and continuing for nearly a year, the Montgomery bus boycott signaled that the civil rights movement had entered the streets. Local people became leaders. Daily injustices of segregation had become a *cause célèbre*. Thousands of people became infuriated by the incomprehensible brutal lynching of Emmett Till only months before and were ready to act. Interracial organizations such as Southern Regional Council (SRC), the YWCA and YMCA, Fellowship of the Concerned (FOC), United Church Women, and the Woman's Division now played a peripheral role as organizations which were predominantly African American swept into the mainstream current of the civil rights movement. History converged on this moment, which was backed by the NAACP's legal attack on segregation, the teachings of nonviolent direct action, and the experience of the Congress of Racial Equality (CORE). African American leadership passed into the hands of those ready to take direct action. The nation watched.

Both hopes for legal action and the presence of political backlash obstructed continuity of momentum for a mass movement generated by the Montgomery bus boycott. Some African Americans still held hope that both the Supreme Court decision for school desegregation and the Eisenhower Administration passage of the 1957 Civil Rights Act would rapidly bring about dramatic changes. Consequently they did not sustain a level of active, organized pressure for civil rights. The backlash from the white political right presented even more of an obstacle. Some states outlawed civil rights organizations. Thousands of people joined extra-legal groups such as the Ku Klux Klan. When desegregation was not forthcoming, CORE and FOR sent out field workers and the SRC spearheaded formation of state and local Councils on Human Rights.

In 1956 orchestrated attempts to suppress the NAACP led to legal injunctions halting its operations in Alabama, Louisiana, and Texas in an effort to break the back of an organization which was lending its strength and support to the Montgomery bus boycott.[44] The NAACP first lost, then slowly regained, legal ground. Its leaders held on in spite of dangerous reprisals. The attack on the NAACP spawned the 1957 formation of the Southern Christian Leadership Conference (SCLC), led by Martin Luther King, Jr. SCLC drew support from African American churches and pastors.

FOR began regional organizing in 1958 by hiring James Lawson, who established a Nashville chapter. Lawson worked closely with the Reverend Kelly Miller Smith and the Nashville Council for Human Rights. By 1960, CORE sent Gordon Carey, one of two field workers, to train students involved in the Greensboro sit-ins in the philosophy and techniques of nonviolence.[45]

Methodist women continued to educate and persuade. They kept civil rights under discussion outside the African American community.

Working to Change Attitudes: World Understanding Teams, Check Lists, and Racial Tensions

Between 1955 and 1957, the Department of CSR initiated programs designed to ease racial tensions and shape racial attitudes of Methodist women. World Understanding Teams proved to be popular. A document called "A Check List on Racial Policies" generated resistance.

World Understanding Teams provided women with experiences that could not be reconciled with theoretical misconceptions and prejudices about race. The first World Understanding Team brought to the U.S. three outstanding Methodist women from Uruguay, India, and Japan.[46] These women represented nations where Methodist women from the United States had sent missionaries and supported mission programs for eighty years and more. For one year they toured the U.S., meeting members of the WSCS and WSG, staying in members' homes, and leading meetings about race and prejudice. The touring women related conditions in the U.S. to situations in their countries. Over ninety-six thousand women attended workshops held in conjunction with the visit of the World Understanding Team, and many others came to open meetings.[47]

Evaluations spoke of benefits which white women discovered by working closely with members of the Central Jurisdiction in planning and attending the workshops. Some women expressed relief at the discovery that "our problems are world problems," and noted that living and eating with people of other races had been meaningful and effective in breaking down racial patterns in some regions. White women found they could discuss their problems with sympathetic people from abroad whose presence challenged them to listen more closely to African Americans.[48]

Three other teams came in 1958, 1961, and 1964. To counter stereotypes about Africans and myths of white racial superiority the Woman's Division brought three women selected for their comparable educational background and similarity with women in the United States to be keynote speakers for workshops.[49]

The 1964–65 World Understanding program created three teams which mixed one international visitor with American women of Native American, African American, Japanese, Eskimo, and Puerto Rican backgrounds. Methodist women began to recognize the racial variety represented by their organization.[50] The personal encounter and interracial dialogue facilitated by the World Understanding programs were among the most effective ways the Woman's Division helped to change

C. L. R. P

attitudes about race.[51] They opened the door to more honest examination of racial discrimination.

Crucial changes began to shape local women's groups in 1957. Autherine Lucy's attempt to study at the University of Alabama, fresh in the news, underscored the need for change.

Although the Check List on Racial Policies served as a central discussion and action aid, a new theme and study book helped pave the way. The 1957 program began innocuously enough with a study on the theme "Christ, the Church, and Race." Methodist women throughout the nation read Liston Pope's book, *The Kingdom Beyond Caste*, which illustrated points of racial stress, examined the roots of prejudice, offered a strategy for integration, and emphasized the involvement of churches in ending segregation. Pope declared that "The place to begin [integration] is in one's own personal relationships and in the circles, especially the voluntary groups, in which one moves."[52] Women studied the text, discussed it, and implemented its suggestions to varying degrees.[53] One society returned all its copies of the book with a note that said they did not want to study the book.[54]

The 1957 Check List on Racial Policies drew the most fire of any Woman's Division program yet initiated. The check list was designed to assess the progress of local women's societies in implementing the Charter of Racial Policies. Strongest negative reactions came from Woman's Societies dominated by members of the White Citizen's Council.[55]

The Check List on Racial Policies solicited reports to the Woman's Division from thirty-two thousand local, district, and conference officers. Local officers were asked whether and how their woman's society or guild had worked to eliminate racial discrimination or segregation in employment, housing, transportation, public schools, public buildings, hotels, restaurants, and barber shops. The questionnaire asked about segregation and discrimination in the local church.

Either the records containing the results of the Check List on Racial Policies were lost, or the results were never compiled, perhaps because the resistance to the check list was so massive that the subject was dropped in the Woman's Division. As long as the Methodist women didn't need to account for their work on civil rights, they were willing to read, study, discuss, and be exposed to new ideas. Probably most women joined the WSCS or WSG for friendship, spiritual nurture, and support, not because faith called them to help change their local community.

Leadership and Structural Changes in the Woman's Division

Changes in the Woman's Division began to reflect a commitment to the principles of the Charter of Racial Policies. Dorothy Weber, associate executive secretary, left CSR/LCA in 1953 and was replaced by Ethel L. Watkins, an Alabama native and graduate of Clark College. Theressa Hoover, who for ten years had been a field worker for the Woman's Division, interpreting and leading its programs, followed Ethel Watkins in 1958. Margaret Bender and Theressa Hoover worked closely with Thelma Stevens. Responsibility for chairing the CSR passed from Cora Ratliff to Sadie (Mrs. J. Fount) Tillman in 1952, then to Mrs. A. R. Henry in 1956 when Tillman became president of the Woman's Division. The Woman's Division began to make efforts to see that more women of color were elected to membership in the Woman's Division.[56]

In 1956 "Local Church Activities" moved out of the Department of Christian Social Relations and into the Section on Education and Cultivation. This change increased the ability of the Department to focus on Christian social relations and helped clarify the need for action on social issues at the local level.[57] The Woman's Division integrated its mission schools and leadership training programs in 1959, eleven years before the denomination integrated.

Race and The Methodist Church: Moderates, Critics, and Allies

The Methodist Church, by virtue of its own segregation, had chosen not to step into the lead in race relations. White Methodist pastors and church leaders were noticeably absent, not showing support for the Montgomery bus boycott. Peter Murray noted:

> Anyone who hoped or believed that southern white moderates would lead the South into a new era of justice and harmony could not find a shred of evidence to support this view from the bus boycott.[58]

The changing social climate, represented by desegregation of the armed forces and, officially, if not yet in practice, public schools, demanded a reevaluation of church policy.

Progress in race relations in The Methodist Church was abysmally absent. The Central Jurisdiction and the Woman's Division memorialized the 1956 General Conference to abolish the Central Jurisdiction and all racial barriers. Methodist women believed that the church needed to re-examine its own life "in the light of the gospel." The Woman's Division petitioned the conference to establish a Study Commission on Racial Policies to assess progress toward desegregation. Through a series of petitions the women asked the church to live up to principles and practices they had set for themselves in the Charter of Racial Policies.[59] Women at the 1956 General Conference suggested that the ultimate goal for the church should be "the full acceptance of any Christian into any local church."[60]

The General Conference, perplexed by the church's race problems, took a moderate position. Delegates adopted a statement on race, reaffirmed freedom of the pulpit and asked churches to sustain clergy who proclaimed the gospel in the face of criticism.[61] But what would they do about segregation? Peter Murray has suggested that the bishops of the church did not know how to lead on this issue. The conference decided, a la *Brown*, to abolish segregation and discrimination with "reasonable speed."[62] They adopted a cumbersome method whereby portions of the Central Jurisdiction could be merged with the geographical jurisdictions. Amendment IX, as this constitutional provision was called, relied on the principle of voluntary acceptance of integration. In contrast to the Woman's Division, the actions of the 1956 General Conference attempted to straddle the polarization and tension that American society was experiencing. Tensions in the church led Methodists to seek like-minded allies. General Conference decisions also kindled the anger of ardent segregationists.

The position of the 1956 General Conference and the impending recommendations of the Commission to Study and Recommend Action Concerning the Jurisdictional System were too much for some Methodists to swallow. Approximately fifteen hundred critics met in 1959 and organized the Mississippi Association of Methodist Ministers and Laymen to prevent integration of the church.

The association, headed by Judge M. F. Pierce, vowed to defend the jurisdictional structure. It established committees to investigate any and all church funds being spent to support integration and examined church school literature for propaganda on integration. A committee of lawyers was formed to inquire into the legal status of church properties, should the church end segregation and the people consequently wish to withdraw their congregations.[63] The association attacked the report of the Study Committee, raising the spectre of racial mixing at meetings of Methodist Youth Fellowships.[64] Although the Association survived only through 1964, conservative Methodists have formed organizations under other names to defend their traditions and have repeated some of the same tactics.

Methodist women made a new ally in The Methodist Church after the 1952 General Conference formed the Board of Social and Economic Relations. CSR initiated conversations with the new board's general secretary, Dudley Ward, concerning mutual interests in social issues. The two organizations sponsored a series of eight Regional Leadership Conferences on race relations from 1955 to 1959. The Leadership Conferences used demographics and economic information to help people understand local situations.

Growing national concern over race relations led the Board of Social and Economic Relations of The Methodist Church and the Woman's Division to sponsor the first national Conference on Human Relations.[65] Seven leaders of the Woman's Division, including Thelma Stevens, were selected by the Committee on Racial Policies to participate in the planning.[66] Ten boards and agencies of The Methodist Church co-sponsored the conference where seventy-five staff, workers, and members of the Woman's Division were to be among fifteen hundred delegates.[67] The Woman's Division encouraged each conference to send three additional delegates to the August 1959 gathering at Southern Methodist University in Dallas. The conference was the first to discuss Methodist attitudes about race on a denomination-wide basis and issued moderate pronouncements to forward the cause of civil rights by declaring segregation evil.[68]

For the nation, fractious days lay ahead. The limited school desegregation and changes in federal housing regulations accomplished in the 1950s served as harbingers of vital changes in social patterns and political power which needed to come in the 1960s. Civil rights legislation had stalled again in Congress.

Behind the 1957–1958 Backlash: Working in Secret

The backlash to desegregation did not stop Methodist women. Leaders maintained a steady stream of activities in the area of civil rights, the most risky of which were done secretly. In declining to submit an article for publication Dorothy Tilly wrote to Esther Meeker, editor of *The Methodist Woman*:

> I did promise to have [for] you an article on what the Southern Church women are doing to allay the tensions of the South. At the

present state of affairs, I believe it is not possible to give publicity to what they are doing. Since my conversation with you the tensions have grown greater. The women are still meeting and working but are giving no publicity to what they are doing. They are very bravely trying to work, in spite of opposition so great that it might affect their husband's business—and in some instances, it has already affected their standing in the community.[69]

Many aspects of Methodist women's work were almost invisible to the public eye. One woman wanted to introduce her pastor and "some of the men of the church" to her African American friends.[70] Other women refused to be intimidated: they integrated youth camps and worked to prevent local Methodist churches from running segregated private schools. Some women intervened in voter registration problems or wrote to political officials.[71]

Methodist women continued a program of visits with local sheriffs and police chiefs designed to help overcome racial biases. They distributed copies of a brochure on "Race and Law Enforcement." Each team of women signed and submitted reports documenting what they learned in these conversations about their concern for "able and impartial enforcement of the law."[72]

Joy Bates, secretary of Children's Work for the South Central Jurisdiction of The Methodist Church took a stand of civil disobedience by refusing to comply with the provisions of the Bennett Ordinance, a law designed to harass civil rights work. For example, she deliberately failed to submit to the State of Arkansas a list of members of the SRC in Arkansas.[73] As secretary of Children's Work, Bates encouraged Methodist women to hold meetings to deal with the impact of racial tensions on children and to integrate junior camps of The Methodist Church which served grades 4–6.[74]

Fear gripped many people who previously had met interracially and now did not. Dorothy Tilly wrote that in Alabama, south Georgia, and South Carolina

good people . . . are so paralyzed with fear they no longer dare to express their convictions. . . . While at Junaluska, [on] Monday, Bess Jones told me that no longer, anywhere in Columbia could be held an interracial meeting. . . . This fear is not confined to white people. In fact it is frightfully real to the Negroes. In Birmingham, Noreen Dunn located one of the neighborhood meetings of the World Day of Prayer in a Negro church. When the day came, the white women were there but the only Negroes were the Pastor's wife and the president of the women's work of the church.[75]

As the times grew more violent and fear mounted, a hardy network of Methodist women refused to be cowed. In 1958 Dorothy Tilly asked her friend Ruth Robinson from Gallatin, Tennessee, to look into the situation in Prince Edward County, Tennessee, where Methodist churches supported segregation by opening alternative schools for white children.[76] Tilly asked Mrs. Robert L. Wilcox, the secretary of CSR of the WSCS at The Methodist Church in Maryville, Tennessee, to investigate a report that Negroes were prevented from voting in Shelby County; the investigation aided "the defeat of a liberal governor."[77] Faith had led thus far: it would not work to turn back.

As the 1950s came to a close, no political majority favoring civil rights for all Americans held sway. Yet those Methodist women who had caught the vision of a multiracial future and joined in the work toward bringing it into being were now dedicated enough to withstand the heat of focused attack. Margaret Mead has said "Never doubt that a small group of thoughtful committed citizens can change the world; indeed, it's the only thing that ever has."

Resistance to integration hardened, creating a social pressure cooker. Defenders of segregation organized in increasingly devious and illegal ways against the losses that come with change. But for supporters of integration, the old ways had been hurtful for too long. They were not willing to pay the price of waiting any longer.

A phenomenon of the present situation is that God seems to be working through secular institutions—the law or civil rights groups—to confront Christians with the necessity for greater faithfulness.

—Peggy Billings
The Methodist Woman
(July–August 1965), 15

CHAPTER 12

Desegregating Society in the 1960s:
Not Fast Enough Nor Far Enough!

Americans were determined. Determined to integrate, determined to resist integration, or determined to keep peace in the household: there was no way to have it all. Little is left to wonder that a subculture of hippies wanted to drop out of the main culture.

In extraordinary times, people take extraordinary measures. Such were the 1960s. Leaders of the 1960s violated segregation customs, city ordinances, federal mandates, and police orders. They appealed to higher authority and spent time in jail. Methodist women continued their broad interest in advancing public policies supporting civil rights but they also focused on a specific human relations project where racial hatred was endemic: the Mississippi Delta.

Methodist women, serving as stage crew for a drama, had surprising connections that helped to shape the ideology and development of the civil rights movement. As if it were reviewing a play, history has tended to focus on the primary actors. With the stage lighting of biblical mandates for justice, behind the scenes grassroots support, and an appreciative audience of thousands in local communities across the nation, the unfolding civil rights drama commanded the nation's attention. Martin Luther King, Jr.'s, appeal to the moral conscience of the nation struck a chord because the instruments were there. Methodist women helped provide the instruments.

In 1962 Thelma Stevens challenged Methodist women: "Changes have come—but not fast enough nor far enough! . . . The Church, including The Methodist Church, has not always been *out front* where the going is hard. Maybe the time has come not only to take stock of the progress over the past decade but to 'determine to move' forward *now* as the New Decade confronts us."[1]

Many white Methodist women felt threatened when the leadership of the civil rights movement was in the hands of African American leaders who agitated for change. Many feared what might happen if the government and the power to influence local decisions were in the hands of African American leaders. Some were alarmed to see youth and young adults asserting leadership.[2] When Viola Liuzzo was shot to death, some white Methodist women thought that the Selma to Montgomery march was "no place for her to be."[3]

The mood of the nation had changed. James Lawson, a leader of the Nashville movement, summed it up. "When people are suffering they don't want rhetoric and processes which seem to go slowly. . . . When they are suffering and they see their people suffering, they want direct participation."[4]

Sit-ins, Vanderbilt University, and Methodists

By 1963, which marked one hundred years since the Emancipation Proclamation was issued, African Americans wanted more than ever before to be free from the twin oppressions of segregation and discrimination. The arrival of 1960 brought with it a sense that time was running out, that injustices had been tolerated too long, and that segregation which had been imposed on a class of people must be resisted by a class of people. A new era opened with broad-based African American support of an African American-led movement that began with a sit-in at a lunch counter in Greensboro, North Carolina.

The spontaneity of Rosa Parks' determination to resist one more insult had sparked the 1955–56 Montgomery bus boycott. Now, in 1960, the decision of four North Carolina Agricultural and Technical College students in Greensboro to stage a sit-in at a Woolworth's lunch counter on February 1 grew out of their frustration with the injustices of segregation. Neither event was planned or organized to kick off a new phase of the civil rights movement. Both forms of resistance to segregation emerged from the context of widespread discussion in the African American community and from connections with the National Association for the Advancement of Colored People (NAACP) and the Fellowship of Reconciliation (FOR) which was working to overturn segregation using nonviolent direct action. Parks had participated in an educational workshop at Highlander Folk School and at least one of the four Greensboro students had read a FOR comic book on nonviolence, "Martin Luther King and the Montgomery Story."

Neither the students nor Parks was pioneering in their actions. Others had gone before them and been arrested. In both situations, the organizational work of the local community and supportive network of people who thought that the action was right and the time had come, galvanized around the symbolic act.

The effective boycott of Montgomery buses appealed to African Americans not to use a service to which all were entitled. This attacked the economic foundation of the public bus service and challenged white public authority.

The sit-ins, on the other hand, required African Americans to position themselves in a place that had not been theirs, but which by custom had been reserved for whites. Sit-ins put people's physical well-being on the line in stores where races mixed to shop, and where a dime spent by an African American would buy candy but no place to sit down for a ten-cent cup of coffee. African Americans who participated in sit-ins were seen, taunted, threatened, abused, and injured. Businesses felt the economic impact of the sit-ins when shoppers stayed away from trouble spots.

Sit-ins relied on the willingness of young African Americans to put themselves physically, yet nonviolently, on the line so that their suffering would arouse the conscience of the nation. Within ten days the Greensboro sit-in ignited a rash of similar sit-ins in five states and fifteen cities.[5] The instantaneous response rose up from a deep longing, a sense of urgency, and careful groundwork laid by organizers.

One of the organizers was James Lawson, a Methodist student at Vanderbilt School of Theology in Nashville who was preparing for ministry. Lawson grew up in The Methodist Church, attending and giving leadership to national conferences of the Methodist Youth Fellowship. As had James Farmer before him, Lawson absorbed social gospel tenets that all persons, created in God's image, deserve to be treated with respect and dignity. Inspired in part by Methodist women such as Thelma Stevens, Lawson came to believe in using peaceful methods to resolve conflicts and took a stand of conscientious objection to participation in the Korean War. When given the option of service other than military duty, he asked what opportunities for service were open through his church.

Perhaps sensing his strength of character and knowing that nonviolent African American leaders were needed in the struggle against segregation, Thelma Stevens provided Lawson with an experience that profoundly influenced the civil rights movement. She arranged for the Woman's Division to engage Lawson for a three-year stint as a missionary to India to study Gandhi's movement, teachings, and methods for nonviolent change.[6]

Lawson returned to the U.S. ready to engage Gandhian principles in the African American struggle. He took a position as field secretary of FOR to engage in organizing work in the South based on nonviolent direct action. Under Lawson's tutelage a strong group formed in Nashville. Lawson continued his position with FOR while undertaking seminary studies at Vanderbilt University's School of Theology. Only a short time later he guided Student Nonviolent Coordinating Committee (SNCC) in the development of its ideology.[7]

Diane Nash

In 1959 Diane Nash transferred as a sophomore from Howard University in Washington, D.C., to Fisk University in Nashville because she wanted to experience what it meant to live in the South. She was unprepared emotionally for the impact of segregation. Nash immediately joined a group of students led by Lawson who met weekly to prepare themselves to lead civil rights actions. Not only did they read the available literature about nonviolence, but they also engaged in role-plays of lunch counter sit-ins. As "white" role-playing hecklers used obscenities, insults, and violence, the "demonstrators" practiced ignoring abuse, controlling their anger, and rolling into a human ball for protection.[8]

Civil rights leaders Nash, Lawson, C. T. Vivian, Kelly Miller Smith, Johnetta Hayes, Dolores Robinson, and others totalling approximately twenty persons participated in a workshop sponsored by the Nashville Christian Leadership Council and held in a local African American Methodist Church. Together they discussed what it meant to love one's opponents. Nash concluded that systems, not people, are the enemy, and that attitudes of individuals could be changed.[9] Throughout the fall of 1959, the Nashville group tested various businesses in the city to find out where and how a successful campaign could be run to desegregate public facilities.[10]

When the spontaneous action of four students in Greensboro ignited a chain reaction of supportive sit-ins, civil rights leaders mobilized responses from numerous southern communities. Lawson, Nash, and others organized sit-ins in Nashville.[11]

Vanderbilt School of Theology administrators decided to crack down on Lawson. Administrators of this Methodist-owned school believed that its reputation was being damaged and its southern white financial base undermined because the Vanderbilt students had incubated and hatched leadership for this attack on segregation. Leaders of student demonstrations were making disturbing news with stories of their arrests and imprisonment. The school expelled Lawson in March 1960 despite supportive testimony of the faculty who believed that Lawson was acting on sound Christian principles and who knew that white hecklers at the demonstrations perpetrated the violence. Four-

220

teen of sixteen faculty members signed a statement which said, in part, " . . . we believe that Mr. Lawson has endeavored to follow his Christian conscience and we see no adequate reason for his expulsion from the divinity school."[12]

The Woman's Division became directly involved at this point. The women sent a telegram to the chancellor of Vanderbilt University and dean of the School of Theology "expressing profound regret over the expulsion . . . and urging his immediate reinstatement."[13] Elaborating on the reasons for its action, the Woman's Division asserted its belief that the church and its institutions have a responsibility to uphold individual freedom of conscience and freedom of speech for all persons, and that God's love and justice make no reference to race.

By the time of the Woman's Division meeting in March 1960, students from eleven states and at least twenty-seven colleges and universities had held sit-ins. Between February 10 and March 16, 935 students, most of them black but some white, had been arrested.[14] For 79 students arrested in Atlanta, bail had been set at $300 each (enough to pay a year's tuition at a state university) and convictions could result in a fine of $1000 or a year in jail. The price was high. The policy of arrests and fines was aimed toward intimidation of demonstrators.

Sit-ins were conducted primarily by students. They risked the threat of violence, physical injury, arrest, imprisonment, fines, expulsion from school, and disruption of their studies. However, they were not jeopardizing an entire family's income or childcare arrangements as would have been the case for wage-earners or parents who joined sit-ins and picket lines. That commitment came later.

The Department of Christian Social Relations (CSR) encouraged Methodist women to read and duplicate a "Letter to Christian Students in the United States" which was being circulated widely among student groups. The open letter gave reasons why Christian teachings supported nonviolent demonstrations against segregation policies. The Woman's Division also invited Methodist women to contribute to the "Legal Aid and Scholarship Fund for Arrested or Expelled Students" set up by the National Student Christian Federation.[15]

Sit-ins met corporate resistance. Large national chain stores had said that they would not change their local policies until local public opinion changed. Woolworth, Kress, Kresge, and Grant companies vowed that as corporations they were "outsiders" and they refused to change local customs. The CSR report asked Methodist women, "Can't we all help to effect the change of public opinion?"[16]

The Nashville civil rights group increased pressure by leading a pre-Easter boycott of downtown businesses. The sit-ins and boycott during one of the year's biggest commercial seasons tipped the economic scale. Businesses began to indicate a williness to enter negotiations for concessions to the African American community. The movement was forcing change. Lawson reported that "the movement itself was the thrust that forged the transformation of the power levers in such a fashion that the merchants negotiated in good faith and were willing to take the risk to do some things."[17]

The Woman's Division was concerned about helping Methodist women understand the background and reasons behind these events which brought apparent chaos into normally orderly southern cities. Many women who believed that the legal system worked for them and who had seen that they could influence federal policies could not fathom why reform was not an adequate response now.

The Committee on Student Work of the Woman's Division did not view the sit-ins as isolated instances of racial anger but as part of a broad picture of international change in which people of color from colonialized nations and people of color long discriminated against in the United States were struggling together to obtain long-delayed access to basic human rights. At the national level the Woman's Division took a sympathetic stance toward sit-ins:

> These non-violent sit-in demonstrations have occurred, however, at a time when colleges and universities, in fact our total society, are confronted with momentous issues that are a part of the worldwide revolution. Therefore, anyone who is sensitive to the earth-shaking disturbances of our social order finds himself understanding these students and why they are doing what they are doing. In fact, a sensitive Christian not only understands but also sympathizes. Christian students are involved in the demonstrations and Christian students everywhere must take a stand.[18]

The Woman's Division voted to "endorse the method of non-violence which many students are practicing in the 'sit-in' demonstrations."[19] The Woman's Division gave its assent to guidelines for nonviolent sit-ins and demonstrations which had been developed by the Nashville group from earlier Congress of Racial Equality (CORE) experiences.[20]

The Woman's Division, while not directly issuing any call to students or women to join sit-ins, interpreted demonstrations as making a Christian witness:

> We believe these demonstrations offer to all Christians in this disturbed hour an opportunity for Christian witness. We urge Methodist women everywhere to study the facts which will enable

them to understand, interpret, and undergird these students. We believe that every local church should seek in the context of the Gospel to clarify its position on the race issue.[21]

White Methodist women did not enlist women to participate in the sit-ins. Perhaps the Division felt the pressure of trying to hold together a large, diverse organization. Or possibly some women participated in the boycotts, where participation was less visible. Here and there white Methodist women marched and aided those in jail, usually acting from individual conscience rather than as members representing their church or women's group.

Women's society members held different points of view. The dynamic often immobilized groups from taking action but left individuals with latitude to link up with others in their community. Yet women who told their husbands and friends that they would not shop in downtown Nashville because they were afraid of violence effectively supported the boycott. Many domestic servants lost their jobs because they participated in a march, sit-in, or demonstration. In spite of boycotts and demonstrations, numerous white churchwomen continued to keep domestic workers on the payroll, providing an important form of assistance to African American women involved in the struggle for change.[22] The Woman's Division hoped that families were a little less fearful of demonstrations because they had helped people understand them in terms of their Christian faith and a changing world context. Some Methodist women's groups fulfilled this hope.

Some southern white Methodist women assailed prejudice in church committee meetings, rather than on marches or at sit-ins, where they confronted their friends or their pastor, not police. An example from the 1970s shows how some Methodist women made important inroads on attitudes during the civil rights years. Bobbie Kearns Roberts served on a district parsonage committee when the first African American district superintendent was appointed to her district. Roberts argued that the location of the new district parsonage should not be determined according to the color of the district superintendent. Although Roberts' local church, Belmont United Methodist Church in Nashville, produced an unusual number of leaders who worked for integration, she depended on groups of people beyond the local church to sustain her when she was criticized for being outspoken. Conference, jurisdictional, and national leaders of the Woman's Division provided this kind of support. Support from friends ameliorated, but did not eliminate, emotional abuse and personal sacrifice experienced by dedicated Christian women like Roberts. Emotional ruptures of the decade left scars

223

which, though buried with passing time, still evoke grief and painful memories.[23]

Women in African American congregations of The Methodist Church, who represented approximately 4 percent of all Methodist women, responded quite differently than women in white churches.[24] In these congregations many members of the Woman's Society of Christian Service (WSCS) and Wesleyan Service Guild (WSG) participated in demonstrations and marches and provided assistance to members of the congregation and the community who were jailed.[25]

One example of this took place at Asbury Temple Methodist Church in Durham where the pastor and members of the congregation had started lunch counter sit-ins in the 1950s. Reverend Douglas Moore guided the members of the youth department of the Sunday school and the members of the Methodist Youth Fellowship who conducted a sit-in at the Royal Ice Cream Company.[26] When students were jailed, Margaret Minor, the teacher of the senior high Sunday school class and a member of the Woman's Division who had helped write the Charter of Racial Policies, went to the jail and helped get the youth out on bail.[27]

In creative ways, the Woman's Division continued to use the tactics of education and persuasion in its campaign for civil rights. The Division expressed concern about the ways demonstrators were being treated by observers. Women could see that police tended to side with business establishments. The women affirmed their belief that "equal protection under the law should be given to the demonstrators and to those against whom the demonstrations are made."[28] The Woman's Division called all Methodist women to contact local law enforcement officers about discouraging intimidation and violence. Working with community groups and police, Methodist women could help to ensure that the rights of students to protest would be protected.

Churchwomen encouraged people to patronize businesses that desegregated. The Woman's Division recommended that women speak in person with managers of local public eating places to offer consumer support. In the case of chain stores with national offices, Methodist women urged local members to write to these companies about their patronage and support for more inclusive policies.

Methodist women explored new racial understandings which grew out of the civil rights movement. They studied Dwight W. Culver's book *We Can and We Will!* and used it as a guide for the Quadrennial Program on Race. Culver pointed out a major difference between desegregation and integration.[29] Desegregation was the removal of barriers which kept people separate and segregated. Integration involved interaction in a nonsegregated environment. Desegregation established the con-

224

ditions under which integration was possible, but whether or not integration occurred depended on the attitudes and voluntary responses of people.[30]

The Woman's Division continued to support Methodist women's local efforts to secure human rights for all. The Department of CSR asked Methodist women to contact leaders in city or county government who were in positions to enact local ordinances in support of basic human rights so that discrimination based on custom would lose its power. Some cities had a Mayor's Committee on Human Relations or a Human Relations Council, and if one were lacking, Methodist women could help form one. Where effective state or local organizations for human relations existed, the local society could provide memberships in these organizations for their leaders in CSR, making both groups stronger by uniting their efforts.[31] Thus, in the midst of social turmoil and sit-ins, Methodist women continued to play to their strength as educators and experts in grassroots coalition building and political work for human relations. They also continued to press for changes in public policy.

Working to End Discrimination in Public Policy

The Woman's Division advocated extension of civil rights through federal legislation and executive branch administration of programs. Advocating legislation represented a disengagement from full-fledged organizational participation in direct action, yet it engaged the Woman's Division in the dynamic and sustained use of public pressure on the federal government to rectify long-standing patterns of injustice and racial discrimination. This approach held the voluntary membership of the organization intact without major losses through a period of social conflict.

The Woman's Division focused its efforts on public policy changes designed to outlaw the poll tax, increase voter registration, require equal pay for equal work, provide protection through civil rights legislation, and end housing discrimination.

Attempts of the Woman's Division to influence votes on civil rights issues before Congress in the 1960s had less impact than in previous years. Methodist women did not have as much power to help deliver an election victory as they had for Truman in 1948. Moral arguments carried little weight in a political campaign. The rise of the military industrial complex in the 1950s changed lobbying so that contributions to campaign coffers seemed to influence votes more than arguments about the rights of poor and minorities. Election campaign costs sky-rocketed. The National Council of Churches (NCC), no longer viewed by political leaders as an authority to be reckoned with, was a voice lost in the wind, speaking to a nation reluctant to re-examine decaying principles of its faltering social order.[32]

In 1960, the Woman's Division pushed for new national policies opposed to racial discrimination. The Division asked Congress to enact civil rights legislation to permit federal action in cases of lynchings both when states had not apprehended and convicted the perpetrators and in all cases of bombings and unauthorized transportation, possession, or use of explosives. The Woman's Division proposed as minimum standards for civil rights legislation a Fair Employment Practices Law and the establishment of a permanent Commission on Civil Rights. The Division agreed that a Commission on Civil Rights should have the power to obtain evidence and enforce the law in the case of the denial of voting rights. Southeast Jurisdiction leaders of Christian Social Relations sent a telegram to newly elected President John F. Kennedy requesting that he use the one-hundredth anniversary of the Emancipation Proclamation to broaden civil rights in the United States.[33] Again filibusters delayed congressional action.

In 1963, the Woman's Division alerted Methodist women to the urgent need for Congress to adopt pending civil rights legislation. The Civil Rights Act guaranteed to all citizens equal access to public facilities, authorized the attorney general to "initiate appropriate legal proceed-ings for carrying out Supreme Court decisions for desegregation of public schools," provided for federal funds to be withheld "where racial discrimination is practiced," and renewed and expanded the Civil Rights Commission.[34] *The Methodist Woman* provided a legislative up-date on the progress of the civil rights bill and its provisions so that Methodist women could lobby for its passage and generate local support.[35]

Voting Rights and Methodist Women

In 1958, the Woman's Division launched a program designed to cultivate churchwomen as citizens more active in local politics. Meth-odist women gathered friends from various neighborhoods and churches around their community to attend programs about public housing. By 1962 these Citizenship Brunches turned their focus to upcoming elections, education about political candidates and issues, and problems

Citizenship
Brunches

226

related to voting. Women shared information about how to register to vote, discussed impediments to voting, and explored what could be done to expand voting rights.

In 1962 Congress was debating a proposed Twenty-fourth Amendment to the Constitution that would outlaw the poll tax and literacy tests that were frequently used to block the registration of African American voters in some southern states. Partly in response to the Methodist women's mission study on "The Christian and Responsible Citizenship," the Woman's Division supported voting rights. They endorsed legislation that provided for federal prosecution of anyone threatening or depriving citizens of the right to register, vote, or have their votes counted. Where states limited voting rights, Methodist women called for federal registrars to register voters.[36]

The Woman's Division encouraged Methodist women to help voters register. In 1962 Thelma Stevens, a member of the FOC, led the Woman's Division when it took a strong stand on voter registration by calling on Christian women to "open doors" to thousands of black citizens who had been deprived of their voting rights. Some Methodist women read two publications of the Woman's Division, *Register Christian Opinion* and *Christian's Primer on Political Action*, which interpreted the new emphasis on voter registration. Some women became actively involved in this aspect of Christian witness.

The Woman's Division cooperated with voter registration programs, especially those sponsored by the Southern Regional Council (SRC) and the FOC. In 1962 the SRC, on behalf of a group of agencies including the American Friends Service Committee, National Jewish Committee, NAACP, and the NCC, received a $325,000 grant for a two-year voter registration program.[37] Members of the FOC supported the voter education project of the SRC and quietly served "in crisis areas such as Mississippi," working with groups which took an active role in the 1964 Mississippi Summer Project of the Voter Education Project.[38] Leaders of the Woman's Division remained active in the SRC. Sadie Tillman, president of the Woman's Division of Christian Service, served as a member of the executive committee of SRC in 1965.[39] Dorothy Tilly remained at the helm of Women's Work for SRC and coordinated programs of the FOC. Methodist women had been concerned about voting rights and worked for more than two decades to end discriminatory practices at the polls.

At last, Congress passed the Voting Rights Act of 1965. The voting rights bill ended literacy testing and authorized federal voter registration in states where less than half of the adult population was registered to vote in 1964.

The Civil Rights Act of 1964 and the Voting Rights Act of 1965 struck a heavy blow against white supremacy in the United States. Although plenty of work remained to be done to ensure that these rights were exercised in law and in action, civil rights had turned an important corner: the law now said that racial discrimination was illegal. The Woman's Division, which had worked for many years so that people of color in the United States would have access to public facilities, schools, housing, and jobs, now had many gains to celebrate. At last, American attitudes about race were shifting.

Implementing Civil Rights Laws

Joy was short-lived. In 1964 resistance to the new Civil Rights Act hardened. It would have been easy for the civil rights victory to become a defeat, either through failure of the new legislation to be implemented or by the dismantling of the organizations which had worked for the Civil Rights Act. Instead, civil rights organizations and the Woman's Division carried out 1964 legislation at the local level.

John Hannah, chair of the United States Commission on Civil Rights, issued an invitation to the Woman's Division to send representatives to a conference to be held in Washington on January 28, 1965. The purpose of the conference was to deal with the implementation of the Civil Rights Act of 1964, Title VI, requiring nondiscrimination in programs receiving federal government assistance. The Woman's Division sent Peggy Billings and three others to attend the conference and bring back ideas for Methodist women.[40]

Ever optimistic, Thelma Stevens believed that if Methodist women understood the meaning of the Civil Rights Act they would cooperate with carrying out the new laws of the nation. Misinformation abounded. Some people mistakenly thought that white people who were selling a house would be required to sell to someone who was African American. Some thought that white children would be sent to formerly all-African American schools. Some believed that quotas were established for hiring African American employees and that white persons would be fired to make room for them. In all of these instances, Stevens set the record straight. The Civil Rights Act did not cover sales of houses nor did it set job quotas. It did not require busing, but rather an end to segregation.[41]

The Woman's Division joined the 1965 march from Selma to Montgomery by sending its energetic new staff member, Peggy Billings.

228

This last large demonstration of the civil rights movement inscribed an indelible mark in the lives of white participants. White liberals, adults and students, turned out in numbers larger than for any previous march: this was an indication that they recognized the power of nonviolent demonstrations.[42] Billings saw the Selma march as a turning point which could crystalize in Methodist women a new sense of urgency to work on the familiar "old" issues of peace, justice, human dignity, and freedom with a new sense of urgency and decisiveness.

Methodist women could do many things to help. Stevens wrote: "Public-minded citizens in the community can band together to create a climate of understanding of the [Civil Rights] act and to support the law enforcement powers in the community."[43] Such community groups, she coached, needed to be racially inclusive and representative of the racial make-up of the community. A local group working quickly with courage and facts in hand could make "outside" help unnecessary if action were taken with no delay. Volunteers trained and placed by the Woman's Division stood ready to help communities implement the Civil Rights Act. Race relations had reached a crisis point. Apprehensively, Thelma Stevens declared, "Time has long since passed the midnight hour!"[44]

Facing Racial Tensions

The failure of the nation to quickly implement fair practices following the passage of civil rights legislation contributed to discontent among a growing contingent of young African American civil rights leaders who were not convinced that the nonviolent policies of Dr. Martin Luther King, Jr., were effective and efficient in moving the nation toward racial justice. During 1966 and 1967, resistance to full implementation of the Civil Rights Act of 1964 and the Voting Rights Bill of 1965, together with government pressure that subdued the civil rights movement at Selma in 1965, provoked a rising level of anger and rage within the African American community. Civil rights groups became aware of growing resistance to civil rights laws. More African American children were in segregated schools than in 1954. More African American males were unemployed.[45]

The nation stood on the brink of a period of destructive racial violence. Riots in Los Angeles and other cities dramatized the need for long-term solutions to urban problems, meaningful employment, and a response to the depersonalization of life in the ghetto.[46] Inner-city areas experienced a drain of leadership and money, creating urban problems of such magnitude that new public policies were needed to resolve them. Department of CSR leaders saw that new middle-class minorities who had left the cities for the suburbs needed to be welcomed and consciously integrated into the life of suburban communities. However, systems of law and justice still discriminated between races. Twenty-eight murders related to civil rights had occurred in 1964–65 alone without any conviction.[47] In cities, police sometimes abused their authority.[48]

People in white churches felt a lot of confusion about new developments in the African American freedom struggle. The Woman's Division used meetings to gather people to interpret events, clarify objectives, and work on problem areas. In 1966 and 1967 alone, they participated in seven conferences. The most significant of these was the Frogmore Conference, designed to help train leaders for integration in The Methodist Church and society at large.

The Woman's Division designed a ten-day training experience for sixty Methodist women, six of them coming from AME, CME, and AME Zion churches.[49] These volunteers would work to create "*a climate to facilitate transfers and mergers of annual conferences of the Central Jurisdiction*," to implement inclusive racial policies in boards and agencies of the church and in local churches, and to assist communities in protecting and delivering constitutionally guaranteed civil rights to all citizens.[50] They made commitments to work in areas of racial tension and respond to the national crisis.[51] Held in Frogmore, South Carolina, February 1–11, 1966, the consultation emphasized the need to press on toward human reconciliation through direct confrontation of Christians standing in the way. Leaders assumed that The Methodist Church had "much unfinished business in race relations."[52] At least one participant thought that members of the women's society were among the last to move on crucial issues. The Frogmore Conference was to be augmented by a series of regional training programs for women who lived in areas of racial tension and were volunteering to guide Methodist women in implementing the Charter of Racial Policies, the General Conference mandates on race, and the Civil Rights Act of 1964.[53]

Evidence bore out the church leaders' concern that racial issues needed to be a national priority. African Americans, whose hopes had been raised by President Lyndon B. Johnson's administration, the Civil Rights Act, and anti-poverty programs, were finding that promises failed in the delivery. Passage of civil rights legislation had not secured social justice. The Frogmore Conference challenged responsible government agencies at all levels to enforce the new laws."[54]

Ten years after the school desegregation decision, over 90 percent of African American public school students in the South remained in segregated schools while *de facto* segregation functioned in the North.[55] The conference deplored the slow desegregation of public schools and the tenacity of segregation. Delegates called on the Department of Health, Education, and Welfare to establish strong guidelines to speed full public school integration.[56]

Public pronouncements and pressure on federal agencies helped shape public policies, but so did a pilot project in the Mississippi Delta funded by the Woman's Division.

The Delta Ministry

The NCC, a participant in the Voter Education Project coordinated by SRC, believed that the economic, health, and social conditions of poor people in Mississippi needed a long-term solution. As short-term volunteers of the 1964 Mississippi Summer Project left and SNCC, which had also been involved in voter registration, pulled out, NCC launched the Delta Ministry.[57] The Delta Ministry served as a combination of a cooperative, a church engaged in social ministries, and a civil rights movement. Its identity was interracial, ecumenical, intergenerational. Both ministers and lay persons served as staff. Where racism was deeply entrenched, a small piece of the civil rights movement came with the intent to stay. Methodist women became involved.

The Woman's Division already had its eye on Mississippi. In 1965 they gave $2000 to the Legal Defense Fund of the Commission on Religion and Race of the NCC. That group had provided legal counsel for over four hundred civil rights cases in Mississippi alone, plus hundreds of others. CSR reported, "Numerous Methodists, both lay and cleric, were involved in these cases, specifically in St. Augustine and Mississippi, some of which are still on the docket."[58]

The Delta Ministry, inspired by a plea for help from some African Americans, quickly attracted the attention of its neighbors. One eviction or other form of harassment followed another. The program of the ministry took its cues from immediate needs that presented themselves. In 1965, Larry Walker, a staff member, visited with people as he delivered Christmas turkeys. The African Americans he spoke with did not know they were allowed to vote and called a meeting to learn more about this. Even though the landowner threatened the tenant who hosted the meeting, one meeting led to another as people learned about voting rights, citizenship, African American history, and how to read.[59] Wages on the plantation were unbearably low, and some people began to discuss a strike. Mississippi Freedom Labor Union, the Washington County Employment Committee, and other groups and activities formed out of these gatherings.

The Delta Ministry worked cooperatively with many volunteers and agencies. Some leaders came from SNCC, the Council of Federated [civil rights] Organizations, the NAACP, and the Mississippi Freedom Democratic Party. The Delta Ministry found its identity in strengthening the hand of people involved in projects that had potential to improve living conditions in the region. Delta Ministry volunteers helped seventy thousand African American voters to register, trained candidates to run for office against white candidates, housed and supported workers involved in a plantation strike, overrode the governor's veto by establishing Head Start programs in Mississippi, and arranged for public distribution of surplus foods to two hundred thousand people who had been denied these benefits.[60] The Mississippi United Church Women provided a nurse for the Delta Ministry. This program was so resented that the front porch of the home of United Church Women President Jane Schutt was bombed.

The Delta Ministry provided the center for a storm of controversy. It was denounced by the Circuit Riders, a group of Mississippi Methodist clergy who defended segregation. Even the North Mississippi Conference permitted churches to cut off their contributions to the NCC.[61] The Methodist Board of Missions caught the brunt of the attack, with southern conferences of the church threatening to split the denomination. NCC, which had counted on a substantial contribution from Methodists for the Delta Ministry, did not receive Methodist mission funds. When the ministry proved to be this controversial, the WCC, in a precedent-setting move, solicited donations from other nations.

It was then that Methodist women attending the Frogmore Conference decided that the urgent needs of the times demanded a new set of priorities for missional spending and recommended that funding of the Delta Ministry be reconsidered.[62] Thelma Stevens and Peggy Billings provided fundamental and crucial initiation, support, and discussion of this kind of thinking. They believed that the power distribution between races in the United States needed to be realigned to create a more equitable situation. Methodist women challenged the church to be part of this redistribution of power and redesignating of priorities for funding. They urged the church to include minority leaders at all levels.

The Woman's Division made a large commitment to a controversial ministry and an investment in an impoverished area of the nation where racial tension was extreme.[63] In 1966, the Woman's Division committed $54,900 each for two years to the Delta Ministry, and the Board of Missions $20,000. The Woman's Division also gave $30,000 per year in 1968 and 1969. An extraordinary time had invoked an extraordinary response.

In the summer of 1967, ghetto riots erupted in Newark, making a clear statement that new directions had to replace former systems. Urban poverty and discrimination had reached crisis proportions. Perhaps the kind of organizing that was making changes in the Mississippi Delta could be used in urban areas. It would require massive funding as well as ecumenical and interracial cooperation.

The Reverend James Lawson, addressing the Methodist women's national seminar, provided analysis of the problems of urban ghettos over the summer just ending and probed church leaders to examine their own responses to the events. Repeatedly delegates to the seminar heard from speakers and news sources that "business as usual" would not be an adequate response to the burning and rioting in the cities.

The civil rights movement, the Delta Ministry, and urban riots were forcing Methodist women to re-think their beliefs and their Christian responsibilities. In September 1967, the NCC issued a call for a radical Christian response:

> We must leave other things undone, at least for the immediate future. . . .
>
> It means working to change the climate of hostility among whites to the legitimate demands of the suppressed people of the inner cities of this land. It means the acceptance of change in established practices and procedures, the building of new kinds of institutions, the establishment of new channels of communication, new ways of participating in the democratic process, a sharing of power.[64]

The time had come to share power.

African Americans Interpret Black Power

During a march from north to south through Mississippi following the attempted assassination of James Meredith in June 1966, Stokely Carmichael presented the new face of African American leadership. He seized media attention for leading marchers in chanting "Black Power!" Black power echoed in a growing swell from people who took pride in calling themselves "black" rather than "Negro" as a way of claiming that the time had come for African Americans to take power over their own lives and political affairs. Some Methodist women chilled with fear at the rising tide of hatred toward white power. Others understood the roots of black anger in the history of racial oppression. The Woman's Division interpreted the new movement in the light of other liberation movements and the Christian task of reconciliation. Methodist women related their responsibilities to biblical perspectives on justice and contemporary efforts for decolonialization. Peggy Billings challenged Christians not to abandon the struggle for human rights or give in to white resistance. She discouraged women from engaging others in a war of words about race. She urged women to work for effective reconciliation by taking action to solve problems related to schools, housing, unemployment, and urban decay.[65] Simply contributing to the traditional Brotherhood Sunday offering was not enough.

The call for black power could be interpreted as a response to the prejudice and systemic violence that had been perpetuated against African Americans over many years. Billings wrote that African American citizens were "losing their preoccupation with acceptance by the white majority. They no longer care a great deal whether majority America approves of them or not. They will be themselves."[66]

Methodist women turned to African American leaders for help in understanding the changing social phenomena and the next steps in opposing racism. The National Committee of Negro Churchmen wrote a "Black Power" statement to interpret the restlessness and dissatisfaction among African Americans, and this was shared with Methodist women. Advocates of black power criticized the "gross imbalance of power" between African Americans and whites. While white people freely invoked white-biased laws, police, military forms of authority, or physical, extra-legal power to get what they wanted, they expected African Americans to appeal to white conscience or use persuasion to effect change. The inequity corrupted both systems. Whites, meeting little resistance to their abuse of power, took arrogant positions. African Americans, unable to gain justice, resorted to self-surrender.[67]

The African American church leaders attributed the breakdown of the social fabric in African American communities to a failure of American leaders over many years to address problems that created ghetto walls, unemployment, poverty, and discrimination. These leaders, whom they now challenged, had failed "to use American power to create equal opportunity *in life* as well as *in law*. . . ."[68] Integregation could not be complete or meaningful without the capacity to "participate with power," by exerting political, economic, and personal influence in social institutions.[69] Just as African Americans had been oppressed as a group, the response to oppression needed to be a group action. The ultimate goal would not be racial isolationism or domination of whites, but reconciliation which recognized that "[o]ur history and destiny are indissolubly linked."

The Woman's Division called upon Methodists to find common beliefs and aspirations for justice contained in the statement on Black Power by the National Committee of Negro Churchmen. While white Americans might respond with violence and hatred or feel that they had been betrayed, Methodist women could respond with action directed toward eliminating segregation and discrimination from within The Methodist Church and by uniting with others working for decent education, housing, jobs, and voter rights for all citizens.[70]

Pauli Murray, the attorney who prepared *States' Laws on Race and Color*, also interpreted the times for *The Methodist Woman*. The Board of Missions of The Methodist Church published Murray's 1967 book entitled *Progress in Human Rights in the United States Since 1948*. Here Murray advanced suggestions about the tasks which lay ahead in the movement for civil rights.[71]

Americans needed to prepare to live together as one people. Discrimination needed to be halted and assistance provided to overcome the inequalities established by past discrimination. Murray listed minimum conditions needed to achieve reconstruction of racial attitudes and institutional change. These included democratically controlled long-range social planning. For example, rather than issue social services and jobs on the basis of demonstrated poverty, these would be given to all people. She urged the nation to take responsibility for vital resources; inculcating her philosophy of sharing for the common good, protecting individual rights, planning sound economics, and committing to resolve racial problems. Murray concluded, "Only a radical transformation of American society through imaginative and concerted effort can produce the conditions which will eliminate the causes of racial conflict."[72]

In the 1960s the Woman's Division spent its efforts on public policy interface doing what it did best—educating and continuing the public dialogue about racial attitudes. Methodist women related the gospel to social issues, especially civil rights, voting rights, poverty, and the Black Power movement. They helped some women know how to work for inclusive and fair public policies and work to improve human relations in their own communities. They played an important interpretive role across generational lines, first in the case of sit-ins and protest marches, and later in helping whites to understand the rise of the Black Power movement. While the nation erupted in violence, represented by the 1967 ghetto riots and the assassinations of Dr. Martin Luther King, Jr., and Robert Kennedy in 1968, The Methodist Church entered a merger with racial implications. The Woman's Division concentrated its efforts on ending the segregated jurisdictional system in The Methodist Church, racially merging Methodist jurisdictional and conference women's societies and bringing to birth The United Methodist Church.

We cannot stop the momentum nor change the direction toward freedom. We can influence the climate and make the process of change worthy of a democracy and even more basic, worthy of the Christian gospel which we profess to believe.

—Thelma Stevens,
Margaret R. Bender, and Theressa Hoover
The Methodist Woman (November 1963), 27

CHAPTER 13

Desegregating The Methodist Church: We Must Act Together— But We Must Act!

Surrounded by sit-ins and marches, school desegration, racially motivated murders, church-burnings, and the flowering of the civil rights movement of the early 1960s, The Methodist Church belatedly studied race relations and developed position statements and strategies for desegregation. Predominately male-led, the church acted as though racial issues could be resolved legislatively. Unlike the women's organization, which had always been concerned with how the gospel shone a light on people's attitudes, the denomination as a whole focused on the mechanics of how the church could desegregate.

Desegregation of The Methodist Church by merger brought both advantages and drawbacks. On the positive side, the Central Jurisdiction structure provided places of service for African Americans at all levels of the church structure except positions as executive staff for boards and agencies. That hurdle of desegregation had only been crossed in a few places. Seasoned black leaders (bishops, district superintendents, jurisdictional officers, and even clergywomen) entered the new denomination at least theoretically on a par with other leaders. Desegregation of local churches, on the other hand, could proceed extremely slowly under the delusion that integrating membership on national, jurisdictional, and conference committees might constitute achievement of genuine racial harmony.

Desegregation turned out to be less complete than full racial integration. At every corner new aspects of the unfinished business of race relations work popped up. Even among Christians who were committed to racial integration, the racism inherent in church structures proved to be a challenge. The church, in its encounter with its own institutional racism, began to glimpse the broad scope of institutional racism inherent in the culture.

As had happened with the 1939 merger, Methodist women looked to leaders of the black caucus to help them understand and interpret ethical dilemmas involved in decisions surrounding the 1968 merger. As allies of a liberation movement, they listened to the voices of those most directly affected by discrimination.

Once again, the process of merging highlighted for women the ways in which they themselves, as a group, were underrepresented and not taken seriously. Because of their growing awareness of institutional racism and sexism in the church, Methodist women set about forming two new structures within The United Methodist Church: the Commission on Religion and Race, to advocate for and monitor the denomination's progress in racial integration; and the Commission on the Status and Role of Women, to advance the church's integration of women into all aspects of its life and work.

The story of the Commission on the Status and Role of Women is not told here, for it was formed in 1972, four years after this chapter closes. The rising consciousness of women's issues in the context of the civil rights movement, however, was an essential ingredient of this period.

As a prelude to all of these structural changes and to the unveiling of institutional racism disclosed by the 1968 merger, the 1960s opened with a restructuring of the Woman's Division voted in by the predominately male Board of Missions of The Methodist Church. The decisions, engineered by men, reminded some women of the way the Board of Missions of the Methodist Episcopal Church, South, (MECS) had treated the Women's Missionary Council (WMC) in 1910.

Déjà vu: Restructuring and Reflections on Gender

In 1960 the Board of Missions decided to restructure the relationship of the Woman's Division to the Board. With men outnumbering women at least two to one, the Board decided to replace the collegial leadership system of the Woman's Division. The Board secured Ann Porter Brown, a former YWCA national treasurer from Kansas, for the position of associate general secretary of the Woman's Division, to provide one executive in charge who would replace the rotating leadership previously provided by the departmental executive officers of the Woman's Division. With one chief executive instead of four, the Woman's Division now had only one voice in the General Conference.

The Division adjusted to a less shared style of internal leadership and faced increased pressure from the Board of Missions to follow its directives.[1] Due to their collegial style of administration, the Woman's Division had enjoyed a numerical majority when the executive heads of the divisions of the Board of Missions had met. Under the new arrangement, two of the top five positions were to be occupied by women.

Changes in the structure of the Woman's Division placed Christian Social Relations (CSR) at the center of the organization in 1964. The Board of Missions merged the Woman's Division's departments of Home and Foreign Missions with their own Home and Foreign Missions programs and assumed administrative responsibility for all of them. The merger made no provision for attending to the special needs of women that had been served by the women's missions, for using the Woman's Division's superior ability to manage the institutions, or for taking action on the continuing discrimination against women in the Board of Missions. This left CSR at the heart of the women's mission program as its missional identity and primary task. The Woman's Division restructured with three sections: CSR, Finance, and Program Education for Missions. The Section on CSR created a portfolio on racial issues and transferred primary responsibility in this area from Thelma Stevens to Peggy Billings.[2]

In 1964, when the Board of Missions selected Ann Porter Brown for the post of general secretary she became the first woman ever to head a board or agency of The Methodist Church. The church was beginning to look at gender issues.

Most of the time, Methodist women simply ran their own organizations, making no complaints about gender limitations. Yet some were aware of their origins rooted in discrimination; of ongoing restrictions to full ministerial credentials (until 1956); of inequities in voice and representation in the church; and of particular end-runs around Methodist women by the General Conference or various church agencies from time to time. From 1926 on, the WMC and its successor, the Woman's Division, maintained a standing committee on the Status of Women and monitored the treatment of women by church and society. Methodist women paid attention to changing understandings of women and their social roles.

They saw themselves as inheritors of a women's missionary movement, temporarily entrusted to them, and to be passed on to the next generation. They took seriously their Christian faith: they regularly attended worship; engaged in prayer; studied the Bible and social issues; and gave many volunteer hours to the life of their local churches. Their biblical understanding of the inherent worth and interrelatedness of all persons, as demonstrated in the life and teachings of Jesus, provided for Methodist women a more powerful motivation for breaking down racial barriers than did all other arguments. Methodist women, who first viewed themselves as a moral influence on their communities, came to see themselves as shapers of opinion and public policy as well.

The biblical understanding held by many Methodist women did not circumscribe them with gender limitations. Consequently they were freed by the gospel to do that to which they were called by God. When the women were not comfortable with culture or customs that served as barriers to their full inclusion in society they called on this higher religious authority. On the other hand, the women's organizations within which they worked gave them more freedom than was available in mixed-gender settings. Women rarely questioned whether the domestic duties that they expected of themselves, or that culture expected of them, were fair. Rather, they questioned why women did not serve on juries and why police departments did not hire more women. Some women were incensed that the men of the Board of Missions required the Woman's Division to restructure, but most were task-oriented. When there was work to be done, and where Methodist women saw the need, they found a way. They cited Galatians 3:28: "There can be neither Jew nor Greek, there can be neither bond nor free, there can be no male and female: for ye all are one in Christ Jesus."

The Methodist Church and Race, 1960–1964

Methodist women made a commitment to spend four years, from 1960 to 1964, studying race as a component of the theme "Our Mission Today."[3] This decision led the entire denomination to study racial issues.

Unlike Methodist women who had been studying racial issues since 1914, prior to the 1960s The Methodist Church had never sponsored a study of racial issues for the whole church and had provided little leadership for its members in the areas of race relations and civil rights. Yet, like the Woman's Division, one of the denomination's strengths was its capacity to use its connectional system to educate people and organize programs of outreach and service to meet needs in local communities.

In 1960 the Woman's Division initiated a proposal for a denomination-wide study of racial issues. They invited the Board of Christian Social Concerns to co-sponsor a quadrennial emphasis on racial issues with the goal of helping Christians "to work with greatly accelerated speed *to help resolve racial tensions throughout our nation*."[4]

The quadrennial program was launched with a conference in Louisville, Kentucky, in 1961. It planned to prepare congregations to welcome persons of all races by helping church members "[r]ecognize that the Church is the house of God and thereby open to the whole family of God in its worship, fellowship, and membership."[5] Methodist women proposed that in implementing the quadrennial program church members could work together across racial lines to organize workshops for parents and youth involved in school desegregation.

The conference urged local churches to respond to the civil rights movement. Conference participants implored Christians to meet the leaders of nonviolent demonstrations, learn their objectives, and "determine their moral obligation to participate in and support nonviolent protest movements."[6]

For both clergy and laity the conference participants made suggestions that replicated what Methodist women already had been doing, but which were new for the church as a whole. For example, clergy could visit students confined in jail and church members could offer financial assistance. Local church members could help citizen committees hold workshops in human relations for law enforcement officers, business leaders, and other concerned citizens. Local church Commissions on Christian Social Concerns might publish the requirements for voting, the procedures for voter-registration, and a summary of local voting conditions; provide information on the motives and practices of hate groups; and report violations of human rights laws to state and federal agencies that enforce civil rights. They offered specific suggestions for bishops, pastors, and congregations; the church press; and church agencies, boards, and annual conferences to help church members prepare to welcome people of all races into the life of the church.

Thelma Stevens, still with a driving passion to overcome racial barriers, encouraged Methodists to become active in the civil rights movement. As one of the conference leaders she urged white Christians to "quietly and naturally" take their place among blacks who were desegregating buses, trains, lunch counters, and restaurants and to patronize merchants who integrated their businesses.

The leadership on racial issues now coming from the Board of

243

Christian Social Concerns dramatically changed the activity profile in The Methodist Church. For example, church periodicals ran articles on racial issues and provided tips to church leaders and pastors. Consequently, more ministers began to preach about racial issues.

The Woman's Division continued to work through General Conference for racial integration in the church. In 1960 Thelma Stevens and an *ad hoc* group helped fund publication of a new book by Philip Wogaman entitled *A Strategy for Desegregation in The Methodist Church*. The Woman's Division distributed copies to its members and all delegates to General Conference.[7]

In 1960 the General Conference took three decisive steps. A new position on race was adopted from the statement issued by the 1959 Conference on Human Relations which claimed, "The House of God must be open to the whole family of God."[8] The conference mandated the formation of a Commission on Christian Social Concerns in each local church, and created the Commission on Interjurisdictional Relations, charged with deciding how "to abolish the Central Jurisdiction, promote interracial brotherhood . . . and achieve a more inclusive church."[9] The new local church structure enabled national leaders of the denomination to have more direct influence in local churches.

Much had changed in the past decade. Many Methodist women now knew that racism was imbedded in many cultures and across the U.S., not just in the South, which is why international and ecumenical ties were critical for efforts to end racism. The Woman's Division was building a United Nations Church Center. On a regular basis Methodist women worked ecumenically for civil rights, especially through Church Women United. Thelma Stevens had guided that group in setting "Assignment: Race" as their emphasis from 1961 to 1966.[10]

With an expanded "team" of denomination, Church Women United, and international connections, Methodist women reexamined their goals concerning racial issues.

The Charter of Racial Policies—1962

In 1962 Methodist women commemorated the tenth anniversary of the Charter of Racial Policies. The Woman's Division issued to conferences and local societies a revised "Charter of Racial Policies of the Woman's Division—1962" for adoption. The 1962 charter reaffirmed the 1952 theological and ethical rationale for racial inclusiveness with minimal changes.

The time had now come to work with renewed effort on the fourth point of the charter: demonstrating within the life and ministry of the church the sacred worth of all persons by providing opportunities for "fellowship and service, for personal growth, and for freedom in every aspect of life. . . ."[11] Thelma Stevens, Margaret R. Bender, and Theressa Hoover, the executive staff of CSR, wrote, "'Christian social relations' means all of us working together, maybe in different ways—*to rid our churches and our society of racial bigotry in any form. . . . We must act together—but we must act! Somebody must take the lead*."[12]

The new charter outlined twelve commitments involving Methodist women, local societies, and the Woman's Division in action around community and national issues. Methodist women pledged to create inclusive attitudes in local churches, to change patterns of segregation, and to work for federal policies that protected the rights of all people in the nation. Thelma Stevens called for women to make a personal commitment to support basic human rights, gather facts, and join with other like-minded persons to support the cause of freedom for all people in the church and community.[13]

local

Personal

Some societies found it easier to hold regular meetings than to deal with racial problems of the 1960s. Sadie Tillman, former president of the Woman's Division, wrote about this problem. She asked:

> Are we going on as usual, "putting on" programs that have no bearing on the agony we are in, making reports on ordinary affairs while closing our eyes to racial upheavals? Are we studying about our "wonderful missionaries" instead of making a mighty effort to put into practice the truth that we send them to proclaim to others?[14]

Indeed, some members of Woman's Societies of Christian Service (WSCS) and Wesleyan Service Guilds (WSG) had never heard of the Charter of Racial Policies.[15] Where injustice is concerned, silence does not have the last word.

Preach?

Working with The Methodist Church, King's Dream, and the Charter

In 1962 the Woman's Division and Board of CSR began preparations with nine other cooperating Methodist agencies for the Second Quadrennial Conference on Human Relations set for August 26–30, 1963, in Chicago.[16] Their dates were selected well before civil rights leaders began to plan the March on Washington for the same weekend.

At the planning meeting, representatives from across The Methodist Church joined the Woman's Division in asking for the elimination of the Central Jurisdiction. The women had made this request every four years since 1940. Now they requested that the General Conference complete the necessary mergers and transfers by 1968.

The Second Quadrennial Conference on Human Relations called for the removal of all discriminatory practices in all institutions of The Methodist Church, including appointment of pastors.[17] They honored Thelma Stevens and six other Protestant, Catholic, and Jewish leaders for national leadership in civil rights. In reaction to churches that closed their doors when African Americans showed up to worship, they asked churches to welcome all persons and asserted the right of all persons to be welcomed at worship regardless of their reasons for coming. The conference challenged churches to prepare their members to live in integrated neighborhoods. Delegates spoke to the need for national job training programs to offset the conditions created by the segregated school systems and challenged employers to offer jobs without discriminating in wages.

At the same time that Methodists gathered in Chicago for the Second Quadrennial Conference, a coalition of major civil rights organizations led the 1963 March on Washington in which the coalition demanded that Congress pass important new civil rights legislation. Six persons delegated by the conference, including Thelma Stevens and Theressa Hoover, and thirty other volunteers from the Methodist gathering, traveled to Washington, D.C., to participate in the March on Washington.[18] The Methodists carried a message from the conference which said:

> Our support of this March comes from our desire: (1) to witness the concern of the American people to the national moral issue of racial injustice and (2) to give support to justice implemented through civil rights legislation.[19]

Those at the conference pledged to work within The Methodist Church to fulfill the objectives of the march. The 1963 March on Washington left an indelible impression on Thelma Stevens. She appealed for people to work for freedom now in every part of the United States to reduce the threat of violence.[20]

Belatedly, in 1964, the church finally affirmed the right of minorities who are oppressed to engage in public protests. Orderly, responsible demonstrations, the church stated, "can serve to bring a better order into being," while violence by demonstrators, onlookers, or police was not constructive. "[T]he blame for violence should be placed on the violent, and not on the peaceable demonstrators."[21] The church could no longer ignore the civil rights movement.

Yet, for Methodists, some of their core work on racial issues during this decade of upheaval came along with preparation for a merger with the Evangelical United Brethren (EUB) Church in 1968. In June 1963, Thelma Stevens challenged Methodist women to be specific and take immediate action toward implementing the Charter of Racial Policies goal which called women to work "with all groups in the church toward eliminating in The Methodist Church all forms of segregation. . . ."[22] With General Conference approaching and racial policies a major agenda item, she claimed that Methodist women could be influential in creating a climate of opinion favorable to changing the church's racial policies, especially by cultivating an "informed constituency *in local churches* across the nation."[23] The Woman's Division sent every woman delegate three pamphlets that mounted a combined argument for desegregating the church.

The Devilish Details of Church Desegregation, 1964

The stakes about racial issues were high at the 1964 General Conference, not only because the nation was in midst of the civil rights movement, but also because that General Conference would set guidelines for the delegation that would negotiate the 1968 merger, including matters relating to race. The Commission on Interjurisdictional Relations authorized by the 1960 General Conference prepared a plan for the elimination of the Central Jurisdiction. Twelve women from the Woman's Division and the WSCS, including President Sadie Tillman, served as members of the Commission.[24] Preliminary plans called for the creation of committees to facilitate the merger of various annual conferences of the Central Jurisdiction into annual conferences of the geographical jurisdictions.[25]

The Central Jurisdiction named a Committee of Five to respond to the proposal, to ensure that Central Jurisdiction concerns were heard, and to formulate recommendations and plans for specific steps to eliminate that jurisdiction. The committee's report recommended that local African American churches simply join the geographical annual conference and jurisdiction where they were located. They noted that the African American pastors would need equal opportunities for employment and advancement. They pointed to the need to employ lay and clergy volunteers in all levels of church life.

247

The Woman's Division disagreed with the Commission on Interjurisdictional Relations' reliance on the voluntary cooperation from annual conferences. The Woman's Division worried that mandates for action would not be implemented in a timely manner. For this reason the Woman's Division presented procedures leading to the elimination of the Central Jurisdiction that were more specific than those presented to the General Conference by the Committee on Interjurisdictional Relations.

 Ultimately, the Woman's Division's platform relied heavily on recommendations from the Committee of Five. By listening to the voices representing the minority group, Methodist women were made aware of places where the church still needed to grow in its understanding.

Each of the Woman's Division's proposals helped protect African Americans from a particular aspect of discrimination. For example, Methodist women called for: transferring bishops of the Central Jurisdiction into geographical jurisdictions; retaining African American leadership from the Central Jurisdiction in agencies of The Methodist Church; establishing a Temporary General Aid Fund to cover unfunded pension liabilities so that the pensions of white pastors and African American pastors could be equalized; and providing protective measures so that impoverished congregations could meet reasonable goals for benevolent and connectional funding obligations. The Woman's Division commended the Committee of Five and encouraged the General Conference to consider the committee's memorials along with the report of the Commission on Interjurisdictional Relations.[26]

The Woman's Division called for the General Conference to adopt for The Methodist Church specific policies on the subject of race and to make explicit in the *Discipline* principles that were implicit in the recommendations of the Committee of Five. The Woman's Division wanted statements in the *Discipline* to make church policy clear. For example, all local Methodist churches were to be racially inclusive. Conferences and jurisdictions should not be segregated or practice discrimination. Ministers transferred from one annual conference to another would retain membership in full connection. Standard fair employment policies would apply to the entire denomination and all of its agencies. The Woman's Division called for withholding of general church funds from any program or agency "failing to operate their program in keeping with the policy of fair employment practices and non-discriminatory services and programs," and mandated all institutions owned by The Methodist Church to operate without racial discrimination or segregation in service or employment.[27] Further, the Woman's Division asked General Conference to change its policy so that no Methodist colleges would have a racial label and all Methodist colleges would have the same relationship to the denomination.

The Woman's Division called on the 1964 General Conference to designate some of its World Service benevolence funds to meet needs created by the racial crisis in the United States and The Methodist Church. The Woman's Division proposed that the General Conference set up one fund which would make possible "biracial and/or interracial ministries in local churches," where such ministries could generate creative solutions to racial tensions, and another fund to subsidize ministers who, because of their convictions and actions on race, suffered economic reprisal. The Woman's Division recommended that the denomination provide bonds "for persons jailed because of attempted entry into a local Methodist church for worship."[28] Finally, the Woman's Division requested the General Conference to prepare "mediation teams" who could be sent anywhere to assist The Methodist Church in times of crisis. Already the Woman's Division had placed three missionary field workers in places of racial tension.[29]

As if a log jam had broken loose, The Methodist Church began to move forward with a flood of statements and new positions. As a direct result of the work of the Woman's Division and the 1963 Conference on Human Relations, the 1964 General Conference adopted strong new commitments to racial inclusiveness in a revised resolution on "The Methodist Church and Race."[30]

The 1964 General Conference took several steps toward healing wounds of interracial conflict. It established a Racial Witness Relief Fund to provide for Methodist ministers left destitute by their witness to a racially inclusive church. Methodist women publicized the fund, and when donations lagged, they acted to revive it.[31] The Woman's Division backed the new Student Interracial Ministry summer program for placement of seminary interns across racial lines. They invited Methodist women to seek white Methodist churches who would be willing to use seminary students in their programs. Women worked hard to recruit African Americans and foreign students for the Student Interracial Ministry.[32]

The 1964 General Conference chose an unusual way to deal with the church's racism. Instead of writing in details and protections for integration, the conference instructed the Commission on Union with the EUB to omit from the draft of the constitution any reference to racial structures. A special session of General Conference was called in 1966 to vote on the new constitution, and if it were ratified, the end to racial structures as authorized by the constitution would be adopted.

The General Conference adopted measures which clarified "that all local Methodist churches *are open* to all persons without discrimination based on race, color, nationality or economic status."[33] The church encouraged full participation of all persons in the life of the church, at least until new categories for discrimination came to light. Annual conferences, likewise, were expected to extend full participation to all persons and eliminate racial discrimination. All institutions and agencies of The Methodist Church were mandated to extend their services and establish employment practices without discrimination. Nevertheless, responsibility for the church's national level program on race fell to the Woman's Division and the Board of Christian Social Concerns. As a crowning jewel recognizing the pioneering work of Methodist women, The General Conference adopted the Charter of Racial Policies of the Woman's Division and recommended it to churches for implementation.[34]

"Discovering" Racism and Creating the Commission on Religion and Race

Thelma Stevens was not satisfied that the church had done its job. The witness of The Methodist Church would have more integrity when its structures and congregations were racially inclusive. However, when Stevens compared the position of the Woman's Division on race relations in 1944 with issues being confronted in 1964 she found that "The world has changed . . . but the *revolution within the church* has not kept pace with the *revolution in the world*!" She claimed that Methodist women had an "urgent responsibility" to work on problems related to race in their local societies and guilds.[35] Even more important, from Stevens' perspective, every local church should witness to Jesus' inclusive gospel.

Leaders of CSR began to help Methodist women look beyond desegregation and integration to the larger problem of racism. Racism set up social barriers to human fulfillment. Searching for new directions in race relations, the Section on CSR convened about twenty African American women to examine the relevance of the church's program for African American women and explore opportunities to confront contemporary social issues. They began to help the Woman's Division understand institutional racism. Racism was present in the assumptions underlying the policies and practices of organizations and it pervaded The Methodist Church.

The Woman's Division rose to defend interests of African American Methodists whom the uniting committee tended to overlook in its concern for the EUB Church and The Methodist Church. The women noticed glaring financial disparities.

The Division recognized the difference in income and cost of transportation between women's organizations in geographical jurisdictions and those in the former Central Jurisdiction and agreed to provide funds to ensure the participation of former Central Jurisdiction officers at the annual meetings of the geographic jurisdictions.[36] Likewise, a huge gap existed between the salaries provided for white pastors and black pastors. In the new church, salary schedules applied to all pastors, regardless of race.

Leaders of Methodist women noticed a loss of leadership positions held by persons of color due to the merger of structures based on race with those established on geographical terms. The Section on Christian Social Relations asked the Woman's Division to establish guidelines for mergers and bring the matter to the attention of conference and jurisdictional presidents and their executive committees.[37]

The Woman's Division, correctly anticipating that a similar situation would develop in the church at large, began advocating for intentional inclusion of ethnic minorities in positions of leadership across all areas of church life.[38]

With the transition to the new United Methodist Church at hand and jurisdictional conferences about to take place where new bishops would be elected and members of general church boards and agencies chosen, Theressa Hoover feared that members of the abolished Central Jurisdiction might be excluded. She pointed to the carefully established quota system for inclusion of former EUB members in episcopal leadership and board membership. The Methodist Church was more than ten times larger than the EUB Church. The former Central Jurisdiction, strongest in the South, had 245,968 members, about one-third the number of EUB members.[39] Theressa Hoover poignantly wrote that since the South Central and Southeastern Jurisdictions had among the fewest former EUB members, and the most former Central Jurisdiction members, and since "the Plan of Union provides for a 13 percent across-the-board representation of former Evangelical United Brethren members, I would ask myself the question: 'Can we do less for former Central Jurisdiction members of The Methodist Church?'"[40] Where former Central Jurisdiction members outnumbered former EUBs, there was no provision for their representation on church boards.

Overall, conference mergers made little difference in the life of local churches. Peggy Billings noted, "Those churches that have made progress were churches that even before merger had some degree of interracial experience."[41]

As plans for the 1968 merger of The Methodist Church with the EUB Church made no reference to race, the constitution of The United Methodist Church contained no plan or deadline for the final merging of the twelve conferences of the Central Jurisdiction with the geographical conferences. Legalistic compliance with the 1964 *Discipline* of the church had created a loophole for segregation. The South Central Jurisdiction decided to proceed with racial merger under the condition that it would occur only when it was deemed that the merger was mutually agreeable, without a deadline. The Judicial Council, the highest judicial body in the denomination, approved the constitutionality of that legislation. The Methodist Church had settled for voluntary desegregation.

The General Conference had never set a deadline for annual conferences to complete mergers related to ending the Central Jurisdiction. The Woman's Division voiced to the General Conference its concern for immediate abolition of racially segregated church structures in a petition which called for completion of this task "in 1968 as The United Methodist Church is created." Instead the conference set a target date of 1972 and left execution of the merger to occur on a voluntary basis.

Disappointed leaders of the Woman's Division pressed ahead to get the church to commit to form a Commission on Religion and Race, an agency with responsibility to monitor progress in race relations, to lead the denomination forward in that area. The Woman's Division had been the church's bellwether on the issue of race relations for many years. When the church established the Commission on Religion and Race, the commission accepted the task of monitoring the church and holding it accountable for its own racism.

Methodist Women Desegregate Annual Conferences

The merger of the Central Jurisdiction and its annual conferences with other conferences and jurisdictions of The Methodist Church meant that the Methodist women's organizations of the WSCS and WSG in each of these areas also went through mergers. Knowing that the merger with the EUB Church also spelled merger of racially segregated annual conferences and women's organizations, the Woman's Division wanted to guide conferences through a smooth transition. To provide a model for other conferences, Mrs. J. J. Johnson, Jr., former vice-president of the Central West [Missouri] Conference, described how her conference had prepared for the interracial merger.[42]

Three conferences separated the Methodist women of Missouri. Missouri East and Missouri West divided white women into two groups, and the remnants of the Central West Conference of the Central Jurisdiction, which once had included Missouri, Colorado, Kansas, Nebraska, and Illinois, served African American Methodist women. The General Conference had provided that the Central West Conference would continue to function while the two white conferences prepared for a merger that would split the Central West Conference between the white conferences.

White woman's society leaders took the initiative to meet African American woman's society officers prior to the merger. Some white women decided to hold monthly luncheon meetings, and soon found that many African American women were employed and could not attend regular luncheons. One woman formed a group for weekly prayer and fellowship with six to eight wives of pastors from the three conferences. For some it was the first time they had chosen to experience more than superficial communication with women of a different racial group. Out of their meetings grew the idea of planning a retreat which brought together Methodist ministers' wives for a two-day gathering.

Conference presidents who began talking with each other about the merger soon had other conference and district officers talking and planning together. When they learned that the merger was scheduled for May 1965, the women of the Central West Conference planned and held a last annual meeting in April to provide closure. For the first time they participated in joint Schools of Christian Mission with the other two conferences.

Twice the merger was delayed. The women were confounded in their attempts to coordinate with the interracial merger taking place between their conferences, but they went ahead in their own way. In 1966, women of the Missouri East Conference invited women of the Central West Conference (eastern portion) to attend their annual meeting. The conference officers from Central West voted in the executive and conference meetings. The annual meeting recommended that they vote in district meetings as well, prior to the merger. Women from the Central West Conference who were added to the nominating committee appreciated being included.

When the ceremonies uniting the three annual conferences occurred on May 31 and June 13, 1966, and when Bishops Eugene Frank and Matthew W. Clair, Jr., clasped hands to symbolize the union, Mrs.

Johnson and other Methodist women felt that their union had already taken place.[43]

Black Methodists for Church Renewal

African American Methodists, facing the elimination of the Central Jurisdiction with the upcoming July 1968 formation of The United Methodist Church, needed to create a new channel for unity and communication. In an unprecedented action, the Woman's Division gave $2000 toward the expenses of the National Conference of Negro Methodists scheduled for February 1968. About three hundred persons at the conference founded Black Methodists for Church Renewal (BMCR).[44] The conference united African American Methodists in solidarity as the time of the merger approached. Minnie Stein, representing CSR, attended the conference and reported that African American Methodists were concerned about their future in the new United Methodist Church that was about to be formed. African American Methodists were looking for ways to nurture and sustain themselves, maintain integrity and influence in the new denomination, and enlarge the church's vision and understanding in the arena of race relations.

BMCR had serious reservations. How would the church deal with the discrimination and segregation that remained deeply entrenched in local custom, policies, and practices? Black Methodists would be watchful and active in guiding the outcome, but the whole church needed to share in this task.

The 1968 Merger: Discrimination by Race and Gender, Again!

The leaders planning the 1968 merger of The Methodist Church and the EUB Church, as late as one year prior to the proposed church union, had not solicited any information from the Woman's Division concerning the proposed objectives or structure of the 1.5 million member women's organization participating in the merger.[45] The Woman's Division asked its president, Virginia Laskey, to appoint a committee to study the church union proposal and its implications for the relationship of a woman's organization to the total church.[46]

The issue of church union raised the familiar question of whether a separate organization was needed for Methodist women. Sarah Cunningham, writing in *The Methodist Woman*, argued that even if no prejudice stood in the way of women, a woman's organization would be an important dimension of church life just as church school, youth groups, and other constituent groups were. Women who wanted to work together for common causes needed the freedom to determine their own program. Christian women around the world needed "ways of pooling their resources, means of ministering to one another, [and] channels for relating their inner needs and inner callings to a world mission. . . ."[47]

As the date approached for the formation of The United Methodist Church, the Woman's Division focused its attention on the merger. Methodist women had to deal with structural changes at many levels of their organization. The EUB Women's Society of Work and Service merged with the Methodist Woman's Society of Christian Service. Local United Methodist women's groups were renamed the Women's (no longer Woman's) Society of Christian Service. The Woman's Division became the Women's Division. The Section of Christian Social Relations reorganized with three areas of responsibility—International Affairs, Racial Justice, and Public Policy and National Climate—each with a designated chair from the membership of the Women's Division.

The Women's Society of Work and Service of the EUB Church brought into the Women's Society of Christian Service of The United Methodist Church 2,919 local societies and 105,420 members who in 1967 had contributed $1,353,000 for their mission programs and organization.[48] In 1968, the Women's Division selected Theressa Hoover to be its associate general secretary, the head of the new organization. The former Methodist Church contributed over 1,500,000 members in more than 33,500 societies and guilds with an annual budget of $11,000,000.[49] The new organization, in 1972 renamed United Methodist Women, was the largest organization of women in the United States.

Thelma Stevens reflected on the uniting conference which had just taken place. The United Methodist Church now replaced the EUB Church and The Methodist Church. She observed that the new church, which claimed to have united branches of Wesleyan heritage, did not include the African Methodist Episcopal Church, the Christian Methodist Episcopal Church, the African Methodist Episcopal Zion Church, the Free Methodist Church, or the Wesleyan Methodist Church.[50] The task of uniting Methodists was not complete and ending denominational division based on race remained unfinished business.

The time had come for the church to resolve immediate problems associated with completing the merger of the Central Jurisdiction.

Beyond that, The United Methodist Church would need to continue working toward eliminating institutional racism, developing attitudes of racial inclusiveness among its members, and shaping public policies without racial bias. The denomination was preparing to share responsibility for racial issues that Methodist women had come to understand were part of their Christian responsibility.

A ll of us are builders of a supportive community that reaches from a neighborhood in any place, U.S.A., to neighborhoods anywhere and everywhere on the globe.

—Thelma Stevens
Legacy for the Future, 122

CHAPTER 14

Fellowship of Love:
Lessons from the Journey

Methodist women who spent two generations changing American racial attitudes accomplished several other things as well. They came to a deeper understanding of their experience as women in a male-dominated culture, of the mission of the church, of the process of social transformation, and of the spiritual lessons it held for them. Life calls for attitude changes from people who are part of a fellowship of love.

Methodist women of the Central Jurisdiction paid tribute to the Department of Christian Social Relations of the Woman's Division for its work against racism:

> It was CSR/LCA, headed for 28 years by Miss Thelma Stevens as executive (staff) secretary, which mobilized Methodist women of all ethnic identities into one of the most sustained campaigns against racism ever witnessed in America.[1]

Between 1920 and 1968, organized Methodist women made substantial changes in racial attitudes, especially in the South. Indeed, they had helped change racial attitudes of many ordinary Americans over two generations. With changed attitudes had come integration of public services and schools, the 1964 Civil Rights Bill and 1965 Voting Rights Act, and desegregation of The Methodist Church.

Along the way, Methodist women felt the sting of sexism. Although it had not stopped them, by 1968 they were much more conscious of it and the ways it was imbedded in church and culture. Methodist women didn't lead the cultural revolution of the feminist movement that followed the civil rights movement, but for reasons evident in their history, many quickly began to ready, study, think, and lead their communities in using inclusive language and seeking more opportunities for women. Based on their experiences they understood the linkages between "isms" of race, gender, and class, and others yet emerging.

259

Changing Concepts of Mission

In substantial ways, Methodist women had helped shape their denomination's concept of mission. In the 1800s many people believed that mission meant doing good deeds for others and being kind to those less fortunate than themselves.

Methodist women began the 1900s by organizing and operating institutions designed to do charitable work in a systematic way. They founded schools and built hospitals and orphanages. By the early 1920s, Methodist women had made commitments to cooperate across racial lines in working for racial justice and ending lynching. Mission called them to reach across social barriers and relate to other human beings. By the 1930s, Methodist women came to see that the work of meeting human needs should be shared. They were helping those less fortunate gain access to public benefits. Mission included self-help, cooperation, and reciprocity. Mission was coming to mean working with others to alleviate problems of injustice. God called people to work for good human relations within institutions as well as between individuals.

In the 1940s, Methodist women began turning to African American women for self-definition and understanding of the systems that needed to be changed to improve interracial relationships. They knew that mission meant educating the public and working for passage of laws that provide equal rights and justice for all. By the 1950s the price of prejudice and intolerance was clear to more white women than ever before. Methodist women began to accept a share of the responsibility for the social climate that fostered these attitudes.

By the 1960s, Methodist women had grasped that the church was called to help improve the quality of life for all people. Decision-making power, program design, leadership, and implementation needed to be shared. In truth, those who came to help others were themselves helped to understand more about human relations. What women learned from their experiences in mission helped the larger denomination grow in its own understanding of its purpose and task.

Religion and Social Transformation

Embedded in the narrative of Methodist women changing racial attitudes is information and analysis about the process of social transformation and the role of religion in that process. Change comes when people hear and recognize a higher calling to do something different than they have been doing. Change also occurs when people believe

260

that their presence in this new way will make a significant difference. Change happens when people have an invitation to think or act differently. But change requires a sense of safety; this implies that the higher calling and the invitation must come from trusted sources. When the invitation can be trusted, people will try thinking and acting in new ways, even when those thoughts and behaviors break with religious or social conventions.

Often the higher calling is grounded in a religious myth or metaphor that serves as an organizing principle. Thus the interpretation of religious texts has power beyond the printed page because it carries the "genetic" imprint for life attitudes that unfold in many dimensions.

Methodist women selected two powerful metaphors: they chose to emphasize that all people are created "in God's image" and that the litmus test for their actions would be Jesus' life and teachings. "In God's image" meant that every person bears a reflection of that which is most sacred and deserves to be treated with respect.

Jesus' exemplary life guided Methodist women. Jesus' life and teachings centered around acceptance of difference, presence with and concern for the social underdog, and an invitation to enhance human relationships. Jesus left judgment to God. Repeatedly, Jesus invited people to look at life in a new way, with a fresh attitude, and with a concern for people who were poor, strangers, foreigners, disabled, or outcast. Jesus was attentive to the needs of women and children, and often was present with them.

Passionate engagement with social transformation requires hopefulness and far-sightedness. Perhaps because key Methodist women leaders came from families where multiple generations had been in leadership, and where they could see the results of thirty or sixty years of effort, they pinned their hope on God's ultimate time rather than on immediate short-term deadlines. At no time did this long-distance view detract from the sense of urgency that things must be done now, but the long perspective sustained hope through times of harassment, backlash, and delay. How one views evil and obstacles to relational wholeness and fulfillment is crucial. It affects attitudes, choices, and the means used to reach the objectives. Dorothy Tilly felt that she could use prayer and quality of character to offset impediments. She set a record player beside her telephone so that when harassing phone calls came, she could play a familiar musical arrangement of "The Lord's Prayer" for the harassers to hear.

Thelma Stevens repeatedly wrote and spoke about "overcoming racial barriers," taking the "next steps," and "following the example of Jesus." Stevens wrote, "*Powers oppress* and *walls divide*. The poor even unto this day must bear the brunt of the seeds of *oppression* and *racism* that have been nourished through the centuries."[2] She called Christians to engage in self-examination, follow the example of Isaiah who gave prophetic leadership to his nation, and eliminate racial walls that divide church members by race.

For Diane Nash, workshops held in Nashville shaped key concepts of nonviolence. She believed in loving one's opponents. "People are never the enemy. The system is the enemy. Attitudes, racism and sexism are the enemy. Racist people could change. Their attitude was the enemy."[3] Not only were the leaders of Methodist women nonviolent; they also did not use words to hurt or abuse. When attacked with bitterness and a vituperative spirit, people whose character and identity were grounded in love had the capacity to refuse to be consumed by a spirit of anger. This ability made them stronger in their cause.

Invitation and presence are crucial aspects of social transformation. Presence gives hope. Invitation leads us out of complacency and habit.

One summer day in 1930, Dorothy Tilly, a diminutive and genteel forty-seven-year-old woman, arrived at Paine College in Augusta, Georgia.[4] Tilly was on the faculty of the Christian Leadership School being sponsored by women of the Colored Methodist Episcopal Church (CME). Well-versed in women's missionary society work as an officer of the Woman's Missionary Council of the Methodist Episcopal Church, South, (MECS) Tilly had come to teach in one of the South's premier programs for continuing education in religion then available to black women. The summer school program for CME women was co-sponsored by women of the MECS and CME Church as part of a continuing relationship between these sister Methodist groups. Tilly thought that leadership development for black women would help unlock the closed door of racial discrimination.

Thelma Stevens, the twenty-eight-year-old director of the Bethlehem Center in Augusta, also arrived for the summer school session. Since witnessing a lynching and vowing to spend her life working to overcome racial barriers, Stevens had completed a master's degree and immersed herself in the nation's racial and cultural struggle. She had lived and worked in the black community adjacent to Paine College for two years. She had broken segregation taboos by holding interracial meetings, sponsoring interracial day camps for children, and eating in interracial settings. When Stevens attended Augusta's white MECS church, she felt the sting of being socially shunned.

As these two women left a morning class session one summer day, Stevens asked Tilly if she was ready for lunch. Stevens suggested that they eat at the Paine College cafeteria where women attending the summer school session were dining. Tilly hesitated. "Why, Thelma, I never ate with Negro people in my life!"

"Well, you don't mind, do you?" Stevens replied.

"No, I don't mind," Tilly responded. "I just never have done it."[5]

Stevens was proposing to go with Tilly through her introduction into a new experience, one solidly grounded in their religious faith. Like many Methodists, these women often sang "In Christ There Is No East or West" at church. They believed the claim of John 3:16 that God loved all the world's people. They took to heart Paul's words in Galatians 3:27 that old divisions fall away, for all are united in Christ. They believed the claim of Genesis 1:26 that all people are part of one human family for all bear the imprint of God's image. So Tilly was not unwilling to associate with African Americans, she just hadn't considered breaking the social taboo. Her thinking was confined by tradition so she would not have taken the initiative.

Not only did Stevens and Tilly have a fine lunch, but Tilly's relationship with black women became more collegial after that day. Stevens reported, "She was just a part of the community after that."

Thelma Stevens used the power of invitation to work for social change. The invitation to communion, to be reconciled across gaps that are enlarged by fear and prejudice; this invitation to face personal and corporate fears and live in community with one another; this is the life of faith, ministry, and mission to which she called Christians.

Power of Invitation.

Stevens extended an invitation to Tilly that engaged her in fellowship and conversation: a simple, yet culturally subversive action. Appealing to a higher calling of Christian faith, Stevens encouraged Tilly to overcome her fear of breaking a racial taboo, and accompanied her in the experience. This simple pattern of exposure to a new perspective through a radical experience came from a heartfelt personal appeal to integrity higher than that practiced under segregation.

This became the model of social transformation used by both Tilly and Stevens as they helped lead Americans on one of the largest projects ever attempted to change American attitudes about race. The kind of love that can see beyond the present to a hope-filled vision of what could be is essential for persuading people to change their attitudes. Methodist women set out to create places where that fellowship of love could be nurtured.

During the course of the twentieth century, Methodist women came to a greater realization that people are interdependent. They came to believe that the ways we classify and group people by observable differences provide an obstacle to the religious journey. God calls people to live in one human family that shows respect for all persons.

Racial segregation, they concluded, subverts God's greater truth that not only do human beings depend on God, but they also depend on each other, on shared social systems, and on a shared planet for life and nurture. Methodist women came to understand that humans live in mutual interdependency. Methodist women worked to overcome hatred, to surmount fear, to diligently guard justice and equality, and to show respect and concern for all. Organized Methodist women hoped that one day the whole world would become one fellowship of love.

Report of the Study Group on Unification of the Woman's Missionary Council, 1937

Your committee agrees that the plan is less than ideal; that it leaves much to be desired if the Methodist Church is fully to represent the Kingdom of God on earth. For Methodist churches in the same city to be related to each other only through a General Conference that meets once in four years seems consistent neither with Methodist connectionalism nor with Jesus' concern that "they all may be one." . . .

Your committee believes that certain provisions of the plan represent an advance in interracial respect and co-operation [autonomy, election of bishops, black delegates to General Conference and the Central Jurisdictional Conference]. The inadequacy of the plan lies in its failure to provide for co-operation between white and colored Methodists in annual and jurisdictional conferences and in local communities. We think we may safely say that the Commission on Unification did not make provision in the plan for more direct relationship between white and Negro Annual Conferences and white and Negro local churches because our churches as a whole are not yet ready for such cooperation. . . .

There remains the question what can we do to set in motion forces that will build up a desire for co-operation between white and colored Methodist churches in our own communities? We think we have already found the answer in our increasing fellowship with the Colored Methodist Episcopal Church. It was about ten years ago that we began working together as missionary women in Leadership Schools for colored women. Many of us, through participation in these schools, have grown in our knowledge and experience of God and have found joy in a broader and more satisfying Christian fellowship than we had ever known before. . . . Can we not extend this type of co-operation to the Negro groups of the M.E. Church within the bounds of our annual conferences?

We are not suggesting a procedure identical to this, but we are suggesting that we become aware of the Negro congregations in our midst, especially of the M.E. connection, and that we seek to find ways of co-operating with them in the good work of the Kingdom. Let us seek to know their leaders in the missionary societies and let us ask our pastors to go with us in this adventure in Christian understanding. As we find work that we can best do together, let us undertake it together. Let us sometimes worship with one another. Those of us who have had such worship experiences will testify that they have brought us new visions of God and of his love for all men. Is not this the practical way to do our part toward building a great church in which men of all races and nations may find fellowship, in which we may all learn to build together the Kingdom of God?

We as women know the value of having an organization of our own, in which we may do things our own way, with our own leaders, meeting at times that are convenient for us. There is room in the world for organizations by age groups, by sex, by occupations, by special interests, by races, by geographical areas, for the pursuit of special objectives. But the Church of God must include all such groups, excluding none and discriminating against none, but uniting all and relating each to all for the sake of the Kingdom. . . .

We believe that we have a great opportunity to help to solve the race problem in America in a Christian way through strengthening the church ties between white and colored Methodists. We believe that such a Methodist connectionalism transcending race and nation and economic class will be better able to create in us the mind which was in Christ Jesus who taught us of one God who is the Father of all and in whom we are all brothers one of another.

APPENDIX B

Charter of Racial Policies—1952

WE BELIEVE

1. We believe that God is the Father of all people of all races and we are His children in one family.

2. We believe that the personality of every human being is sacred.

3. We believe that opportunities for fellowship and service, for personal growth, and for freedom in every aspect of life are inherent rights of every individual.

4. We believe that the visible church of Jesus Christ must demonstrate these principles within its own organization and program.

5. We believe that the Woman's Division as an agency of The Methodist Church must build in every area it may touch, a fellowship and social order without racial barriers.

6. We believe that progress may be advanced by declaring emphatically those policies on which the Woman's Division is determined to move in order to come nearer the ideal.

POLICIES

1. Persons to fill positions within the official body or staff of the Woman's Division of Christian Service shall be selected on the basis of qualifications without regard for race.

The Committee on Nominations of the Woman's Division shall consider all openings for service in the Division or staff on this principle giving due consideration to circumstances which will offer opportunity for fruitful and happy service.

2. The institutions and projects of the Division are instruments by which we may translate the Christian ideals and attitudes of this charter into action.

    a. We will employ all missionaries, deaconesses and other workers regardless of racial or national background, on the basis of qualifications, and the promise they show for effective work in the field to which they will be sent.

267

b. The facilities and opportunities offered by our projects and institutions shall be open to all people without discrimination because of racial or national background.

c. Where law prohibits or custom prevents the immediate achievement of these objectives, workers and local boards are charged with the responsibility of creating a public opinion which may result in changing such laws and customs.

3. All promotional plans of the Woman's Division must take into account the various racial groups within its organization pattern and related to its program emphases.

4. Special guidance toward the integration of all groups into the life and work of the church shall be given to the auxiliary societies of the Woman's Division.

5. Summer Schools of Missions and Christian Service of both Jurisdictions and Conferences are urged to seek increasingly to establish a working relationship across racial lines in planning and carrying out all phases of the programs, taking into account geographical accessibility of groups involved.

6. Summer school subsidies provided for or by any Jurisdiction or Conference should be available when requested for use at the school most accessible to the person receiving the subsidy.

7. Workshops, seminars, and institutes should be set up on a geographical basis with full opportunity for initial participation by all racial groups in the making and execution of the plans.

8. Local Societies and Guilds should give increased emphasis to the working together of all racial groups and study and action that affect the life of the church and community.

9. All Jurisdiction and Conference Societies are urged to work for the enactment of policies at all Methodist Assembly grounds that will enable the full participation of any racial group in any phase of the assembly program.

10. The Woman's Division has consistently observed its established policy for holding its meetings in places where all racial groups can have access to its facilities without discrimination in any form. To further extend this policy Jurisdiction and Conference Societies are urged to work for its implementation as a basic step toward building a Christian fellowship within the organization and toward an impact on the community as a whole.

THE WOMAN'S DIVISION OF CHRISTIAN SERVICE CALLS WITH NEW URGENCY ON THE JURISDICTION AND CONFERENCE WOMAN'S SOCIETIES OF CHRISTIAN SERVICE TO STUDY THE PRINCIPLES AND POLICIES IN THIS CHARTER, LOOKING TOWARD EARLY RATIFICATION BY EACH JURISDICTION AND CONFERENCE. SUCH A RATIFICATION WILL CONSTITUTE A COMMITMENT TO WORK FOR THE SPEEDY IMPLEMENTATION OF THOSE PRINCIPLES AND POLICIES WITHIN THE BOUNDS OF A RESPECTIVE JURISDICTION OR CONFERENCE.

A Response to Criticism of School Desegregation

The Department of Christian Social Relations
and Local Church Activities
April 26, 1955
Mrs. J. Fount Tillman

In giving this report, there are certain statements I feel should be made. This department presents many social issues of a controversial nature in various areas of life and thought, as well as issues involving different problems of adjustment in the several geographical centers.

As a Woman's Division of the Board of Missions it is our responsibility to set the highest ultimate goals of Christian life and thought as objectives for all efforts. We recognize that there are varying stages of progress in different areas. On one problem, one group may be far in advance of another because there is no acute concern in that situation. On another problem, the reverse may be true.

Because of the wide range of interests we represent, we must make our objectives so inclusive that they permit all groups to advance toward fuller realization of Christian ideals. . . . However, any deviation from an expression of the highest Christian concern in the rights and privileges of all men would be disastrous in its effect.

We must recognize, however, that there are these varying degrees of progress toward the realization of the ideal in our own country. Each woman on the Division should be an interpreter in her own area, as well as an encourager of all efforts toward fulfillment of the ideal.

As a case in point, there is the Supreme Court decision on segregation in the schools. Extreme yet sincere fears as to the decrees on implementation of this decision may prove to be entirely unjustified.

We recognize that much of the opposition is based on prejudice. Prejudice expresses itself in various ways. Both discrimination and segregation are outgrowths of prejudice. In one state prejudice might be expressed by discrimination; in another state, by segregation. For example: There may be a zoning ordinance in one and a "Jim Crow" law in another. In some states integration of schools and churches is an accomplished fact; in others it may mean long and painful adjustments

269

involving changing social and economic patterns. Leaders of several races and nationalities involved, whether white, Negro, Mexican, Indian, or others, must work out steps of progress in terms of local conditions.

The Division, throughout the years, has acted on the basis of establishing the Christian ideal and of suggesting possible procedures toward the realization of the ideal. As women representing varied sections of the country, we accept responsibility for interpreting these ideals in understandable terms in our home areas. The glory of the enterprise is in our united effort. We move in the same direction, recognizing the differences in backgrounds but realizing the joy of a common goal.

APPENDIX D

Statement on School Integration
September, 1958

Integration—As responsible Christian citizens living in these days of national racial tensions we share the guilt for all the hurts and fears that have afflicted the peoples in all the places where human dignity has been violated and bigotry has held sway. We must also share the responsibility for upholding law and order in Little Rock and Chicago, or Montgomery and New York and throughout the nation, thereby achieving a greater measure of freedom, justice and unfettered opportunity for all people in our nation. Our voices and the voices of our fellow Christians throughout the land must be heard with new determination to remove every pattern of enforced segregation from our churches, communities and nation.

The Woman's Division has noted with gratitude to God the unswerving support of law and order by many Christian and Jewish leaders in Little Rock and elsewhere. In these days of tension, when state officials, in some cases, have used the power of their high office to circumvent the law of the land, it is imperative that responsible citizens unite their efforts to restore respect for and observance of the Federal laws.

The Woman's Division of Christian Service of The Methodist Church records its gratification for the ruling of the Supreme Court of the United States on September 12, 1958. This ruling unanimously affirmed a lower court decision on school integration in Little Rock which said:

"The time has not yet come in these United States when an order of a Federal Court must be whittled away, watered down, or shamefully withdrawn in the face of violent and unlawful acts. . . ."

This was in substance also a reaffirmation of the 1954 decision of the Supreme Court for school integration and the 1955 directive to "move with all deliberate speed" toward that end. This new decision upholds and strengthens our faith in our democratic form of government and its fundamental recognition of the basic equality of every person. As Christians we rejoice in this new evidence of the acceptance

271

of the principle that we are "one nation under God" obligated to protect the rights of all people.

The Woman's Division calls upon Methodist women everywhere to pray for God's guidance and strength to stand firm in these trying times. *It Is Recommended*: That Methodist women join with other like-minded groups in their community and nation seeking together and as individual Christians to work for:

    a. Compliance with the Supreme Court decision for integration in public schools.

    b. Open occupancy housing policies in their communities.

    c. Fair employment policies and practices in all phases of the community life.

    d. "A fellowship without barriers" in their local churches.

APPENDIX E

A Charter of Racial Policies—1962

WE BELIEVE

1. *We Believe* that God is the Father of all people and all are His children in one family.

2. *We Believe* that the personality of every human being is sacred.

3. *We Believe* that opportunities for fellowship and service, for personal growth, and for freedom in every aspect of life are inherent rights of every individual.

4. *We Believe* that the visible church of Jesus Christ must demonstrate these principles within its own organization and program.

5. *We Believe* that the Woman's Division as an agency of The Methodist Church must build a fellowship and social order without racial barriers in every area it may touch.

WE WILL

1. *Commit* ourselves as individuals called by Jesus Christ to witness by word and deed to the basic rights of every person regardless of cost.

2. *Unite* our efforts with all groups in the church toward eliminating in The Methodist Church all forms of segregation based on race whether in basic structure or institutional life.

3. *Create* in local churches opportunities for inclusive fellowship and membership without restriction based on race.

4. *Act* with other groups and agencies to involve families in new experiences with other races and cultures.

5. *Share* in creative plans that challenge youth, students and young adults of all races to new understanding of the Church's mission and ministries.

6. *Interpret* and strengthen recruitment and employment practices of the Woman's Division consistent with our belief in the oneness of God's family.

7. *Open* the facilities and services of all Woman's Division institutions without restriction based on race and make such policies clearly known.

8. *Establish* all Schools of Missions and Christian Service and all leadership development and enrichment programs on a regional basis without restriction based on race.

9. *Seek* to change community patterns of racial segregation in all relationships including education, housing, voting, employment and public facilities.

10. *Work* for national policies that safeguard the rights of all the nation's people.

11. *Support* world-wide movements for basic human rights and fundamental freedoms for peoples everywhere.

12. *Join* with others who seek in church and community justice and freedom for all members of the family of God.

As we begin this new decade, the Woman's Division of Christian Service calls with new urgency on the Woman's Society of Christian Service and Wesleyan Service Guild to study the principles and goals stated in this Charter, looking toward early ratification. Such ratification will constitute a commitment to work for the speedy implementation of those principles and goals within jurisdiction, conference, district and local society or guild.

Notes

Notes to Preface

1. John Oxenham, "In Christ There Is No East or West," *The Methodist Hymnal* (Nashville: The Methodist Book Concern, 1935), 507.

Notes to Chapter 1

1. This continued into the twentieth century. In 1950 Methodists and Baptists together ranged from a low of 70 percent to a high of 80 percent of all church members in each of eleven southern states. Samuel S. Hill, Jr., *Southern Churches in Crisis* (New York: Holt, Rinehart and Winston, 1966), 39.

2. Donald Mathews found that colonial ministers were designated "to report to authorities at the capital the vital statistics, state of moral government, and general vitality of the parish." The relationship of the two functions of civil servant and moral authority required leaders who could support the "conventions and beliefs upon which [the society] relied for social harmony. . . . Consequently, religious dissent was looked upon not as a mere difference of opinion, but as a challenge to authority and therefore a disruption of community." Donald G. Mathews, *Religion in the Old South* (Chicago: University of Chicago Press, 1977), 5. See also E. Brooks Holifield, *Gentlemen Theologians: American Theology in Southern Culture, 1775–1860* (Durham, NC: Duke University Press, 1978).

3. Jean Miller Schmidt has identified within American Methodism a series of leaders who have addressed social issues and personal piety in "Reexamining the Public/Private Split: Reforming the Continent and Spreading Scriptural Holiness," Russell E. Richey and Kenneth E. Rowe, ed., *Rethinking Methodist History, A Bicentennial Historical Consultation* (Nashville: Kingswood Books, An Imprint of The United Methodist Publishing House, 1985), 75–88.

4. Methodists in the new United States decided that their objective was to "reform the continent and spread scriptural holiness throughout the land." *Discipline of the Methodist Episcopal Church*, 1784, iii.

5. William B. Gravely, "Methodist Preachers, Slavery and Caste: Types of Social Concern in Antebellum America," *Duke Divinity Review*, Vol. 34, August 1969, 213.

6. *Discipline* of the Methodist Episcopal Church, 1808, Section IX, Of Slavery.

7. Ralph E. Morrow, *Northern Methodists and Reconstruction* (East Lansing: Michigan State University Press, 1956), 45. Donald G. Jones, *The Sectional Crisis and Northern Methodism: A Study in Piety, Political Ethics, and Civil Religion* (Metuchen, NJ: Scarecrow Press, 1979).

8. Emory Stevens Bucke, *The History of American Methodism*, Vol. III (New York: Abingdon Press, 1964), 422.

9. Estimates of the number of slaves imported vary widely. Gary B. Nash has indicated that between 1601 and 1810 358,000 slaves were brought to colonies which became part of the continental United States. This number represented about 4.5 percent of the total slave trade. Gary B. Nash, *Red, White, and Black* (Englewood Cliffs, NJ: Prentice-Hall, Inc., 1982), 148. Armet Francis cited much larger numbers of slaves brought to American shores: 900,000 in the sixteenth century, 2.75 million in the seventeenth century, 7 million in the eighteenth century, and over 4 million in the nineteenth century. Based on estimates that five slaves died en route for every one that reached the western hemisphere, the population lost to Africa may have been 60 million. Cited by a photography exhibit of Armet Francis, "The Black Triangle, The People of the African Diaspora," Woodruff Library, Atlanta University, 1988.

10. George D. Kelsey, *Racism and the Christian Understanding of Man*, (New York: Charles Scribner's Sons, 1965). In a few instances, slaves were owned by free African Americans or by Native Americans.

11. See Thomas Virgil Peterson, *Ham and Japheth, The Mythic World of Whites in the Antebellum South* (Metuchen, NJ: The Scarecrow Press, Inc. and The American Theological Library Association, 1978).

12. Everett Tilson, *Segregation and the Bible* (New York: Abingdon Press, 1958), 29–312; and George D. Kelsey, *Racism and the Christian Understanding of Man*, 82–83.

13. See chapter 15, "Reconstruction: Struggle, Hope, and Betrayal (1865–1877)," Vincent Harding, *The Other American Revolution* (Los Angeles: Center for Afro-American Studies, University of California, and Atlanta, GA: Institute of the Black World, 1980).

14. Ibid., 75.

15. Ibid., 68.

16. C. Vann Woodward, *The Strange Career of Jim Crow* (New York: Oxford University Press, 1957), 104.

17. Ibid., 55.

18. Eighty African American men, women, and children were lynched during 1915. "Lynching and the N.A.A.C.P.," in Herbert Aptheker, ed., *A Documentary History of the Negro People in the United States, 1910–1932* (Secaucus, NJ: The Citadel Press, 1973), 143.

19. C. Vann Woodward, *The Strange Career of Jim Crow*, 81.

20. African American leader Booker T. Washington accepted segregation. Rayford W. Logan, *The Betrayal of the Negro from Rutherford B. Hayes to Woodrow Wilson* (New York: Collier Books, 1954), 9. Morton Sosna has described the years between 1890 and 1920 as "in many ways the grimmest that blacks had faced since the end of slavery." Morton Sosna, *In Search of*

the Silent South, Southern Liberals and the Race Issue (New York: Columbia University Press, 1977), 11.

21. Lerone Bennett, Jr., *Before the Mayflower: A History of Black America* (New York: Penguin Books, 1982), 344.

22. C. Vann Woodward, *The Strange Career of Jim Crow*, 65.

23. J. W. E. Bowen, ed., *Africa and the American Negro* (Atlanta, 1896), 195.

24. Ridgely Rorrence, *The Story of John Hope* (New York: Macmillan, 1948), 114.

25. W. E. B. DuBois, *The Souls of Black Folk* (Chicago: A. C. McClurg & Co., 1903; repr., Cutchogue, NY: Buccaneer Books, Inc., 1976), 50; See also August Meier, Elliott Rudwick, and Francis L. Broderick, eds., *Black Protest Thought in the Twentieth Century* (Indianapolis: Bobbs-Merrill Education Publishing, 1971), 44; and Edgar A. Toppin, *Blacks in America: Then and Now* (Boston: The Christian Science Publishing Society, 1969), 48.

26. Cited by Edgar A. Toppin, *Blacks in America: Then and Now*, 51.

27. Ray Stannard Baker, *Following the Color Line* (Doubleday, Page & Company, 1908; repr., New York: Harper & Row, Publishers, 1964), 19.

28. Patricia R. Hill, *The World Their Household, The American Woman's Foreign Mission Movement and Cultural Transformation, 1870–1920* (Ann Arbor: The University of Michigan Press, 1985).

29. Anne Firor Scott, *The Southern Lady, From Pedestal to Politics 1830–1930* (Chicago: University of Chicago Press, 1970), 37.

30. Mabel Howell, *Women and the Kingdom, Fifty Years of Kingdom Building by the Women of the Methodist Episcopal Church, South, 1878–1920* (Nashville, TN: Cokesbury Press, 1928), 46–47.

31. Suzanne Lebsock, *The Free Women of Petersburg, Status and Culture in a Southern Town, 1784–1860*, (New York: W. W. Norton & Co., 1985), 249.

32. Deaconesses were Methodist women missionaries in the United States who were certified by the Woman's Missionary Council and assigned to mission posts after completing a two-year course of training. Lucy Rider Meyer of the Methodist Episcopal Church first developed this channel of service for women in 1885. *First Annual Report of the Woman's Missionary Council of the Methodist Episcopal Church, South, 1910–1911* (Nashville, TN: Publishing House of the Methodist Episcopal Church, South, 1911), 15; and *Fourth Annual Report of the Woman's Missionary Council, 1914*, 74. (Henceforth such annual reports will be abbreviated with *WMC*).

33. Virginia Shadron, "The Laity Rights Movement, 1906–1918" in Rosemary Skinner Keller, Louise L. Queen, and Hilah F. Thomas, eds., *Women in New Worlds, Historical Perspectives on Wesleyan Tradition* (Nashville: Abingdon Press, 1982), 265, citing Mary Helm to Nellie N. Somerville, August 29, 1910, Somerville-Hopworth Collection, Schlesinger Library, Radcliffe College, Cambridge, MA.

Early men's views and women's views of these events are widely different. James Cannon, III, wrote in *History of Southern Methodist Missions*, (Nashville: Cokesbury Press, 1926), 59: "[Bishop W. R. Lambuth] introduced many forward-looking policies. Perhaps the most notable of these was the reorganization in 1910 of the Board of Missions so as to include the two Women's Societies." Initiated in 1906, the change was consummated at the General Conference of 1910. For the first time in the history of missionary societies, all the agencies of a single denomination, both home and foreign, general and special, men's, women's, and children's, were consolidated in one General Board of Missions.

Belle Harris Bennett wrote, "At the General Conference of 1910 more than one hundred thousand women, working in two distinct organizations for the evangelization and social uplift of races and peoples in widely different lands, working under different laws and with different methods, accepted from a ruling body of lawmakers without a woman in it a crude and radical plan of readjustment and consolidation, and for three years have worked under it and through it without an appreciable loss of members or decrease in collections." *Fourth Annual Report of the WMC, 1914*, 74.

Notes to Chapter 2

1. Walter Rauschenbusch, *Christianity and the Social Crisis* (New York: The Macmillan Company, 1907). Torchbook edition edited by Robert D. Cross (New York: Harper & Row, Publishers, Inc., 1964), 143.

2. Ibid., 247.

3. John Patrick McDowell, *The Social Gospel in the South: The Woman's Home Mission Movement in the Methodist Episcopal Church, South, 1886–1939* (Baton Rouge: Louisiana State University Press, 1982), 1. See also Charles H. Hopkins, *The Rise of the Social Gospel in American Protestantism, 1865–1915* (New Haven, 1940), 320–27.

4. Institutional churches were congregations which, in response to the urban crises and social gospel, became community centers. Large classroom buildings with gymnasiums housed expanded weekday programs. Institutional churches sponsored basketball leagues, classes in sewing, parenting, nutrition and health care, well-baby clinics, labor colleges, instruction in trades, Boy Scouts, Girl Scouts, youth clubs, and children's clubs.

5. John Patrick McDowell, *The Social Gospel in the South*, 15, citing Mrs. R. W. [Tochie] MacDonell, "Home Mission Reading Course," *Our Homes*, vol. XIX, November 1910, 5.

6. Ibid., 31.

7. Ibid., 76, 85, 87.

8. Ruth Bordin, *Woman and Temperance, the Quest for Power and Liberty, 1873–1900* (New Brunswick: Rutgers University Press, 1990), 76, 79.

9. Ibid., 84, citing *Union Signal*, 10 December 1891, 10.

10. Sara Estelle Haskin, *Women and Missions in the Methodist Episcopal Church, South* (Nashville: Publishing House of the Methodist Episcopal Church, South, 1921), 195.

11. Also in 1913 the Southern Sociological Congress first met to make a concerted attempt to deal with southern racial issues.

12. Atticus G. Haygood, *Our Brother in Black: His Freedom and His Future* (Nashville: Southern Methodist Publishing House, 1887), 148.

13. Ronald Cedrick White, Jr., "Social Christianity and the Negro in the Progressive Era, 1890–1920," (Ph.D. diss., Princeton University, 1972).

14. Prior to 1910, these three leaders of the Woman's Home Missionary Society of the MECS frequently met in the home of MacDonell in Nashville where they studied reports of labor, commerce, immigration, and conditions in other countries. Helm published information from these reports and discussions in *Our Homes*. These women were already familiar with sociological methods and social service. Belle Harris Bennett's life slogan, "Eternal life for the individual, the kingdom of God for humanity," espoused a social gospel theme. Tochie MacDonell (Mrs. R. W.), *Belle Harris Bennett, Her Life Work* (Nashville: Board of Missions, The Methodist Episcopal Church, South, 1928), 88–89.

15. Mary Helm, *The Upward Path: The Evolution of a Race* (Cincinnati: Jennings & Graham, 1909), 173.

16. The term "southern Methodist" is used to refer to members of the Methodist Episcopal Church, South, prior to the 1939 merger and does not include southern members, African American or white, of the Methodist Episcopal Church or members of The Methodist Church.

17. Mary Helm, *The Upward Path*, 203.

18. Ibid., 19, 89.

19. Ibid., 40–41.

20. Ibid., 68

21. Ibid., 82.

22. Ibid., 87.

23. Ibid., 88.

24. Lily Hardy Hammond, *Southern Women and Racial Adjustment* (Lynchburg, VA: J. P. Bell Co., Inc., printers, 1917), 30.

25. Lily H. Hammond, *In Black and White: An Interpretation of Southern Life* (New York: Fleming H. Revell, 1914), 196.

26. Ibid., 23.

27. Ibid., 80.

28. Ibid., 91–92.

29. Jacquelyn Dowd Hall, *Revolt Against Chivalry: Jessie Daniel Ames and the Woman's Campaign Against Lynching* (New York: Columbia University Press, 1979), 74.

30. Ibid., 217.

31. Ibid.

32. Elizabeth Fox-Genovese, *Within the Plantation Household: Black and White Women of the Old South* (Chapel Hill: The University of North Carolina Press, 1988), 336.

33. John T. Kneebone, *Southern Liberal Journalists and the Issue of Race, 1920–1944* (Chapel Hill: The University of North Carolina Press, 1985), 85.

34. Ibid., 203.

35. Gunnar Myrdal and associates described a gradual change, which occurred after the Civil War, from a caste system in which all white citizens belonged to an upper class and all black citizens to a lower class to a double scale of three economic classes with categories of upper, middle, and lower class ascribed to both races. The greatest sense of competition came between the lower-class whites and the middle-class blacks whose economic means were similar. Upper-class blacks, professionals serving the black commu-

nity, had the least contact with whites. Lower-class blacks had the most contact with upper- and middle-class whites but did not provide a threat because of the great disparity in economic means. The impact of the formation of a new black middle class on interracial attitudes was described by Robert E. Park: "The distances which separate the races are maintained, but the attitudes involved are different. *The races no longer look up and down: they look across*." Robert E. Park, "The Bases of Race Prejudice," *Annals of the American Academy of Political and Social Science* (November, 1928), 20, cited by Gunnar Myrdal, Richard Sterner, and Arnold Rose, *An American Dilemma, The Negro Problem and Modern Democracy* (New York: Harper & Row, Publishers, 1944), 691. [Italics added by Myrdal.]

36. Jacquelyn Dowd Hall, *Revolt Against Chivalry*, 80.

37. For additional identifications, see note 46 below.

38. Jacquelyn Dowd Hall, *Revolt Against Chivalry*, 86.

39. Ibid., 86.

40. Mary McCrorey to Lugenia Hope, 6 July 1931, Neighborhood Union papers, cited by Jacquelyn Dowd Hall, *Revolt Against Chivalry*, 86.

41. Although this new movement emerged in 1920, in every historical period some white persons have protested the use of slavery in North America.

42. Morton Sosna, *In Search of the Silent South, Southern Liberals and the Race Issue* (New York: Columbia University Press, 1977), 21–22.

43. Jacquelyn Dowd Hall, *Revolt Against Chivalry*, 63.

44. Ibid., 87.

45. The Woman's Missionary Council of the Methodist Episcopal Church, South, was a segregated organization for whites.

46. I have provided the woman's given name rather than the husband's given name for women, where known. Noted affiliations are as follows: Janie Porter Barrett, founder of the Locust Street Social Settlement in Virginia, was superintendent of Virginia Industrial School in Peak's Turnout, VA; Mary McLeod Bethune, founder and president of Bethune-Cookman College in Daytona Beach, FL; Charlotte Hawkins Brown, founder and president of Palmer Memorial Institute in Sedalia, NC; Lugenia Hope, founder and director of the Neighborhood Union in Atlanta; Lucy Laney, founder and president of Haines Normal and Industrial Institute in Augusta, GA; Mary J. McCrorey's husband was president of Johnson C. Smith University in Charlotte, NC; Jennie Moton's husband was president of Tuskegee Institute; Margaret Washington's husband was founder and first president of Tuskegee Institute; Marion Raven Wilkinson, president of the South Carolina Federation of Colored Women's Clubs; and Mrs. M. L. Crosthwaite, registrar of Fisk University.

47. "Background of the Memphis Conference," Jessie Daniel Ames Papers, Southern Historical Collection, University of North Carolina, Chapel Hill, NC. Carrie Parks Johnson edited out of the statement a crucial plank calling for voting rights and a demand for African American women for "all the privileges and rights granted to American womanhood." The cautious approach of the Methodist women created frustration for Lugenia Hope. Jacquelyn Dowd Hall, *Revolt Against Chivalry*, 96, note 115.

48. Elizabeth Haynes' husband, George Edmund Haynes, professor of sociology and economics at Fisk University, wrote a mission study book used

by Methodist women: *Trend of the Races* (New York: Council of Women for Home Missions and the Missionary Education Movement of the U.S. and Canada, 1923).

49. Jessie Daniel Ames Papers. See also Wilma Dykeman and James Stokely, *Seeds of Southern Change, The Life of Will Alexander* (Chicago: University of Chicago Press, 1962), 89–96; Jacquelyn Dowd Hall, *Revolt Against Chivalry,* 87–95; Gerda Lerner, *The Majority Finds Its Past: Placing Women in History* (New York: Oxford University Press, 1979), 109–10; Arnold Shankman, "Civil Rights, 1920–1970," *Women in New Worlds*, vol. 2, ed. by Rosemary Skinner Keller and others (Nashville: Abingdon Press, 1982), 213–17.

50. *Eleventh Annual Report of the Woman's Missionary Society of the Methodist Episcopal Church, South, 1921,* 38. George Edmund Haynes wrote the FCC report.

51. Carrie Parks Johnson, "Women and Their Organizations," an address presented to the Commission on Interracial Cooperation, YMCA Auditorium, Atlanta, GA, 7 October 1921, p. 5. Jessie Daniel Ames Papers. Johnson said, "These women [on the program] from the Presbyterian, Disciples, Episcopal, Baptist, Methodist Churches, the Young Woman's Christian Association and the Woman's Clubs represented more than 1,000,000 members of their organizations, while Mrs. Brown, who is with us today, represent [*sic*] 100,000 colored women."

52. Jacquelyn Dowd Hall, *Revolt Against Chivalry*, 100.

53. Ibid., 102.

54. In the 1920s towns usually did not have any public rest rooms to serve African Americans. African Americans who traveled to town to shop or to market farm goods were inconvenienced.

55. *Thirteenth Annual Report of the WMC, 1923,* 136, cited by Annie Laura Winfrey, "The Organized Activities of the Women of Southern Methodism in the Field of Negro-White Relationships, 1886–1937," Master's thesis, Scarritt College for Christian Workers, June 1938, 94.

56. *Sixteenth Annual Report of the WMC, 1926,* 22.

57. *Eighteenth Annual Report of the WMC, 1928,* 142.

58. *Seventeenth Annual Report of the WMC, 1927,* 119.

Notes to Chapter 3

1. W. E. B. DuBois, *The Negro Artisan* (Atlanta University Publication No. 7, 1902), 169–70, cited in Marc Karson and Ronald Radosh, "The American Federation of Labor and the Negro Workers, 1894–1949" from Julius Jacobson, *The Negro and the American Labor Movement* (Garden City, NY: Anchor Books, Doubleday & Company, Inc., 1968), 157.

2. August Meier and Elliott M. Rudwick, *From Plantation to Ghetto, An Interpretive History of American Negroes* (New York: Hill and Wang, 1966), 198–99.

3. Sumner M. Rosen, "The CIO Era, 1935–55," in *The Negro and the American Labor Movement*, 188.

4. Ibid., 205.

5. Ralph Bunche, *The Political Status of the Negro in the Age of FDR*, ed. Dewey W. Grantham (Chicago: The University of Chicago Press, 1973), 24.

6. John T. Kneebone, *Southern Liberal Journalists and the Issue of Race, 1920–1944* (Chapel Hill: The University of North Carolina Press, 1985), 54.

7. Ibid., 135.

8. Jessie Daniel Ames, *The Changing Character of Lynching: Review of Lynching, 1931–1941* (Atlanta: Commission on Interracial Cooperation, Inc., 1942), 61–62.

9. John T. Kneebone, *Southern Liberal Journalists,* 169–70. About two hundred African American delegates attended the conference.

10. Anthony P. Dunbar, *Against the Grain, Southern Radicals and Prophets, 1929–1959* (Charlottesville: University Press of Virginia, 1981), 189, 190.

11. Ralph Bunche, *The Political Status of the Negro*, xxvii.

12. Jessie Daniel Ames to Mrs. Julian McKey, 3 January 1931, ASWPL Papers, Trevor Arnett Library, Atlanta University, Atlanta. Cited by Jacquelyn Dowd Hall, *Revolt Against Chivalry: Jessie Daniel Ames and the Woman's Campaign Against Lynching* (New York: Columbia University Press, 1979), 162, note 7.

13. "Arthur Raper, 1899–1979—A Life Looking 'for the Heart of the Thing,'" Interview by Cliff Kuhn, *Southern Changes*, 9:6, June/July 1987, 6.

14. Lugenia Hope, Charlotte Hawkins Brown, and Mary McLeod Bethune argued at length but to no avail with Jessie Daniel Ames.

15. Jacquelyn Dowd Hall, *Revolt Against Chivalry*, 165.

16. *Twentieth Annual Report of the WMC, 1930*, 137.

17. Some of these black women were college educated. Jacquelyn Dowd Hall noted that many of the white women in leadership positions in the Association of Southern Women for the Prevention of Lynching were "among the first generation of women college graduates in the region and had acquired the altered self-perceptions associated with economic autonomy." Since white leadership overlapped among the ASWPL, the Women's Committee of the Commission on Interracial Cooperation, and the Woman's Missionary Council, one would expect to find some carry-over to the YWCA as well. This was true for Louise Young. Jacquelyn Dowd Hall, *Revolt Against Chivalry*, 185.

18. Minutes of the Pre-Conference Meeting, Commission on Interracial Cooperation, Inc., Wesley Memorial Methodist Church, Atlanta, GA, 17 March 1931, Jessie Daniel Ames Papers, Southern Historical Collection, University of North Carolina Library, Chapel Hill, NC. These women were affiliated with institutions as follows: Brown, president of Palmer Memorial Institute in Sedalia, NC; Barrett, superintendent of Virginia Industrial School, Peak's Turnout, VA; Moton, wife of the president of Tuskegee Institute, Tuskegee, AL; Bethune, president of Bethune-Cookman College, Daytona Beach, FL; Derricotte, staff member of the National Student Council of the YWCA, and later dean of Women at Fisk University, Nashville, TN; Hope, director of the Neighborhood Union (Atlanta) and wife of the president of Atlanta University; Burroughs, corresponding secretary of the National Baptist Woman's Convention and president of the National Training School for Women and Girls, Washington, DC; Coleman, presi-

dent of the Woman's Missionary Connection, CME Church; McCrorey, wife of the president of Johnson C. Smith University, Charlotte, NC; and Stewart, president of the National Federation of Colored Women, Evansville, IN.

Of these women, none held membership in the MECS and only Bethune belonged to the MEC. Although the racial stand of the MECS had effectively alienated prominent black women, they worked with white churchwomen through women's organizations.

19. Church Woman's Conference, Tuskegee Institute, AL, 10–11 June 1933, Jessie Daniel Ames Papers.

20. *Twenty-first Annual Report of the WMC, 1931*, 129.

21. ASWPL, Appendix F, Digest of Discussion [November 1, 1930] 14, Jessie Daniel Ames Papers.

22. Woman's Missionary Council, *Report of Commission on Woman's Place of Service in the Church* ([Nashville]: Woman's Missionary Council, Methodist Episcopal Church South, 1930), 119–20.

23. *Twenty-third Annual Report of the WMC, 1933*, 137.

Notes to Chapter 4

1. Dan T. Carter, *Scottsboro, A Tragedy of the American South* (New York: Oxford University Press, 1969), 18–19.

2. Ibid., 97.

3. Mrs. J. E. Andrews to Mrs. A. W. Newell, 14 December 1931, Jessie Daniel Ames Papers, Southern Historical Collection, University of North Carolina Library, Chapel Hill, NC.

4. Ibid., 122.

5. Dorothy Tilly, "The Fellowship of the Concerned," *The Woman's Press*, February, 1950, 8.

6. ASWPL, "This Business of Lynching," *Bulletin*, No. 4, January, 1935, cited in the *Twenty-fifth Annual Report of the WMC, 1935*, 143. The ASWPL counted as prevented lynchings incidents in which rumors circulated that there would be a lynching and situations in which a black person apprehended for a crime was taken to another town for safe keeping because of hostility in the local white community. In some cases women helped officers of the peace smuggle black persons accused of a crime out of town.

7. Sociologist John Shelton Reed found that in the 1930s lynchings were 35 percent of what they had been in the 1920s where ASWPL did not work, and 26 percent where they were most active. Ibid., 236. Also ibid., 235, citing Monroe N. Work, ed., *Negro Year Book*, 1937–38, 157; and 1941–46, 309.

8. *Twenty-fifth Annual Report of the WMC, 1935*, 142. See also James R. McGovern, *Anatomy of a Lynching: The Killing of Claude Neal* (Baton Rouge: Louisiana State University Press, 1982).

9. Charles S. Johnson, *A Preface to Racial Understanding* (New York: Friendship Press, 1936), 158.

10. *Twenty-sixth Annual Report of the WMC, 1936*, 124.

11. Ibid., 245.

12. *Twenty-fifth Annual Report of the WMC, 1935*, 140.

13. *Twenty-eighth Annual Report of the WMC, 1938*, 162.

14. Jacquelyn Dowd Hall, *Revolt Against Chivalry: Jessie Daniel Ames and the Woman's Campaign Against Lynching* (New York: Columbia University Press, 1979), 215.

15. Ibid., 233.

16. Ibid., 187, citing Jessie Daniel Ames to Mrs. L. W. Alford, 30 July 1935, ASWPL Papers; JDA Interview. n.d. [1965–66?], Southern Regional Council Papers, Atlanta, GA, and Southern Oral History Program, University of North Carolina at Chapel Hill, NC.

17. Jacquelyn Dowd Hall, *Revolt Against Chivalry*, 186, footnote 65, Hall interview with Louise Young, 13 February 1972. For a similar story, see Arnold Shankman, "Dorothy Tilly of the Fellowship of the Concerned" unpublished manuscript.

18. Ibid., 186.

19. *Twenty-second Annual Report of the WMC, 1932*, 111–12.

20. *Twenty-eighth Annual Report of the WMC, 1938*, 169.

21. Ibid., 145.

22. Ibid., 115–18.

23. Ibid., 167. Anthony P. Dunbar, *Against the Grain, Southern Radicals and Prophets, 1929–1959* (Charlottesville: University Press of Virginia, 1981), 97.

24. *Twenty-seventh Annual Report of the WMC, 1937*, 64.

25. Ibid., 144.

26. *Twenty-third Annual Report of the WMC, 1933*, 127. *Thirtieth Annual Report of the WMC, 1940*, 162.

27. *Twenty-fourth Annual Report of the WMC, 1934*, 128.

28. *Twenty-eighth Annual Report of the WMC, 1938*, 162.

29. *Twenty-second Annual Report of the WMC, 1932*, 134.

30. *Twenty-seventh Annual Report of the WMC, 1937*, 117.

31. *Twenty-eighth Annual Report of the WMC, 1938*, 146.

32. *Twenty-sixth Annual Report of the WMC, 1936*, 120–21.

Notes to Chapter 5

1. *Thirtieth Annual Report of the WMC, 1940*, 163.

2. *Twenty-seventh Annual Report of the WMC, 1937*, 142–43. The full text of this report is provided in Appendix A.

3. *Twenty-seventh Annual Report of the WMC, 1937*, 157.

4. "The Southern church—whatever its representatives on the commission may have thought—would probably have been ready to approve unification without the racial segregation feature." "Southern Methodist Women Ask Searching Questions," *Christian Century* 54 (April 21, 1937), 509; cited by Dwight Culver, *Negro Segregation in The Methodist Church*, (New Haven: Yale University Press, 1953), 76.

5. Ibid.

6. *Twenty-seventh Annual Report of the WMC, 1937*, 158.

7. Ibid., 159.

8. Women in the Methodist Episcopal Church who were ordained as local pastors could baptize and serve Holy Communion in their own church only. They did not hold membership and could not vote in the annual conference, nor were they members of conference boards, agencies, or committees. This ordination was so limited in scope that it was not recognized as granting regular ordination to women.

9. *Twenty-first Annual Report of the WMC, 1931*, 159. Five of ninety-three deaconesses responding to a 1937 WMC survey indicated that they wished to become ministers. *Twenty-seventh Annual Report of the WMC, 1937*, 125.

10. Cited in a letter from the Woman's Missionary Council ("Mrs. W. M. Alexander, *Chairman*; Mrs. Ida R. Groover, *Secretary*") to President F. D. Roosevelt, 10 March 1940. *Thirtieth Annual Report of the WMC, 1940*, 32.

11. *Twenty-seventh Annual Report of the WMC, 1937*, 141.

12. *Twenty-ninth Annual Report of the WMC, 1939*, 170.

13. *Thirtieth Annual Report of the WMC, 1940*, 180.

14. Ibid., 33.

15. *Twenty-ninth Annual Report of the WMC, 1939*, 60, 153, and Alice G. Knotts, "Thelma Stevens' 'Thorns That Fester:' An Oral Biography and Interview," 5–7 December 1983, 102. Mary McLeod Bethune was among the distinguished women present.

16. *Twenty-ninth Annual Report of the WMC, 1939*, 153.

17. Ibid., 125.

18. Ibid., 153. *Thirtieth Annual Report of the WMC, 1940*, 159.

19. *Twenty-ninth Annual Report of the WMC, 1939*, 60.

20. Ibid., 123.

21. Ibid., 124.

Notes to Chapter 6

1. Mamie Lee Ratliff Finger, "Cora Rodman Ratliff, 1891–1958: A Woman of Courage and Vision," 1989, private collection of Mamie Lee Ratliff Finger. Biographical material about Cora Rodman Ratliff comes from this unpublished manuscript.

2. Ibid., 3.

3. Ibid., 4.

4. Ibid., 8.

5. Valera Bailey to Mamie Lee Finger, 1982, citing the Annual Report of the Woman's Society of Christian Service, North Mississippi Conference of The Methodist Church, 1939. Lake Junaluska Heritage Center Archives, Cora Rodman Ratliff Collection, Lake Junaluska, NC.

6. Ibid., 10, citing Lillie Florence Arnold, *Georgia Wesleyan Christian Advocate*, June 1980.

7. Ibid.

8. See p. 159.

9. Ibid., 14, citing Sue Minter. When the Minters eventually had to leave Mississippi, they moved to Texas.

10. Ibid., 19.

11. Prejudice and lack of press coverage muted the voices of courageous African American leaders and intimidated others. White allies of the civil rights movement, including Ratliff, spoke for change in the face of criticism.

12. Ibid., 19.

13. *Christian Advocate*, 11 August 1938, 833.

14. Dr. Frentis Logan, professor of American History, Greensboro Agricultural and Technical College, 16 May 1990.

15. *Journal and Guide* (Greensboro), 11 December 1937, 20. Bennett College Archives, Bennett College Scrapbook, 1947–1949, Bennett College, Greensboro, NC. *Afro-American*, 14 February 1948. *The Future Outlook*, 17 November 1948.

16. Bennett College Scrapbooks, 1936–1962.

17. "Memorial Services for Dr. David Jones," Thomas F. Holgate Library, Bennett College Scrapbook, May 1959–April 1962, 28.

18. Ellease Randall Colston, director of Alumni Affairs, formerly director of Admissions from 1956 to 1986, Bennett College, 16 May 1990.

19. Bennett College Scrapbook, May 1959–April 1962, 28.

20. Grace Lewis, Greensboro resident, 16 May 1990.

21. Interview with Minnie Smith, former Bennett College teacher, Greensboro, NC, May 1990. Bennett College Archives, Box 6, "Old Clippings."

22. Interview with Myra Jones, niece of Susie Jones, Greensboro, NC, 15 May 1990.

23. Mrs. George Simkins, activist and resident of Greensboro, 16 May 1990. Ellease Randall Colston, 16 May 1990.

24. Task Group on the History of the Central Jurisdiction Women's Organization, *To a Higher Glory: The Growth and Development of Black Women Organized for Mission in The Methodist Church 1940–1968* (New York: Women's Division of the Board of Global Ministries, The United Methodist Church, 1978), 103.

25. Alice G. Knotts, "Thelma Stevens' 'Thorns that Fester:' An Oral Biography and Interview," 5–7 December 1983, 103–4.

26. Ibid., 4–5.

27. Ibid., 278–81.

28. Thelma Stevens, "Jesus and the Pharisees," Master's thesis, Scarritt College for Christian Workers, Nashville, 1928, 64.

29. Ibid., 60.

30. Thelma Stevens, "Thorns That Fester," 20.

31. Ibid., 40–41.

32. Thelma Stevens, *Legacy for the Future, The History of Christian Social Relations in the Women's Division of Christian Service 1940–1968* ([New York:] Women's Division, Board of Global Ministries, The United Methodist Church, 1978). Interview with Thelma Stevens by Jacquelyn [Dowd] Hall, 13 February 1972, Southern Oral History Collection, Wilson Library, University of North Carolina, Chapel Hill, NC. Alice G. Knotts, "Thelma Stevens' 'Thorns that Fester.'" The Women's Division of the Board of Global Ministries of The United Methodist Church has an additional taped interview conducted by Hilah F. Thomas.

33. Betty Thompson, "Theressa Hoover, A Woman for All Seasons," *Response*, October 1990, 6.
34. Ibid., and author's interview with Theressa Hoover, 26 October 1987. *Response* cites nineteen churches involved in the coalition.
35. Interview with Theressa Hoover, 26 October 1987.
36. Ibid.
37. Peggy Billings, interview by author, 26 February 1991. Peggy Billings assisted in editing this portion of the chapter.
38. Ibid.
39. Peggy Billings to author, 15 March 1991.
40. Thelma Stevens, *Legacy for the Future*, 8.

Notes to Chapter 7

1. Anthony Lake Newberry, "Without Urgency or Ardor: The South's Middle-of-the-Road Liberals and Civil Rights, 1945–1960" (Ph.D. Diss., Ohio University, 1982), 64.
2. Wilma Dykeman and James Stokely, *Seeds of Southern Change: The Life of Will Alexander* (Chicago: The University of Chicago Press, 1962), 263–64.
3. Ames to Dabney, 10 April 1942, Series 7690, Box V, Dabney Papers, cited by Newberry, "Without Urgency or Ardor," 74
4. Joining Gordon B. Hancock, from Virginia Union University, on the editorial committee were Charles S. Johnson, Fisk University; F. D. Patterson, Tuskegee Institute; Benjamin E. Mays, Morehouse College; Ernest Delpit, president of Carpenters' Local, New Orleans; Rufus E. Clement, Atlanta University; Horace Mann Bond, Fort Valley State College; James E. Jackson, Southern Negro Youth Congress; William M. Cooper, Hampton Institute; and P. B. Young, editor of *Journal and Guide*, Norfolk, VA, and chair of the conference.
5. "A Basis for Inter-Racial Cooperation and Development in the South, A Statement by Southern Negroes," 20 October 1942, cited by Charles S. Johnson, *To Stem this Tide, A Survey of Racial Tension Areas in the United States* (Boston: The Pilgrim Press, 1943), 132.
6. "Statement of Conference of White Southerners on Race Relations," 8 April 1943, cited by Charles S. Johnson, *To Stem this Tide*, 141; citing the Nashville *Banner* (AP release), 12 April 1943.
7. *Journal*, Executive Committee Meeting, 13, 14 March 1945, 33.
8. *Congressional Record*, 76th Congress, 3rd Session, 1940, LXXXVI, Appendix 4546. William C. Berman, *The Politics of Civil Rights in the Truman Administration* (Ohio State University Press, 1970), 11–12.
9. Tom C. Clark to Harry S. Truman, 11 October 1946, Truman Papers, OF 596A, Harry S. Truman Library (HSTL), cited by William C. Berman, *The Politics of Civil Rights*, 53.
10. William C. Berman, *The Politics of Civil Rights*, 84.
11. *Journal*, Executive Committee Meeting, 22 March 1949, 28.

12. *New York Times*, 28 July 1948, 4, cited by William C. Berman, *The Politics of Civil Rights*, 119.

13. Genna Rae McNeil, *Charles Hamilton Houston and the Struggle for Civil Rights* (Philadelphia: University of Pennsylvania Press, 1983), 217, citing Charles Hamilton Houston, "Law as a Career," July 1932, CHH Papers, Howard University and Houston & Gardner firm files, Washington, DC.

14. Ibid., 132, citing Charles Hamilton Houston, "Tentative Statement Concerning Policy of NAACP in Its Program of Attacks on Educational Discrimination," 12 July 1935, 1 C197 NAACP Records.

15. Genna Rae McNeil, *Charles Hamilton Houston*, 134.

16. Ibid., 142.

17. Ibid., 135.

18. Purpose Statement of the Fellowship of Reconciliation, cited by Robert Cooney and Helen Michalowski, ed., Marty Jezer, *The Power of the People: Active Nonviolence in the United States* (Culver City, CA: Peace Press, Inc., 1977), 72.

19. Sudarshan Kapur, *Raising Up a Prophet: The African-American Encounter with Gandhi* (Boston: Beacon Press, 1992), 81. Dericotte and Wilson traveled to India in 1928. The others went in 1935. Sue Bailey Thurman, a national staff member of the YWCA, brought African American and Gandhian perspectives to that organization.

20. Ibid., 55–56; citing Drusilla Dunjee Houston, "That Little Man Gandhi," *Chicago Defender*, 12 December 1931, 14.

21. James Farmer, *Lay Bare the Heart, An Autobiography of The Civil Rights Movement* (New York: New American Library, 1985), 146.

22. Ibid., 102.

23. Ibid., 103–4. Farmer discussed ways his interpretation of the founding of CORE differed from George Houser's version published by August Meier and Elliott Rudwick, *CORE, A Study in the Civil Rights Movement, 1942–1968* (New York: Oxford University Press, 1973).

24. Pauli Murray, *Song in a Weary Throat, An American Pilgrimage* (New York: Harper & Row, Publishers, 1987), 201.

25. Ibid., 114–29, 138–46, 218.

26. *New South*, 1:12, December 1946, 25, 23.

27. *New South*, 2:11, November 1947, 9.

28. *New South*, 3:2, February 1948, 1; *New South*, 3:3, March 1948, 1–2.

29. *New South*, 3:3, March 1948, 1.

30. Ibid., 2, 7.

31. *New South*, 3:6–7, June–July 1948, 3–4.

32. *Smith v. Allwright, 1944*. See also *To Secure These Rights, The Report of the President's Committee on Civil Rights* (Washington, DC: United States Government Printing Office, 1947), 36.

33. *New South*, 3:12–4:1, December 1948–January 1949, 6–7; *New South*, 4:3, March 1949, 5–8; *New South*, 4:9, September 1949, 3–4.

34. Inez S. White (Mrs. William C. White) to Margaret Price, 26 January 1948, Southern Regional Council Archives, Atlanta University Center Woodruff Library Archives Department, Atlanta, Georgia.

35. George D. McClain, "Pioneering Social Gospel Radicalism: An

Overview of the History of the Methodist Federation for Social Action," *Radical Religion* 1980, V:1, 12.

36. Jeanne G. Knepper, "Sacred Rights, Holy Liberties: The Methodist Federation for Social Action and Human Rights," Ph.D. diss. in process, The Iliff School of Theology and the University of Denver. Information about the Federation has been provided courtesy of her research.

37. *Social Questions Bulletin* (henceforth *SQB*) 29:6, June 1939, 4; and 29:7, September 1939, 1–2.

38. *SQB* 30:4; April 1940, 2–4; and 30:9; December 1940, 2.

39. Roy Wilkins, "Jim Crow Democracy," *SQB* 31:4, April 1941, 1–2; and Roy Wilkins, "Negroes in a Fighting Democracy," *SQB* 32:4, April 1942, 1–3.

40. Thelma Stevens, "Methodist Women in Action," *SQB* 32:1, March 1942, 1–3.

41. *SQB* 33:3, March 1943, 4; and Charles C. Webber, "American Fascism—A Case Study," *SQB* 33:6, June 1943, 2–3.

42. C. C. Garner, J. F. McLeod, Jr., J. B. Nichols, A. S. Turnipseed, and J. A. Zellner, *Making Methodism Methodist* (n.p.: Stone and Pierce, 1946, 1947), 3, 45.

43. "Eliminate Discrimination," *SQB* 34:5, May 1944, 1–3; and "Extend Democracy!" *SQB* 34:6, June 1944, 1–3.

44. Thelma Stevens, "Methodist Women Need the Federation," *SQB* 34:7, October 1944, 1.

45. Ibid.

46. Mrs. W. H. Ratliff to Jack McMichael, 30 October 1949. Jack R. McMichael to George Mitchell, 2 November 1949, Mark Chamberlin Papers, University of Oregon.

47. Dwight Culver, *Negro Segregation in The Methodist Church* (New Haven: Yale University Press, 1953), 72; Alice G. Knotts, "The Debates Over Race and Women's Ordination," *Methodist History* 29:1, October 1990, 40.

48. *Twenty-seventh Annual Report of the WMC, 1937*, 142–43.

49. Peter Carlisle Murray, "Christ and Caste in Conflict: Creating a Racially Inclusive Methodist Church," Ph.D. Diss., Indiana University, 1985, 50–52.

50. Dwight Culver, *Negro Segregation.*

51. Ibid., 135–36.

52. Ibid., 140.

53. Ibid., 145–57.

Notes to Chapter 8

1. *Journal*, Annual Report, 1940–1941, 96.

2. The terminology of a "new social order," also occasionally referred to as a "new world order" or a "Christian social order" is taken from the literature of Methodist women and The Methodist Church.

This is the first of many references to the minutes of the Woman's Division of Christian Service of the Board of Missions of The Methodist

Church. Each year's minutes, bound together in one volume, include both the *Annual Report* and the *Journal* of the Executive Committee. Citations come from the quarterly "Report and Recommendations of the Department of Christian Social Relations and Local Church Activities to the Woman's Division of Christian Service of the Board of Missions of The Methodist Church." Since after 1968 all such volumes of the successor organization were entitled *Journal* of the Women's Division of the Board of Global Ministries these annual volumes issued between 1940 and 1968 also are designated as *Journal*. *Journal*, Executive Committee Meeting, 12–15 June 1943, 46, citing *Unity—A Challenge to American Democracy*, 68.

3. Thelma Stevens, *Legacy for the Future*, 25, and Alice G. Knotts, "Thelma Stevens' 'Thorns that Fester:' An Oral Biography and Interview," 5–7 December 1983, 270–72.

4. Thelma Stevens, "Report of the Executive Secretary," *Journal*, Annual Meeting, Department of Christian Social Relations and Local Church Activities, 1940–1941, 98.

5. Thelma Stevens, "Former Things Have Come to Pass and New Things I Now Declare," Isaiah 42:9 (address given to the Methodist Federation for Social Action, Eastern Pennsylvania Conference, Reading, PA, 9 June 1982), 1. Personal papers of Thelma Stevens.

6. Fred L. Brownlee, *These Rights We Hold* (New York: Friendship Press, 1952), 6.

7. Albert C. Knudson, *The Principles of Christian Ethics* (New York: Abingdon-Cokesbury Press, 1943).

8. Thelma Stevens, "Former Things Have Come to Pass," 3–4.

9. At the close of 1945 the Department of Christian Social Relations and Local Church Activities (CSR/LCA) and the Woman's Division agreed that the Social Creed should be used as a point of reference in judging current issues. This stipulation, sent to and adopted by the 1948 General Conference, provided that the Social Creed be read to each local congregation at least once a year. *Journal*, Executive Committee Meeting, 17 September 1946, 13–14.

10. *Discipline of The Methodist Church*, 1940, Paragraph 1712, 769.

11. In 1921 ecumenical leaders formed the Commission on Race Relations of the Federal Council of Churches and organized the World Council of Churches in 1948. The Woman's Division used statements issued by major ecumenical conferences that preceded the formation of the WCC.

12. Peter Carlisle Murray, "Christ and Caste in Conflict: Creating a Racially Inclusive Methodist Church," Ph.D. diss., Indiana University, 1985, 57; citing Frank Samuel Loescher, *Protestant Church and the Negro* (Philadelphia: Association Press, 1948), 17–18.

13. *Discipline of The Methodist Church*, 1948, Paragraph 2026, 601.

14. See the report of a study by Kenneth Clark and Mamie Phipps, *Journal of Experimental Education*, Spring 1940, cited by Juan Williams, *Eyes on the Prize, America's Civil Rights Years, 1954–1965* (New York: Viking Penguin Inc., 1987), 23.

15. Gunnar Myrdal, Richard Sterner, and Arnold Rose, *An American Dilemma, The Negro Problem and Modern Democracy* (New York: Harper & Row, Publishers, 1944), 21–25.

16. The phrase "separate but equal" comes from the Supreme Court decision *Plessy v. Ferguson*, 1896.

17. Democratic language has been discussed by other scholars. J. Philip Wogaman used the term "civil society," to mean one of four sources of human authority from which ethical principles are derived. J. Philip Wogaman, *A Christian Method of Moral Judgment* (Philadelphia: The Westminster Press, 1976), 176. The term "democratic language" also carries the meanings that Robert N. Bellah and associates apply to the republican strand of American thought in *Habits of the Heart, Individualism and Commitment in American Life* (New York: Harper & Row, Publishers, 1985), 30.

18. Thelma Stevens, "A Woman: Who Art Thou?" An address to the Florida Conference of United Methodist Women, 11 October 1972.

19. *Discipline of The Methodist Church*, 1940, Paragraph 1716, 775.

20. *Journal*, Annual Meeting, 1940–1941, 98, 100.

21. *Journal*, Annual Meeting, 28 November–4 December 1944, 18.

22. Members of the Committee on Minority Groups and Interracial Co-Operation (1940–44) were Mrs. David D. (Susie) Jones and Mrs. Paul Arrington, co-chairpersons, Mrs. W. H. C. Goode from the North Central Jurisdiction, Miss Sara A. McConnell from the Southeastern Jurisdiction, Mrs. Mary McLeod Bethune, Miss Louise Young from the South Central Jurisdiction, Miss Mina Klayman, and associate member Mrs. Ruth Muskrat Bronson. *Journal*, Annual Meeting, 1940, 14.

23. Thelma Stevens, *Legacy for the Future*, 38 and *Journal*, Executive Committee Meeting, 14–15 September 1942, 29.

24. *Journal*, Executive Committee Meeting, 12–15 June 1943, 45.

25. Task Group on the History of the Central Jurisdiction Women's Organization, *To a Higher Glory: The Growth and Development of Black Women Organized for Mission in The Methodist Church, 1940–1968* (New York: Women's Division of the Board of Global Ministries, The United Methodist Church, 1978), 78.

26. *Journal*, Executive Committee Meeting, 29 November–4 December 1942, 9.

27. Thelma Stevens, "Departmental Suggestions, The Larger Community," *The Methodist Woman*, July 1943, 16.

28. *Journal*, Executive Committee, 1944, "A Review of the Work of the Quadrennium and the Look Ahead," 186. The report noted that the Department had attempted to reconcile its preaching and practices. Mrs. James [Louise] Oldshue, "Consistency An Imperative," *The Methodist Woman*, January 1948, 22–23.

29. *Journal*, Annual Report, 3 December 1943, cited by Thelma Stevens, "Some Practical Aspects of Brotherhood," *The Methodist Woman*, February 1944, 22.

30. *Journal*, Fourth Annual Meeting, 3–8 December 1943, 4.

31. "Interfaith Declaration on World Peace," cited by *The Methodist Woman*, December 1943, 19–20, reprinted from Information Service, 9 October 1943.

32. "Bill of Rights" or "Nine Freedoms," National Resources Planning Board, cited in "Department of Christian Social Relations and Local Church

Activities, A Review of the Work of the Quadrennium and the Look Ahead," *Journal*, Annual Meeting, December 1944, 188.

33. Thelma Stevens, "A District Institute on Christian Social Relations and Local Church Activities," *The Methodist Woman*, November 1945, 29.

34. Lillian Smith, *Killers of the Dream* (New York: Doubleday and Company, Inc., 1948), 62.

35. Ibid., 64.

36. Ibid., 65.

37. Ibid., *Killers of the Dream*, 15, 18.

38. *Journal*, Annual Report, 1943–1944, 189. This recommendation was repeated to the General Conference in the *Quadrennial Reports to the General Conference*, 1944, 130.

39. Thelma Stevens, "Methodist Women in Action," *SQB* 32:3, March 1942, 1.

40. Mrs. David D. [Susie] Jones, "People Are Getting The Idea," *The Methodist Woman*, February 1947, 24.

41. Sudarshan Kapur, *Raising Up a Prophet, The African-American Encounter with Gandhi* (Boston: Beacon Press, 1992), 123, 163.

42. Task Group on the History of the Central Jurisdiction Women's Organization, *To a Higher Glory*, 78.

43. Ibid., 73, 78.

Notes to Chapter 9

1. Mrs. M. E. [Dorothy] Tilly, "The Christian Woman Influencing the Nation Through Political Action," *The Methodist Woman*, December 1949, 15.

2. *Journal*, Executive Committee Meeting, 14–15 September 1942, 28–29.

3. Thelma Stevens and the Department of CSR/LCA prepared a leaflet which provided specific recommendations for dealing with racial or class differences and defense-industry-related workers. Ibid., 16.

4. Edwin R. Embree, *13 Against the Odds* (New York: The Viking Press, 1945), 23.

5. "Christian Social Relations and Local Church Activities, A Program of Action for 1945," *The Methodist Woman*, January 1945, 16.

6. *Journal*, Eighth Annual Meeting, 2–12 December 1947, 15.

7. *Journal*, Executive Committee Meeting, 17 March 1942, 20.

8. *Journal*, Executive Committee Meeting, 13, 16 March 1943, 3–4.

9. *Journal*, Second Annual Meeting, 1941, 14.

10. *Journal*, Sixth Annual Meeting, 27 November–3 December 1945, 9.

11. *Journal*, Executive Committee Meeting, 13–14 March 1945, 34; and Thelma Stevens, "Department of Christian Social Relations and Local Church Activities," *The Methodist Woman*, March 1945, 19.

12. *Journal*, Seventh Annual Meeting, 2–12 December 1946, 16–17.

13. Ibid.

14. August Meier and Elliott Rudwick, *CORE, A Study in the Civil Rights*

Movement 1942–1968 (New York: Oxford University Press, 1973). In March 1940, the Methodist Federation for Social Service tested the cafeteria, found that it was segregated, and delegated action to the Washington, DC, chapter. Two years later, seeing no change in policy, the Methodist Federation for Social Service made new efforts to integrate the same facility. *SQB*, June 1942, 2.

15. *Journal*, Executive Committee Meeting, 29 November–4 December, 1942, 10.

16. Pauli Murray, *Song in a Weary Throat: An American Pilgrimage* (New York: Harper & Row, Publishers, 1987), 211.

17. "Christian Social Relations and Local Church Activities, A Program of Action for 1945," *The Methodist Woman*, January 1945, 17.

18. Mrs. L. M. Awtrey, Mrs. R. H. McDougall, Mrs. A. A. Hardy, and Mrs. M. E. [Dorothy] Tilly to Ellis Arnall and Members of the Legislature, 19 January 1945, Southern Regional Council Archives, Atlanta University Center Woodruff Library Archives Department, Atlanta, GA.

19. *Journal*, Executive Committee Meeting, 11–14 September 1943, 12.

20. Untitled material submitted for publication in the *North Georgia Review* (which became *South Today* in 1942) accompanied by a letter from Jessie Daniel Ames to Lillian E. Smith, 30 December 1941. Jessie Daniel Ames Papers, Southern Historical Collection, University of North Carolina Library, Chapel Hill, NC. See "Winning the World with Democracy," a symposium by Louis Adamic, Sherwood Eddy, Channing Tobias, Gerald Johnson, Guy Johnson, Jessie Daniel Ames, Ira Reid, Roger Baldwin, Phillips Russell, and Howard Kester, *South Today*, Spring 1942, 7–24.

21. Untitled material submitted for publication in the *North Georgia Review* accompanied by a letter from Jessie Daniel Ames to Lillian E. Smith, 30 December 1941, Jessie Daniel Ames Papers.

22. Jessie Daniel Ames, *The Changing Character of Lynching: Review of Lynching, 1931–1941* (Atlanta: Commission on Interracial Cooperation, Inc., 1942), 66.

23. "Mrs. L. W. Alford, McComb, Mississippi, Completes A Decade's Work Against Lynching," *The Southern Frontier*, July 1941, 2.

24. *Journal*, Executive Committee Meeting, 17 March 1942, 20.

25. *Journal*, Executive Committee Meeting, 17–19 June 1947, 23.

26. "Fact Sheet on Willie McGee Case, October 22, 1949"; Mrs. W.H. Ratliff to Jack McMichael, 30 October 1949; Jack R. McMichael to George Mitchell, 2 November 1949; Methodist Federation for Social Action papers, The United Methodist Archives and History Center, Madison, NJ.

27. *Journal*, Executive Committee Meeting, 17–19 June 1947, 24.

28. Ibid.

29. Lillian Smith, incensed by the inadequate prosecution and punishment of persons involved in lynchings, reported that between 1882 and 1946 "no member of a lynch mob was given a death sentence or life imprisonment. Only 135 persons in the entire United States . . . have been convicted of being members of lynch mobs." Lillian Smith, *Killers of the Dream*, (New York: Doubleday and Company, Inc., 1948), 178.

30. Ibid., 23; *New York Times*, 20 May 1947, 1, 20; *New York Times*, 22 May 1947, 1, 28; Rebecca West, *A Train of Powder* (New York: The Viking

Press, 1955), 77, 113. According to the *New York Times*, Judge J. Robert Martin, Jr., instructed the jury to disregard "any so-called racial issues."

31. *Journal*, Executive Committee Meeting, 17–19 June 1947, 24.

32. Dorothy Tilly, "The Background," Box 1, Folder 6, Dorothy Tilly Papers, Emory University.

33. *Twenty-third Annual Report of the WMC, 1933*, 131. In 1932 Eleanor Roosevelt lent her name and influence to the National Consumers' League at a time when Louise Young served on the board and was offered the position of general secretary of the National Consumers' League, a position she declined. Mary W. Dewson to Louise Young, 15 April 1932; and Louise Young to Mary W. Dewson, 7 May 1932. Louise Young Papers, Scarritt Graduate School Archives, Scarritt-Bennett Center, Nashville, TN.

34. A critic charged that Eleanor Roosevelt should resign from the NAACP. Typescript, undated, 5, Dorothy Tilly Papers, Box 1, Folder 2, Emory University.

35. James R. McGovern and Walter T. Howard, "Private Justice and National Concern: The Lynching of Claude Neal," *The Historian*, December 1980.

36. Thelma Stevens, *Legacy for the Future, The History of Christian Social Relations in the Women's Division of Christian Service 1940–1968* ([New York:] Women's Division, Board of Global Ministries, The United Methodist Church, 1978), 48.

37. President Truman to the President's Committee on Civil Rights, cited by Bettie S. Brittingham, "Christ and the Drama of the World," *The Methodist Woman*, February 1948, 3.

38. Dorothy Tilly to Robert Carr, 28 May 1947, PCCR Papers, Box 7, Tilly Folder, Truman Library; also cited by Anthony Lake Newberry, "Without Urgency or Ardor: The South's Middle-of-the Road Liberals and Civil Rights, 1945–1960" Ph.D. diss., Ohio University, 1982.

39. Anthony Lake Newberry, "Without Urgency or Ardor," 125.

40. *To Secure These Rights, The Report of the President's Committee on Civil Rights* (Washington, DC: U.S. Government Printing Office, 1947), 178.

41. Memorandum, "Programs and Projects Conducted by Organizations" 2, 17, from papers of the President's Committee on Civil Rights, Dorothy Tilly Papers, Box 3, Folder 2, Emory University.

42. Ibid., 23.

43. Transcripts of the proceedings, PCCR, 17 April 1947, 220–21.

44. Ibid., 221, 561, 562.

45. Two thirds of complaints filed with FEPC charged businesses with discrimination, while one quarter found that the government discriminated. Unemployment consistently ran about twice as high for minorities as for whites. The PCCR castigated the practice of restrictive housing covenants for their calculated intent to create and deepen racial and religious divisions. The committee found that enforcement of restrictive covenants hinged on co-opting the court system to enforce these provisions that denied equality of opportunity to citizens. In health care, while African Americans had access to only 1 percent of hospital beds, other citizens had access to 99 percent. Difference in income increased differences in access to health care. Unequal educational opportunities coupled with segrega-

tion meant that the number of African Americans per African American doctor was four times that of whites per white doctor. *To Secure These Rights*, 54, 60, 69, 72.

46. Ibid., 99–100.

47. Ibid., 107–12.

48. Ibid., 133.

49. Ibid., 134.

50. Ibid., 173.

51. Dorothy Tilly to Charles E. Wilson and Robert Carr, 8 September 1947, President's Committee on Civil Rights, Harry S. Truman Library.

52. "To The Two Southern Residents of the Civil Rights (?) Committee" [Mailed from Atlanta 8 February 1948] Dorothy Tilly Papers, Archives, Winthrop College, Rock Hill, SC.

53. *Journal*, Eighth Annual Meeting, 2–12 December 1947, 15.

54. Ibid.

55. Ibid., 16.

56. PCCR distributed 25,000 free copies to the press, organizations, libraries, Congress, and each state legislator. The committee estimated circulation of the report at 963,700 copies. "Public Interest in the President's Civil Rights Program," undated, Papers of Philleo Nash, Harry S. Truman Library.

57. *Journal*, Executive Committee Meeting, 16–18 March 1948, 5.

58. Hanna F. Desser and Ethel C. Phillips, *Here's the Way to Secure These Rights* (Cincinnati: Woman's Division of Christian Service, Board of Missions and Church Extension, The Methodist Church [1948]). The FBI obtained its copy of this book from MFSA and kept it in a file of subversive materials.

59. Ibid., 15.

60. Dorothy Tilly, "The Story of the President's Committee on Civil Rights," (Cincinnati: Woman's Division of Christian Service, Board of Missions and Church Extension, The Methodist Church, 1948).

61. Ibid., 5.

62. Ibid., 7.

63. Transcripts of the President's Committee on Civil Rights, 3 April 1947. Dorothy Tilly Papers, Emory University.

64. Tilly also visited officials in conjunction with her efforts to extend civil rights and bring improvements in the nation's law enforcement and court systems. Tom C. Clark, U.S. Attorney General, to Dorothy Tilly, 28 October 1947. Dorothy Tilly Papers, Emory University.

65. *Journal*, Eighth Annual Meeting, 2–12 December 1947, 16.

66. Channing H. Tobias to Dorothy Tilly, 5 November 1948. Dorothy Tilly Papers, Emory University.

67. The United States resisted all attempts to ratify the U.N. covenants because of a secret political bargain which was struck. At the time the U.N. Covenants were first presented to the U.S. Senate, Senator John W. Bricker had advocated an amendment to the U.S. Constitution which would have required two-thirds of the state governments to ratify any covenants or treaties, taking that power away from the president and the Senate. John Foster Dulles, then U.S. secretary of state and a supporter of ratification of

the U.N. covenants, opposed the amendment but saw that it had a certain amount of popular support. In order to stop the Bricker amendment, Dulles agreed not to present any covenants to the Senate for ratification. Margaret R. Bender, "Human Rights Struggle, 1948–1965," *The Methodist Woman*, November 1965, 31. The genocide covenant was ratified in 1988.

68. The women who founded the Fellowship of the Concerned came from these groups: B'nai B'rith, Salvation Army, the Council of Jewish Women, Methodists, Baptists, Christian Churches, Congregational Churches, Lutherans, Roman Catholics, Presbyterians, the Council of Church Women, YWCA, League of Women Voters, Atlanta Urban League, Labor, and PTAs. They came from Alabama, Arkansas, Florida, Georgia, Kentucky, Louisiana, Mississippi, New York, North Carolina, South Carolina, Tennessee, Texas, and even Cuba. "'The Fellowship of the Concerned' Workshop of Southern Church Women, September, 8–9 1949, Wesley Mem., Bldg, Atlanta Ga." Fellowship of the Concerned file, Southern Regional Council papers, Woodruff Library, Atlanta University; and Dorothy Tilly, "The Fellowship of the Concerned," The Woman's Press, 5 February 1950, 8.

69. Dorothy Tilly to Robert Carr, 8 September 1947, Box VII, President's Commission on Civil Rights (PCCR) Papers, Truman Library; cited by Anthony Lake Newberry, "Without Urgency or Ardor," 125.

70. Arnold M. Shankman, "Civil Rights, 1920–1970," from Rosemary Skinner Keller, Louise L. Queen, and Hilah F. Thomas, eds., *Women in New Worlds, Historical Perspectives on Wesleyan Tradition* (Nashville: Abingdon Press, 1982), 231, and Thelma Stevens, *Legacy for the Future, The History of Christian Social Relations in the Women's Division of Christian Service 1940–1968* ([New York:] Women's Division, Board of Global Ministries, The United Methodist Church, 1978), 70.

Notes to Chapter 10

1. Thelma Stevens, Dorothy Weber, and Margaret R. Bender, "Information and Action," *The Methodist Woman*, November 1951, 25.

2. *Journal*, Annual Report, 17 January 1953, 38.

3. Liston Pope, *The Kingdom Beyond Caste* (New York: Friendship Press, 1957), xv.

4. "Working Toward World Understanding," *The Methodist Woman*, March 1956, 21.

5. Thelma Stevens, Margaret R. Bender, and Ethel L. Watkins, "Information and Action," *The Methodist Woman*, February 1956, 25.

6. *Journal*, Annual Meeting, 8 January 1955, 45.

7. Ibid., 45.

8. Ibid., 46.

9. Fred J. Cook, *The Nightmare Decade, The Life and Times of Senator Joe McCarthy* (New York: Random House, 1971), 34.

10. Ibid., 452, 455.

11. *Journal*, Annual Report of the Woman's Division, 16 January 1954, 54.

12. In keeping with the 1936 agreement of economic leaders reported by Fred J. Cook (*The Nightmare Decade*, 34), efforts to change working conditions, wages, segregation or living conditions of blacks were labeled subversive. See also Jeanne Knepper, "Radicals in Conservative Times: An Investigation of the Strategies and Decisions of MFSS During the Periods 1915–1920 and 1939–1948," Typescript, personal papers, 29.

13. Stanley High, "Methodism's Pink Fringe," *Reader's Digest* 56:134–38, February 1950. See also "Radicalism in the Methodist Ranks," *Christian Century* 67:197, 15 February 1950.

14. Thelma Stevens, Dorothy Weber, and Margaret R. Bender, "Information and Action," *The Methodist Woman*, January 1953, 21.

15. Thelma Stevens to Elwood H. Chisolm (New York NAACP office) 29 March 1957, NAACP Papers, Library of Congress.

16. Thelma Stevens, Eleanor Neff, and Dorothy Weber, "Information and Action," *The Methodist Woman*, May 1950, 25.

17. Ibid., June 1950, 25.

18. Ibid., May 1950, 25; June 1950; July–August 1950, 29; September 1950, 25; October, 1950, 25; November 1950, 21. See also Thelma Stevens, *Legacy for the Future, The History of Christian Social Relations in the Women's Division of Christian Service 1940–1968* ([New York:] Women's Division, Board of Global Ministries, The United Methodist Church, 1978), 59–60.

19. President Truman had failed to support civil rights legislation after proposing it to Congress. *Journal*, Executive Committee Meeting, 9 September 1952, 36.

20. Methodist women worked to ensure human rights by encouraging the U.S. Congress to ratify the U.N. genocide convention and urging the United Nations General Assembly to adopt U.N. conventions on human rights.

21. Ibid., 36.

22. Aldon D. Morris, *The Origins of the Civil Rights Movement: Black Communities Organizing for Change* (New York: The Free Press, 1984), 4.

23. This interpretation is credited to E. Franklin Frazier. Lerone Bennett, Jr., *Before the Mayflower, A History of Black America* (New York: Penguin Books, 1982), 371.

24. Anthony Lake Newberry, "Without Urgency or Ardor: The South's Middle-of-the Road Liberals and Civil Rights, 1945–1960" (Ph.D. diss., Ohio University, 1982), 145.

25. *New South* 9:4–5, April–May 1954, 16.

26. Their journal was published for ten years ending in 1946.

27. Anthony Lake Newberry, "Without Urgency or Ardor," 178.

28. Ibid., 193–94.

29. Ibid., 197.

30. Ibid., 212–13.

31. Robert J. Norrell, *Reaping the Whirlwind: The Civil Rights Movement in Tuskegee* (New York: Alfred A. Knopf, 1985), 37.

32. The courts ruled illegal a gerrymandering of city boundaries purposely to exclude African Americans in *Gomillion v. Lightfoot*. Before the voucher system (the requirement that two, usually white, voters had to vouch for the character of a potential voter) could be found unlawful in

Mitchell v. Wright, county registrars "discovered" that Mitchell was duly registered. Ibid., 60–63, 123–26.

33. Ibid, 144–53. Interview with Ennis Sellers, retired and living in Gulf Breeze, FL, 30 January 1993.

34. Ibid., 148.

35. *New South*, 6:2, February 1951, 2.

36. The basic membership pledge of the Fellowship of the Concerned read: "I am concerned that our constitutional freedoms are not shared by all our people; my religion convinces me that they must be and gives me courage to study, work and lead others to the fulfillment of equal justice under the law. I will respond to calls from the Southern Regional Council to serve my faith and my community in the defense of justice." Cited by Arnold Shankman, "Dorothy Tilly, Civil Rights and the Methodist Church," *Methodist History*, 18, January 1980, 98.

37. Ibid.

38. "Sworn Written Application for Registration" [State of Mississippi] 18 April 1955, Fellowship of the Concerned Files, 1955, Archives of the Southern Regional Council, Atlanta University Center, Woodruff Library, Atlanta, GA.

39. "Gleanings from the Conference of 'The Fellowship of the Concerned'" Southern Regional Council, All Saints' Church, Atlanta, GA, 24–25 February 1955, 4, Archives of the Southern Regional Council.

40. Ibid., 7.

41. Rosemary Skinner Keller, Louise L. Queen, and Hilah F. Thomas, eds., *Women in New Worlds, Historical Perspectives on Wesleyan Tradition* (Nashville: Abingdon Press, 1982). See Arnold M. Shankman, "Civil Rights, 1920–1970," 229.

42. Mrs. John Baker, reporter, "Report of Buzz Group Number 3—Leader, Mrs. Caxton Doggett, Fellowship of the Concerned, Avon Park, September 10–11, 1958," Dorothy Tilly Papers, 1958–1961, Archives of the Southern Regional Council.

43. W. Wilson White, assistant attorney general, Civil Rights Division, by St. John Barrett, second assistant, to Dorothy Tilly, 4 February 1959, Dorothy Tilly Papers, 1958–1961, Archives of the Southern Regional Council.

44. Dow Kirkpatrick to M. G. Lowman, Circuit Riders, Inc., 19 January 1959, Dorothy Tilly Papers, 1958–1961, Archives of the Southern Regional Council.

45. Ibid.

46. Thelma Mills, Houston YWCA, to Dorothy Tilly, 22 December 1958, Dorothy Tilly Papers, 1958–1961, Archives of the Southern Regional Council.

47. The National Council of Negro Women invited key women to discuss desegregation case studies at their annual meeting in 1959. Dorothy Tilly was asked to speak about Atlanta, Mrs. William T. Mason to tell the Norfolk story, and Mrs. Charles White to tell about her experiences on Houston's Board of Education. H. Elsie Austin, executive director, National Council of Negro Women, Inc., to Dorothy Tilly, 18 May 1959, Dorothy Tilly Papers, 1958–1961, Archives of the Southern Regional Council.

48. Interview with Martha Turnipseed of Ramer, AL, 30 January 1993.

Notes to Chapter 11

1. Pauli Murray, ed., *States' Laws on Race and Color* (Cincinnati: Woman's Division of Christian Service, Board of Missions, The Methodist Church, 1950). Pauli Murray prepared the first edition of the book. Verge Lake edited later versions.

2. Thelma Stevens, Eleanor Neff, and Dorothy Weber, "Information and Action," *The Methodist Woman*, June 1950, 25.

3. Ibid., July–August 1950, 29.

4. "Race Relations," *The Methodist Woman*, October 1952, 35.

5. Muriel Day, "Learning to Live Together . . . another article on the home mission theme for 1957–1958 'Christ, the Church, and Race,'" *The Methodist Woman*, April 1957, 13.

6. Thelma Stevens, Eleanor Neff Curry, and Dorothy Weber, "Information and Action," *The Methodist Woman*, September 1950, 25.

7. Pauli Murray reported that Thurgood Marshall provided copies of this book to each member of the NAACP staff and referred to it as the "'bible' during the final stages of the legal attack upon the 'separate but equal' doctrine." Pauli Murray, *Song in a Weary Throat, An American Pilgrimage* (New York: Harper & Row, Publishers, 1987), 289.

8. *Journal*, Executive Committee Meeting, 18 March 1952, 8.

9. *Journal*, Annual Report, 19 January 1953, 31–32. The Committee on Racial Practices recommended that a committee be named to consider how the Charter would be used and to report on the progress of the Woman's Division toward its full implementation.

10. For the text of the Charter of Racial Policies—1952, see Appendix B.

11. "A Charter of Racial Policies," *The Methodist Woman*, April 1952, 22 and September 1954, 22; Thelma Stevens, *Legacy for the Future* ([New York]: Women's Division, Board of Global Ministries, The United Methodist Church, 1978), 64.

12. *Journal*, Annual Report, 8 December 1950, 48.

13. "A Worksheet on Human Rights," *The Methodist Woman*, May 1952, 27.

14. "A Charter of Racial Policies," and "Progress Toward Charter Ratification," *The Methodist Woman*, September 1954, 22–23.

15. Thelma Stevens and Margaret R. Bender, "Information and Action," *The Methodist Woman*, January 1954, 25.

16. *Journal*, Annual Report, 16 January 1954, 54.

17. "'Brotherhood' Is a 'Local Responsibility,'" *The Methodist Woman*, February 1954, 22.

18. Southern Regional Council, *The Schools and the Courts*, cited in "'Brotherhood' Is a 'Local Responsibility,'" *The Methodist Woman*, February 1954, 23.

19. "Affirmations of the Assembly," *The Methodist Woman*, July–August 1954, 43. Thelma Stevens, *Legacy for the Future, The History of Christian Social Relations in the Women's Division of Christian Service 1940–1968* ([New York:] Women's Division, Board of Global Ministries, The United Methodist Church, 1978), 69.

20. Tillman gave valuable leadership, helping Methodist women to

implement the Charter of Racial Policies. From 1956 to 1964 she chaired the Woman's Division, giving priority to the charter and to building the United Nations Church Center.

21. *Journal*, Executive Committee Meeting, 26 April 1955, 16.

22. *Journal*, Executive Committee Meeting, 26 April 1955, 16–17.

23. *Journal*, Executive Committee Meeting, September 1954, 76–77.

24. "Progress in Interracial Practices," *The Methodist Woman*, November 1954, 14.

25. Muriel Day, "Learning to Live Together," 13.

26. *Journal*, Executive Committee Meeting, September 1955, 29.

27. "Five Years' Progress in Meeting the Needs of Children and Youth," *The Methodist Woman*, November 1955, 27, citing *Southern School News*, Southern Education Reporting Service.

28. Ibid., 28.

29. [Thelma Stevens] "Everyone Has the Right," *The Methodist Woman*, February 1957, 28–29.

30. Mrs. Robert L. Wilcox, "Progress in School Integration As Seen by Four Jurisdiction Secretaries, Southeastern Jurisdiction," *The Methodist Woman*, February 1958, 28.

31. Ibid., 29.

32. Alice Knotts, "Race Relations in the 1920s: A Challenge to Southern Methodist Women," *Methodist History*, July 1988, 199–212.

33. Mrs. Robert L. Wilcox, "Progress in School Integration," 28.

34. *Journal*, Annual Meeting of the Woman's Division, 13 January 1961, 52.

35. "After the Tenth Anniversary," *The Methodist Woman*, February 1959, 27.

36. Noreen D. Tatum, "Report of Chairman of Christian Social Relations, United Church Women of Alabama," undated. Dorothy Tilly Papers, 1959–1961, Archives of the Southern Regional Council.

37. Thelma Stevens and Margaret R. Bender, "Department of Christian Social Relations," *The Methodist Woman*, November 1957, 24; *Journal*, Annual Report, January 1958, 71; and *Journal*, Executive Committee Meeting, September 1958, 50–51.

38. *Journal*, Annual Report, January 1959, 93.

39. "Guide for a Workshop on Housing," *The Methodist Woman*, April 1959, 29.

40. "Citizenship Brunches on Housing," *The Methodist Woman*, April 1958, 30.

41. Ibid., 31.

42. *Journal*, Executive Committee Meeting, 18 April 1961, 19.

43. "Guide for a Workshop on Housing," 32.

44. Alden D. Morris, *The Origins of the Civil Rights Movement: Black Communities Organizing for Change* (New York: The Free Press, A Division of Macmillan, Inc., 1984), 31.

45. James Farmer, *Lay Bare the Heart, An Autobiography of The Civil Rights Movement* (New York: New American Library, 1985), 192.

46. Thelma Stevens, Margaret R. Bender, and Ethel Watkins, "Information and Action," *The Methodist Woman*, December 1955, 17.

47. Ibid.

48. Ibid., 18.

49. *Journal*, Annual Report, 12 January 1962, 77.

50. *Journal*, Executive Committee Meeting, January 1965, 40.

51. "What a World Understanding Workshop Could Do for Your Community," *The Methodist Woman*, December 1965, 32.

52. Liston Pope, *The Kingdom Beyond Caste* (New York: Friendship Press, 1957), 103.

53. Mrs. Ringle, unknown to me except that she was a previous owner of my copy of this text, left in her book five handwritten questions selected to guide a discussion of "The Roots of Prejudice."

54. Thelma Stevens, "Address by Miss Thelma Stevens," *Report of Interracial Leadership Conference*, Pittsburgh, PA, 6–7 December 1957, 31.

55. Ibid., 30.

56. Photos of thirty-six newly elected members of the Woman's Division show at least three African American women. *The Methodist Woman*, October 1955, 4–5.

57. Thelma Stevens, Margaret R. Bender, and Ethel Watkins, "Information and Action," *The Methodist Woman*, September 1956, 21, and Dorcas Hall and Maude White Hardie, "Organization and Promotion," *The Methodist Woman*, September 1956, 27.

58. Peter Carlisle Murray, "Christ and Caste in Conflict: Creating a Racially Inclusive Methodist Church," Ph.D. diss., Indiana University, 1985; citing J. Mills Thornton III, *Alabama Review* 33 (July 1980), 232–35; David L. Lewis, *King: A Biography*, 2nd ed. (Urbana: University of Illinois Press, 1978), 83–84.

59. *Discipline of The Methodist Church*, 1952, Paragraph 2027, 652.

60. The 1952 General Conference adopted this wording: "As Christians we confess ourselves to be children of God, brothers and sisters of Jesus Christ. This being true, there is no place in The Methodist Church for racial discrimination or racial segregation." *Discipline of The Methodist Church*, 1952, Paragraph 2027, 651.

61. Ibid., 23.

62. Peter Carlisle Murray, "Christ and Caste in Conflict," 97, 99.

63. *Information Bulletin*, published by the Mississippi Association of Methodist Ministers and Laymen, 7 April 1959, 1–2.

64. *Information Bulletin*, No. 1 Special, April 1960, 1.

65. Theressa Hoover recounts that Thelma Stevens initially proposed the idea of a national Methodist Conference on Race, bringing handwritten rough drafts of a proposal to a Monday morning staff meeting of the Department of Christian Social Relations. Interview with Theressa Hoover, 24 October 1987.

66. *Journal*, Executive Committee Meeting, 9 April 1957, 20.

67. *Journal*, Executive Committee Meeting, 14 September 1958, 31. The request was approved in January 1959.

68. "Celebrations That Will Endure," *The Methodist Woman*, December 1959, 22.

69. Dorothy Tilly to Mrs. C. A. [Esther] Meeker, 11 June 1956. Archives of the Southern Regional Council.

70. Maude Taylor Serelio to Dorothy Tilly, 21 January 1958. Archives of the Southern Regional Council. Other archival sources and interviews confirm that these findings are evidence of activities which had a broader distribution than the sources listed here indicate.

71. A successful voter registration project in a predominantly African American precinct run by Bennett College served as a model for the Woman's Division. Margaret Bender, executive secretary, Department of Christian Social Relations, to Dorothy Tilly, 27 June, 1960.

72. "We, of the Woman's Society of Christian Service of ____ Church, have visited Mr. _____ (Sheriff) (Chief of Police). . . ." 1952, Archives of the Southern Regional Council.

73. Mrs. W. F. Bates to Dorothy Tilly, 28 December 1957. Archives of the Southern Regional Council.

74. Enclosure, a letter to Secretaries of Children's Work, 28 November 1957, ibid.

75. Dorothy Tilly to Thelma Stevens and Mrs. E. U. [Ruth] Robinson, 9 July 1958. Archives of the Southern Regional Council.

76. Dorothy Tilly to Mrs. E. U. Robinson, 15 May 1958. Archives of the Southern Regional Council.

77. Dorothy Tilly to Mrs. Robert L. Wilcox, 14 August 1958. Archives of the Southern Regional Council.

Notes to Chapter 12

1. Thelma Stevens, "Determined to Move," *The Methodist Woman*, February 1962, 25.

2. Martin Luther King, Jr., Stokely Carmichael, James Lawson, John Lewis, Diane Nash, and many prominent leaders were in their twenties or early thirties.

3. Peggy Billings to the author, 26 February 1991.

4. Juan Williams, *Eyes on the Prize, America's Civil Rights Years, 1954–1965* (New York: Viking Penguin, Inc., 1987), 123.

5. Lerone Bennett, Jr., *Before the Mayflower, A History of Black America* (New York: Penguin Books, 1984), 557. The network of preparation, leadership, and communication is described by Alden D. Morris, *The Origins of the Civil Rights Movement, Black Communities Organizing for Change*. (New York: The Free Press, A Division of Macmillan, Inc., 1984).

6. James Lawson, United Methodist minister and former FOR staff member, interview by author, 30 January 1986, Denver. Tape recording.

7. James Farmer, *Lay Bare the Heart: An Autobiography of the Civil Rights Movement* (New York: New American Library, 1985), 193.

8. Diane Nash, civil rights leader, Nashville movement, interview by author, 5 October 1985, Chicago. Tape recording. Juan Williams, *Eyes on the Prize, America's Civil Rights Years, 1954–1965*, 126.

9. Ibid.

10. James Lawson at The Iliff School of Theology, Denver, 1 March 1988.

11. *Journal*, Executive Committee Meeting, 22 March 1960, 35.

12. Ibid.

13. Ibid., 36.

14. During the same period the Southern Regional Council counted 979 arrests. Ibid., 40.

15. Ibid., 41.

16. Ibid., 40.

17. Interview with James Lawson, 30 January 1986, Denver, Colorado.

18. *Journal*, Executive Committee Meeting, 22 March 1960, 40.

19. Ibid.

20. Ibid., 40. The guidelines were as follows:

> Don't strike back or curse back if abused.
> Don't laugh out.
> Don't hold conversations with floor workers.
> Don't leave your seats until your leader has given you instruction to do so.
> Don't block entrances to the stores and aisles.
> Show yourself friendly and courteous at all times.
> Sit straight and always face the counter.
> Report all serious incidents to your leader.
> Refer all information to your leader in a polite manner.
> Remember the teachings of Jesus Christ, Mohandas K. Gandhi and Martin Luther King.
> Remember love and non-violence.
> May God bless each of you.

21. Ibid.

22. Peggy Billings, "A God-Given Second Chance," *The Methodist Woman*, July–August 1965, 14.

23. Bobbie Kearns Roberts, former member of the Woman's Division of Christian Service, interview by author, 29 July 1986, Nashville.

24. Methodist women ranged in age from mid-twenties to senior citizens, usually with families or careers. Assuming that about 60 percent of 350,000 African American Methodists were women and that approximately 31 percent of all women in The Methodist Church (1,500,000 out of 4,800,000) belonged to the WSCS or WSG, then about 65,100 of nearly 1,500,000 women in local women's societies or 4.3 percent were African American.

25. *Journal*, Report and Recommendations of the Section of Christian Social Relations, Appendix A, 1965, 18.

26. Margaret Minor, former member of the Woman's Society of Christian Service, interview by author, 28 September 1986, Durham, NC. See also Taylor Branch, *Parting the Waters, America in the King Years, 1954–63* (New York: Simon and Schuster, 1988), 272.

27. Margaret Minor, interview by author, 28 September 1986, Durham, NC.

28. Ibid.

29. Thelma Stevens, "Excerpts from *We Can and We Will!*" *The Methodist Woman*, February 1962, 25. Dwight Wendell Culver, "*We Can and We Will!*" *A Manual for the Methodist Church Quadrennial Program on Race* (Cincinnati: Woman's Division of Christian Service of the Board of Missions of The Methodist Church, 1961). See also Dwight W. Culver, *Negro Segregation in The Methodist Church* (New Haven: Yale University Press, 1953).

30. Up to this point the terms "desegregation" and "integration" have been used interchangeably, as they were used by the press and the Woman's Division at that time, to provide linguistic variety. Hereafter the terms are used according to the definitions provided by Dwight Culver.

31. Ibid., 36.

32. Wade Clark Roof and William McKinney have identified the decline of the influence of the National Council of Churches as a loss of establishment, and notice a similar decline in the position of individual mainline denominations in exerting cultural influence. For McKinney, the location of the headquarters of the National Council of Churches in Morningside Heights, near the home of President Dwight D. Eisenhower in 1958, stands in contrast to the inability of the National Council of Churches to gain the ear of later presidents. William McKinney, "The NCC in a New Time (I)," *Christianity and Crisis*, 48:19, 9 January 1989, 465.

33. Telegram from Mrs. Robert L. Wilcox, Mrs. David J. Cathcart, and members of the Standing Committee on Christian Social Relations of the Southeastern Jurisdiction Woman's Society of Christian Service of The Methodist Church, *The Methodist Woman*, February 1961, 27.

34. *Journal*, Executive Committee Meeting, 24 September 1963, 39.

35. "The Effect of Changes in Congressional Habits," *The Methodist Woman*, January 1964, 28–29.

36. Ibid., 95.

37. *Journal*, Executive Committee Meeting, 3 April 1962, 44.

38. Annual Report of the Executive Director of the Southern Regional Council, April, 1965, "A Review of Program Activities of 1964," 17. Kelly Miller Smith Collection, Vanderbilt University, Nashville, TN. For SNCC's role in the Mississippi Summer Project see Carson Clayborne, *In Struggle, SNCC and the Black Awakening of the 1960s* (Cambridge, MA: 1981), 102–3, 119, 177.

39. "List of Officers and Members of the Executive Committee of the Southern Regional Council," January 1965. Kelly Miller Smith Collection.

40. *Journal*, Annual Report, January 1965, 36.

41. Ibid., 28–29.

42. Mary King, in 1964 a SNCC staff worker, claims that by the end of 1964 Methodists, Presbyterians, the United Church of Christ, and Episcopalians, as well as other secular organizations, provided "impressive backing" for civil rights efforts. Mary King, *Freedom Song, A Personal Story of the 1960s Civil Rights Movement* (New York: Quill, William Morrow, 1988), 437–38.

43. Thelma Stevens, "'inherent rights of every individual,'" *The Methodist Woman*, February 1965, 29.

44. Ibid., 29.

45. Peggy Billings, "Full and Equal Opportunity Goal for America," *The Methodist Woman*, April 1967, 31. "'Black Power,' Statement by National

Committee of Negro Churchmen," *The Methodist Woman*, 1 December 1966, 40.

46. Ibid., 29.

47. "Some Race Related Deaths in the United States (1955–1965)" *New South*, 20:11, November 1965, 12–13.

48. Ibid., 31.

49. Ibid., 18.

50. *Journal*, Executive Committee Meeting, 18 September 1965, 18.

51. Jointly sponsored by the Woman's Division and the Division of Human Relations and Economic Affairs of the Board of Christian Social Concerns, the conference gathered resource leaders, representatives of other denominations, personnel from both the National and World Divisions of the Board of Missions, and women leaders from 23 conferences. *Journal*, Executive Committee Meeting, 14 January 1966, 63.

52. Peggy Billings, "The Agenda: Old Business and New in Race Relations," *The Methodist Woman*, June 1966, 36.

53. *Journal*, Annual Report, January 1965, 35.

54. Peggy Billings, "The Agenda," 37.

55. Ibid.

56. Ibid., 53.

57. The student wing of the civil rights movement, the Student Non-Violent Coordinating Committee (SNCC), was founded in 1961. Diane Nash and John Lewis served on its steering committee along with many others. COFO, the Council of Federated [civil rights] Organizations, helped with the Mississippi Freedom Summer Project and coordinated weekly rallies.

58. *Journal*, Executive Committee Meeting, 24 April 1965, 20.

59. Bruce Hilton, *The Delta Ministry* (London: The Macmillan Company, Collier-Macmillan Ltd., 1969), 68–70. Interview with Dr. Bruce Hilton and the Rev. Virginia Hilton, who were on the Delta Ministry staff from 1965 to 1967, 30 April 1988, St. Louis, MO.

60. Ibid., 14–15.

61. Ibid., 164.

62. *Journal*, 23 April 1966, 10.

63. *Journal*, Executive Committee Meeting, 22–24 September 1966, 20.

64. "National Seminar Accents Human Rights Year," *The Methodist Woman*, December 1967, 40.

65. Kenneth Clark cited by Peggy Billings, "'Black Power' as Human Power," *The Methodist Woman*, February 1968, 24.

66. Ibid., 25.

67. "'Black Power,' Statement by National Committee of Negro Churchmen," *The Methodist Woman*, December 1966, 40.

68. Ibid.

69. Ibid., 40–41.

70. *Journal*, Executive Committee Meeting, 22–24 September 1966, 21.

71. Pauli Murray, *Progress in Human Rights in the United States Since 1948* (Cincinnati: The Board of Missions of The Methodist Church, 1967).

72. Pauli Murray, "The Civil Rights Movement," *The Methodist Woman*, February 1967, 34.

Notes to Chapter 13

1. Thelma Stevens, *Legacy for the Future, The History of Christian Social Relations in the Women's Division of Christian Service 1940–1968* ([New York:] Women's Division, Board of Global Ministries, The United Methodist Church, 1978), 85, 87. Many church leaders expected women to conform. In the 1960s, when the women of the WSCS made an independent decision with which a pastor disagreed, I remember hearing Methodist ministers discuss this mutual problem and make a typical response, "When are the women going to join the church?"

2. Thelma Stevens, *Legacy for the Future*, 88.

3. The theme "Our Mission Today" listed barriers of race and culture among five "Frontiers that Call Us." *Journal*, Annual Report, 12 January 1960, 12.

4. *Journal*, Executive Committee of the Woman's Division, 23 September 1960, 61–63.

5. "Quadrennial Program on Race—The Methodist Church, 1960–1964," *The Methodist Woman*, June 1961, 30.

6. Ibid., 31.

7. *Journal*, Executive Committee Meeting, 22 March 1960, 21. Conversation with Philip Wogaman, 26 April 1988.

8. *Journal*, Annual Report, 16 January 1960, 51–52. *Discipline of The Methodist Church*, 1960, Paragraph 2026, 705.

9. *The Discipline of The Methodist Church*, 1960, Paragraph 2013, 683, cited by *The Methodist Woman*, February 1961, 25.

10. *Journal*, Annual Report, 12 January 1962, 78; *Journal*, Executive Committee Meeting, 3 April 1962, 43; Bruce Hilton, *The Delta Ministry* (London: The Macmillan Company, Collier-Macmillan Ltd., 1969), 177.

11. "A Charter of Racial Policies—1962" in Thelma Stevens, *Legacy for the Future*, 91; *The Methodist Woman*, April 1962, inside cover.

12. Thelma Stevens, Margaret R. Bender, Theressa Hoover, "Department of Christian Social Relations," *The Methodist Woman*, May 1963, 26.

13. In 1964 the Woman's Division adopted the recommendations of the Department of Christian Social Relations for the implementation of the 1962 Charter of Racial Policies. Suggestions for action were provided to accompany each goal. *Journal*, Executive Committee Meeting, 17 January 1964, 85–87.

14. Sadie Wilson Tillman, "Program Suggestion—For a Program on Race," *The Methodist Woman*, October 1963, 25.

15. Wy Pringley, who was a member of the WSCS, did not hear about the Charter of Racial Policies in the 1960s. Conversation at Grant Park-Aldersgate United Methodist Church, Atlanta, GA, 16 October 1988.

16. *Journal*, Executive Committee Meeting, 3 April 1962, 45. Thelma Stevens was one of four persons from the Woman's Division on the planning committee. *Journal*, Annual Meeting, 12 January 1962, 77; and 11 January 1963, 77.

17. "Methodist Human Relations Conference—1963," *The Methodist Woman*, November 1963, 28.

18. Press Release, Commission on Public Relations and Methodist Information, 27 August 1963. United Methodist Publishing House Archives, Nashville, TN.

19. Ibid., undated.

20. Thelma Stevens, "'I Have a Dream,' Civil Rights and Community Action," *The Methodist Woman*, November 1963, 29.

21. Ibid., 28.

22. Thelma Stevens, "We Will—Unite Our Efforts," *The Methodist Woman*, June 1963, 28.

23. Ibid., 28.

24. *Journal of the General Conference of The Methodist Church* (Nashville: The Methodist Publishing House, 1960), 1706–1708.

25. Thelma Stevens, "We Will—Unite Our Efforts," 28.

26. Ibid., 52.

27. *Journal*, Executive Committee Meeting, 28 February, 3 March 1964, 52.

28. Ibid.

29. Thelma Stevens, "The Methodist Church and Race," *The Methodist Woman*, May 1964, 28.

30. *Doctrines and Discipline of The Methodist Church*, 1964 (Nashville: The Methodist Publishing House, 1964), Paragraph 1824, 684–88.

31. *Journal*, Annual Report, 15 January 1965, 35–36.

32. Ibid., 36.

33. Thelma Stevens, "Mandates for Action, The 1964 General Conference Speaks," *The Methodist Woman*, July–August, 1964, 28.

34. Ibid., 27–28.

35. Thelma Stevens, "The Methodist Church and Race," 28.

36. *Journal*, Executive Committee Meeting, 10 January 1968, 72.

37. *Journal*, Annual Report, 11, 13, 14 January 1967, 39.

38. The Woman's Division petitioned the General Conference to "call upon Annual Conferences to take appropriate steps to insure continuity of full representation of racial minorities in all boards and agencies on all organizational levels." *Journal*, Annual Report, 10 January 1968, 74.

39. Theressa Hoover, "If I Were a Delegate . . . ," *The Methodist Woman*, May 1968, 33.

40. Ibid., 33.

41. "From the 1966 Annual Meeting," *The Methodist Woman*, March 1966, 37.

42. Mrs. J. J. Johnson, Jr., "Our Mission: In Missouri (Merger and Preparation for It)," *The Methodist Woman*, February 1967, 27.

43. Ibid.

44. BMCR still serves United Methodists. The choice of the term "Black Methodists," a subject of debate at the time, represented racial pride and empowerment with which the participants approached their new task. Minnie Stein, "Our Time Under God Is Now," *The Methodist Woman*, February 1968, 18.

45. Thelma Stevens, "The Heritage of Our Women's Organizations: The Methodist Church," *The Methodist Woman*, September 1968, 27.

46. *Journal*, Executive Committee Meeting, 16 April 1967, 19.

47. Sarah Cunningham, "Why a Woman's Organization in the Church?" *The Methodist Woman*, January 1967, 11.

48. Mary McLanachan, "The Heritage of Our Women's Organizations: The Evangelical United Brethren Church," *The Methodist Woman*, September 1968, 26.

49. Thelma Stevens, "Heritage of Our Women's Organizations," 27.

50. Thelma Stevens, "General Conference Report," *The Methodist Woman*, July–August 1968, 25.

Notes to Chapter 14

1. Task Group on the History of the Central Jurisdiction Women's Organization, *To a Higher Glory: The Growth and Development of Black Women Organized for Mission in The Methodist Church, 1940–1968* (Women's Division of the Board of Global Ministries, The United Methodist Church, 1978), 73.

2. Thelma Stevens, "Former things have come to pass and new things I now declare," a message to MFSA Eastern Pennsylvania Conference, Reading, PA, manuscript. 9 June 1982.

3. Diane Nash, interview, 5 October 1985, Chicago.

4. Alice G. Knotts, "Social Transformation and Holy Living: Call, Invitation and Presence." A presentation for the combined meetings of United Methodism and American Culture and the Third Historical Convocation of The United Methodist Church, St. Simons Island, GA, 24–28 August 1995.

5. Alice G. Knotts, "Thelma Stevens' 'Thorns that Fester:' An Oral Biography and Interview," 5–7 December 1983, unpublished manuscript, Women's Division of Christian Service, The General Board of Global Ministries, The United Methodist Church, 291.

Bibliography

Primary Sources

ANNUAL REPORTS, JOURNALS, AND PERIODICALS OF
METHODIST WOMEN'S ORGANIZATIONS

Annual Reports of the Woman's Division of the Board of Missions of The Methodist Church, 1964–1968.

Annual Reports of the Woman's Home Missionary Society of the Methodist Episcopal Church, 1920–1940. Cincinnati: The Methodist Book Concern Press.

Annual Reports of the Woman's Missionary Council of the Methodist Episcopal Church, South, 1911–1940.

Archives of the Section of Christian Social Relations of the Women's Division of The Board of Global Ministries of The United Methodist Church, 1950–1968.

The General Board of Social and Economic Relations. The Methodist Church.

The Methodist Woman. The Woman's Division of The Board of Missions of The Methodist Church, 1940–1968.

Minutes of the Executive Committee of the Woman's Division of The Board of Missions of The Methodist Church, 1940–1963. [Designated in notes as *Journal*.]

Reports of Interracial Leadership Conferences, listed chronologically:
>   Woodlawn Methodist Church, Chicago, IL, 8–9 March 1955.
>   Grand Avenue Temple, Kansas City, MO, 23–24 October 1956.
>   Louisville, KY, 15–16 November 1956.
>   Wesley Memorial Church, Atlanta, GA, 28–29 January 1957.
>   Indianapolis, IN, 1–2 May 1957.
>   St. Louis, MO, 9–10 May 1957.
>   Bethune-Cookman College, Daytona Beach, FL, 10–11 September 1957.

Pittsburgh, PA, 6–7 December 1957.
Methodist Youth Interracial Conference, Detroit, MI, 18–20 April 1958.

Response. The Women's Division of the General Board of Global Ministries of The United Methodist Church, 1968—.

Woman's Home Missions. Woman's Home Missionary Society of the Methodist Episcopal Church, 1920–1940.

PUBLICATIONS AND STUDY BOOKS USED BY METHODIST WOMEN

Bartholomew, Ruth L. *Actions Speak Louder; Making Christian Our Race Relations*. Woman's Division of Christian Service of the Board of Missions of The Methodist Church, 1957.

Brownlee, Frederick Leslie. *These Rights We Hold*. New York: Friendship Press, [1952].

Calhoun, Eugene Clayton. *The Forgiving Forgiven: The Theological Ground for the Mission of the Church in Human Relations*. Cincinnati: Woman's Division of Christian Service of the Board of Missions of The Methodist Church, 1962.

A Christian's Primer of the United Nations. Woman's Division of Christian Service of the Board of Missions and Board of Christian Education of The Methodist Church, 1952.

Culver, Dwight Wendell. "We Can and We Will!" A Manual for the Methodist Church Quadrennial Program on Race. Cincinnati: Woman's Division of Christian Service of the Board of Missions of The Methodist Church, 1961.

Desser, Hanna F. and Ethel C. Phillips. *Here's the Way to Secure These Rights*. Cincinnati: Woman's Division of Christian Service Board of Missions and Church Extension of The Methodist Church, [1948].

The Family in a World of Rapid Social Change, Selected Materials from the National Seminar Held at Bennett College, Greensboro, N.C., July 21–31, 1957. Cincinnati: [Woman's Division of Christian Service of The Board of Missions of The Methodist Church] 1960.

Gallagher, Buell Gordon. *Portrait of a Pilgrim*. New York: Friendship Press, [1946].

A Guide for the Woman's Society of Christian Service. Cincinnati: Woman's Society of Christian Service of the Board of Missions of The Methodist Church, 1952.

Hammond, Lily H. *In Black and White: An Interpretation of Southern Life*. New York: Fleming H. Revell, 1914.

_____. *In the Vanguard of a Race*. New York: Council of Women for

Home Missions and Missionary Education Movement of the United States and Canada, 1922.

_____. *Southern Women and Racial Adjustment.* Lynchburg, VA: J. P. Bell Company, Inc., 1917.

Haskin, Sara Estelle. *The Upward Climb: A Course in Negro Achievement, Developed and Recorded by Sara Estelle Haskin.* New York: Council of Women for Home Missions and Missionary Education Movement of the United States and Canada, 1927.

_____. *Women and Missions in the Methodist Episcopal Church, South, 1878–1920.* Nashville: Publishing House of the Methodist Episcopal Church, South, 1921.

Helm, Mary. *The Upward Path: The Evolution of a Race.* Cincinnati: Jennings & Graham, 1909.

_____. *Why and How, A Descriptive Narrative of the Work of the Woman's Home Mission Society of the M. E. Church, South.* Nashville, TN: Woman's Missionary Council, M. E. Church, South, 1912.

Howell, Mabel. *Women and the Kingdom, Fifty Years of Kingdom Building by the Women of the Methodist Episcopal Church, South, 1878–1920.* Nashville, TN: Cokesbury Press, 1928.

Hoyland, John Somerville. *The Teaching of Jesus on Human Relations.* Adapted by Mary DeBardeleben. New York: Abingdon-Cokesbury Press, n.d.

Human Rights in a World Perspective, Sourcebook for the 12th Quadrennial Seminar of the Woman's Division of Christian Service, Kansas City, MO, August 1–10, 1967. Cincinnati: [Woman's Division of Christian Service of The Board of Missions of The Methodist Church], 1968.

Johnson, Charles S. *A Preface to Racial Understanding.* New York: Friendship Press, 1936.

Mays, Benjamin. *Seeking to Be Christian in Race Relations.* New York: Friendship Press, 1957. Revised 1964.

Murray, Pauli. *States' Laws on Race and Color.* New York: Woman's Division of Christian Service [The Methodist Church], 1951.

Pope, Liston. *The Kingdom Beyond Caste.* New York: Friendship Press, 1957.

The President's Commission on Civil Rights. *To Secure These Rights.* Report of the President's Commission on Civil Rights, 1947.

Speer, Robert E. *Of One Blood, A Short Study of the Race Problem.* New York: Council of Women for Home Missions and Missionary Education Movement of the United States and Canada, 1924.

SPEECHES, ARTICLES, AND BOOKS BY
  METHODIST WOMEN

Ames, Jessie Daniel. *The Changing Character of Lynching: Review of Lynching, 1931–1941*. Atlanta: Commission on Interracial Cooperation, Inc., 1942.

Dunn, Noreen Tatum. *A Crown of Service, Story of Woman's Work in the Methodist Episcopal Church, South, From 1878–1940*. Nashville: Parthenon Press, 1960.

_____. *Women and Home Missions*. Nashville: Cokesbury Press, 1936.

Finger, Mamie Lee Ratliff. "Cora Rodman Ratliff, 1891-1958: A Woman of Courage and Vision." 1989. Unpublished manuscript.

Howell, Mabel. *Women and the Kingdom: Fifty Years of Kingdom Building by the Women of the Methodist Episcopal Church, South, 1878–1920*. Nashville, TN: Cokesbury Press, c. 1928.

MacDonell, Mrs. R. W. [Tochie]. *Belle Harris Bennett: Her Life Work*. Nashville: Woman's Section of the Board of Missions, Methodist Episcopal Church, South, 1928.

Meeker, Ruth Esther. *Six Decades of Service, 1880–1940, A History of the Woman's Home Missionary Society of The Methodist Episcopal Church*. Continuing Corporation of the Woman's Home Missionary Society of the Methodist Episcopal Church, 1969.

Stevens, Thelma. "Address by Miss Thelma Stevens," Report of Interracial Leadership Conference, Pittsburgh, PA, 6–7 December 1957, 27–36.

_____. "A Place of Their Own." *Southern Exposure*. 1976 4 (3): 54–58.

_____. "A Woman: Who Art Thou?" An Address to the Florida Conference of United Methodist Women. 11 October 1972.

_____. "The Color Line in Wartime." *Social QuestionsBulletin*. 32:1:1–3. March 1942.

_____. "Former Things Have Come to Pass and New Things I Now Declare." Address to the Methodist Federation for Social Action, Eastern Pennsylvania Conference, Reading, PA, 9 June 1982.

_____. "Jesus and the Pharisees." Master's thesis, Scarritt College for Christian Workers, 1928.

_____. *Legacy for the Future, the History of Christian Social Relations in the Women's Division of Christian Service 1940–1968*. Women's Division, Board of Global Ministries, The United Methodist Church, 1976.

_____. "Methodist Women Need the Federation." *Social Questions Bulletin*. 34:7:1. October 1944.

_____. "Old Roots Sprout New Branches." Amarillo, TX. 7 October 1983.

Task Group on the History of the Central Jurisdiction Women's Organization. *To A Higher Glory, Growth and Development of Black Women Organized for Mission in The Methodist Church 1940–1968*. Women's Division, Board of Global Ministries, The United Methodist Church, undated. ca. 1976.

Tilly, Dorothy. "The Fellowship of the Concerned." *The Woman's Press.* February 1950.

Winfrey, Annie Laura. "The Organized Activities of the Women of Southern Methodism in the Field of Negro-White Relationships, 1886–1937." Master's thesis, Scarritt College for Christian Workers, 1938.

METHODIST PERIODICALS AND RECORDS, OFFICIAL AND UNOFFICIAL

Annual Reports of the Board of Missions of the Methodist Episcopal Church, South, 1922–1926.

Crum, Mason. *The Negro in the Methodist Church*. New York: Board of Missions and Church Extension, The Methodist Church, 1951.

Discipline of the Methodist Episcopal Church, 1904–1938.

Discipline of the Methodist Episcopal Church, South, 1886–1938.

Discipline of The Methodist Church, 1939–1964.

Discipline of The United Methodist Church, 1968.

Journal of the General Conference of The Methodist Church, 1940, 1944, 1948, 1952, 1956, 1960, 1964, 1968.

Journal of the Uniting Conference, 1939, of the Methodist Episcopal Church; the Methodist Episcopal Church, South; and the Methodist Protestant Church held at Kansas City, Missouri, April 26–May 10, 1939. New York: Methodist Publishing House, 1939.

The Methodist Hymnal. Nashville, TN: The Methodist Book Concern, 1939.

Methodist Student Movement. 1964 Minutes. Atlanta. 14–20 June 1964.

Nashville Christian Advocate. 1920–1968.

Quadrennial Reports to the General Conference, 1944. Nashville: Abingdon Press.

Social Questions Bulletin, 1949–1968.

Social Service Bulletin, 1939–1948.

AUTOBIOGRAPHIES AND BIOGRAPHIES

Farmer, James. *Lay Bare the Heart: An Autobiography of the Civil Rights Movement*. New York: New American Library, 1985.

Knotts, Alice G. "Thelma Stevens' 'Thorns That Fester': An Oral Biography and Interview." 5–7 December 1983.

Murray, Pauli. *Song in a Weary Throat: An American Pilgrimage*. New York: Harper and Row, Publishers, 1987.

Wahlberg, Edgar M. *Voices in the Darkness*. Boulder, CO: Roberts Rinehart, Publishers, 1983.

Wells, Ida B. *Crusade for Justice, The Autobiography of Ida B. Wells*. Ed. by Alfreda K. Duster. Chicago: The University of Chicago Press, 1970.

INTERVIEWS BY ALICE G. KNOTTS

Julia Austin	7 August 1986	Nashville
Peggy Billings	26 February 1991	Trumansburg, NY
Ellease Randall Colston	16 May 1990	Greensboro
Charles Copher	25 July 1986	Atlanta
Rhoda Edmeston	30 July 1986	Nashville
Omar Fink	26 September l986	Durham
Rosemarie Harding	16 July 1985	Denver
Bruce Hilton	30 April 1988	St. Louis
Virginia Hilton	30 April 1988	St. Louis
Leontine Kelly	3 April 1985	Denver
Myra Jones	15 May 1990	Greensboro
James Lawson	30 January 1986	Denver
Grace Lewis	16 May 1990	Greensboro
Frentis Logan	16 May 1990	Greensboro
William McClain	7 August 1985	Denver
Dorothy McConnell	12 May 1984	New York
Margaret Minor	30 September 1986	Durham
Diane Nash	5 October 1985	Chicago
Nancy Webb Pigg	27 July 1986	Nashville
Bette Prestwood	31 July 1986	Nashville
Selma Richardson	25 July 1986	Atlanta
Bobbie K. Roberts	29 July 1986	Nashville
Ellen Rosser	7 August 1986	Nashville
Ennis Sellers	30 January 1993	Gulf Breeze, FL
Minnie Smith	16 May 1990	Greensboro
Thelma Stevens	5–7 December, l983	Hermitage, TN
Martha Turnipseed	30 January 1993	Ramer, AL
Philip Wogaman	26 April 1988	St. Louis
Harriet Wright	28 September 1986	Durham

SPECIAL COLLECTIONS

Ames Papers, Jessie Daniel, Southern Historical Collection, University of North Carolina, Chapel Hill, NC.

Bennett College Archives, Bennett College, Greensboro, NC.

Chamberlin Papers, Mark, Special Collections, University of Oregon, Eugene, OR.

Smith Collection, Kelly Miller, Special Collections, Jean and Alexander Heard Library, Vanderbilt University, Nashville, TN.

Southern Oral History Collection, Wilson Library, University of North Carolina, Chapel Hill, NC. Interview with Louise Young by Robert Hall and Jacquelyn Hall.

Southern Oral History Collection, Wilson Library, University of North Carolina, Chapel Hill, NC. Interview with Thelma Stevens by Jacquelyn Hall, 13 February 1972.

Southern Regional Council Papers, Special Collections, Robert W. Woodruff Library, The Atlanta University Center, Atlanta, GA.

Tilly Papers, Dorothy Rogers, Special Collections Department, Robert W. Woodruff Library, Emory University, Atlanta, GA.

Tilly Papers, Dorothy Rogers, Archives, Winthrop University, Rock Hill, SC.

Truman Papers, Harry S., Harry S. Truman Library, Independence, MO.

United Methodist Publishing House Library and Archives, Nashville, TN.

Woman's Division of the Board of Missions of The Methodist Church, 1950–1972, Archives of the Division of Christian Social Relations.

Young Papers, Louise, Scarritt Graduate School Archives, Nashville, TN.

PERIODICALS AND REPORTS

New South. The Southern Regional Council. Atlanta, GA. 1945–1968.

Social Questions Bulletin. Methodist Federation for Social Action. Staten Island, NY. 1935–1950.

South Today.

To Secure These Rights, The Report of the President's Committee on Civil Rights. Washington, DC: United States Government Printing Office, 1947.

ARTICLES

Braden, Anne. "A Second Open Letter to Southern White Women." *Southern Exposure*. 1977 4 (4): 50–53.

Brown, Robert McAfee. "Further Reflection on Freedom Riding." *Christianity and Crisis*. 21:46–7. 7 August 1961.

Brown, Robert McAfee. "Residential Segregation." *Christianity and Crisis*. 16:90–91. 9 July 1956.

Brown, R. R. "Little Rock and the Churches." *Union Seminary Quarterly Review*. 13:19–27. January 1958.

Chambers, Clarke A. "Varieties of Welfare History," *Reviews in American History*, Vol. 15, No. 3, September 1987.

"Eliminate Discrimination." *Social Questions Bulletin*. 34:5:1–3. May 1944.

"Extend Democracy!" *Social Questions Bulletin*. 34:6:1–3. June 1944.

Fraser, T. P. "Desegregation and the Church." *Union Seminary Quarterly Review*. 11:37–39. March 1956.

Graham, F. P. "Need for Wisdom; two suggestions for carrying out the Supreme Court's decision against segregation." *Christianity and Crisis*. 15:66–72. 30 May 1955.

Hall, Jacqueline. "Reminiscences of Jessie Daniel Ames: 'I Really Do Like a Good Fight.'" *New South*. 1972 27 (2): 31–41.

Hill, Patricia R. "Heathen Women's Friends: The Role of Methodist Episcopal Women in the Women's Foreign Mission Movement, 1869–1915." *Methodist History*. April 1981,19:3.

"Integrated Hierarchy Eludes Methodists." *Christianity Today*. 10:46. 22 July 1966.

Keller, Rosemary Skinner. "Creating a Sphere for Women in the Church: How Consequential an Accommodation?" *Methodist History*. 18:83–94. January 1980.

King, Martin Luther, Jr. "From the Birmingham Jail." *Christianity and Crisis*. 23:89–91. 27 May 1963.

Kirkpatrick, D. "The Methodist Church [and the race problem]:It Reflects Culture as Much as It Reforms It." *Christianity and Crisis*. 18:26–28. 3 March 1958.

Kline, Larry O. "The Negro in the Unification of American Methodism." *Drew Gateway*. 34:128–49. Spring 1964.

Lee, J. O. "Churches and Race Relations; a survey." *Christianity and Crisis*. 17:4–7. 4 February 1957.

McClain, George D. "Pioneering Social Gospel Radicalism: An Overview of the History of the Methodist Federation for Social Action." *Radical Religion*. 5:1. 1980.

McGovern, James R. and Walter T. Howard. "Private Justice and National Concern: The Lynching of Claude Neal," *The Historian*. December 1980.

Mitchell, Norma Taylor. "From Social to Radical Feminism." *Methodist History*. 1975 13 (3): 21–44.

Moore, A. J., Jr. "Methodist General Conference 1960." *Christianity and Crisis*. 20:78–9. 30 May 1960.

Morton, Nelle K. "Toward the Church's Self-Understanding in Race Relations." *Drew Gateway*. 30:10–21. Autumn 1959.

Muelder, Walter G. "Methodism and Segregation: A Case Study." *Christianity and Crisis*. 20:39–42. 4 April 1960.

"Negro Methodists Resort to Courts." *Christian Century*. 54, 17 February 1937.

Raper, Arthur. "1899–1979—A Life Looking 'for the Heart of the Thing.'" Interview by Cliff Kuhn. *Southern Changes*. June/July 1987, 6.

Shankman, Arnold. "Dorothy Tilly, Civil Rights and The Methodist Church." *Methodist History*. 1980 18 (2): 95–108.

"Southern Churches and the Race Question, a symposium on Episcopal, Disciples, Southern Baptist, Southern Presbyterian, and Methodist attitudes." *Christianity and Crisis*. 18:17–28. 3 March 1958.

Stapleton, Carolyn L. "Belle Harris Bennett: Model of Holistic Christianity." *Methodist History*. 21:131–42.

Stevens, Thelma. "A Place of Their Own." *Southern Exposure*. 1976 4 (3): 54–58.

Stewart, J. G. "Civil Rights: How the Bill Was Passed." *Christianity and Crisis*. 24:156. 20 July 1964.

Thomas, James S. "Central Jurisdiction: Dilemma and Opportunity." *Drew Gateway*. 4:119–27. Spring 1964.

Thompson, Betty. "Theressa Hoover, A Woman for All Seasons." *Response*. October 1990.

Thorburn, Neil. "'Strange Fruit' and Southern Tradition." *Midwest Quarterly*. 1971 12 (2): 157–71.

Useem, Michael, and Gary T. Marx. "Majority Involvement in Minority Movements: Civil Rights, Abolition, Untouchability." *Journal of Social Issues*. 1971 27 (1): 81–104.

Valentine, F. "The Court, the Church, and the Community." *Review and Expositor*. 52:536–550. October 1955.

Webber, Charles C. "American Fascism—A Case Study." *Social Questions Bulletin*. 33:6:2–3. June 1943.

White, Ronald C. "'Our Brother in Black': Methodism and Racial Reform in the Progressive Era." *Drew Gateway*. Winter/Spring. 1984.

Wilkins, Roy. "Jim Crow Democracy." *Social Questions Bulletin*. 31:4:1–2. April 1941.

_____. "Negroes in a Fighting Democracy." *Social Questions Bulletin*. 32:4:1–3. April 1942.

_____. "The Color Line in Wartime." *Social Questions Bulletin*. 33:3:1–3. March 1943.

Wood, James R. and Mayer N. Zald. "Aspects of Racial Integration in The Methodist Church: Sources of Resistance to Organizational Policy." *Social Forces*. 1966 45 (2): 255–65.

Secondary Sources

Adamic, Louis, Sherwood Eddy, Channing Tobias, Gerald Johnson, Guy Johnson, Jesse Daniel Ames, Ira Reid, Roger Baldwin, Phillips Russell, and Howard Kester. "Winning the World with Democracy." *South Today*. (Spring 1942).

Alexander, Gross. *A History of the Methodist Church, South, in the United States*. Nashville: Publishing House of the Methodist Episcopal Church, South, 1907.

Andolsen, Barbara Hilkert. *"Daughters of Jefferson, Daughters of Bootblacks," Racism and American Feminism*. Macon, GA: Mercer University Press, 1986.

Aptheker, Herbert, ed. *A Documentary History of the Negro People in the United States, 1910–1932*. Secaucus, NJ: The Citadel Press, 1973.

Baker, Ray Stannard. *Following the Color Line*. New York: Harper & Row, Publishers, 1964. Originally published 1908.

Beard, Mary R. *Woman as Force in History, A Study in Traditions and Realities*. New York: Collier Books, 1946.

Bellah, Robert N., Richard Madsen, William M. Sullivan, Ann Swidler, and Steven M. Tipton. *Habits of the Heart, Individualism and Commitment in American Life*. New York: Harper & Row, Publishers, 1985.

Bennett, Lerone, Jr. *Before the Mayflower, A History of Black America*. Harrisonburg, VA: R. R. Donnelley and Sons, Co., 1982.

Berman, William C. *The Politics of Civil Rights in the Truman Administration*. Columbus: Ohio State University Press, 1970.

Bordin, Ruth. *Women and Temperance, the Quest for Power and Liberty, 1873–1900*. New Brunswick: Rutgers University Press, 1990.

Bowen, J. W. E., ed. *Africa and the American Negro*. Atlanta: 1896.

Branch, Taylor. *Parting the Waters, America in the King Years 1954–63*. New York: Simon and Schuster, 1988.

Brewer, Earl D. C. and Clyde W. Faulkner, Jr. *Attitudes Toward Inclusiveness in Local Methodism*. Ohio: Board of Missions, The Methodist Church, 1968.

Brisbane, Robert H. *The Black Vanguard, Origins of the Negro Social Revolution 1900–1960*. Valley Forge, PA: Judson Press, 1970. Second Printing, 1970.

Bucke, Emory Stevens, gen. editor. [and others] *The History of American Methodism*. Volumes II, III. New York: Abingdon Press, 1964.

Bunche, Ralph. *The Political Status of the Negro in the Age of FDR*. ed. Dewey W. Grantham. Chicago: The University of Chicago Press, 1973.

Cameron, Richard M. *Methodism and Society in Historical Perspective*,

Vol. I. Edited by the Board of Social and Economic Relations of The Methodist Church. New York: Abingdon Press, 1961.

Campbell, Barbara E. *United Methodist Women: In the Middle of Tomorrow*. Women's Division, The Board of Global Ministries, The United Methodist Church, 1975.

Carmichael, Stokely and Charles V. Hamilton. *Black Power, The Politics of Liberation in America*. New York: Vintage Books, A Division of Random House, 1967.

Carr, Robert K. *The House Committee on Un-American Activities*. Ithaca, NY: Cornell University Press, 1952.

Carroll, Berenice A., ed. *Liberating Women's History: Theoretical and Critical Essays*. Urbana: University of Illinois Press, 1976.

Carter, Dan T. *Scottsboro, A Tragedy of the American South*. New York: Oxford University Press, 1969.

Carson, Clayborne. *In Struggle: SNCC and the Black Awakening of the 1960s*. Cambridge, MA.: Harvard University Press, 1981.

Chafe, William H. *Civilities and Civil Rights: Greensboro, North Carolina, and the Black Struggle for Freedom*. New York: Oxford University Press, 1980.

_____. *Women and Equality, Changing Patterns in American Culture*. New York: Oxford University Press, 1977.

Chambers, Clarke A. "Varieties of Welfare History." *Reviews in American History*. Vol. 15, No. 3. September 1987.

Clayborne Carson, David J. Garrow, Vincent Harding, and Darlene Clark Hine. *Eyes on the Prize, America's Civil Rights Years, A Reader and Guide*. New York: Penguin Books, 1987.

Conrad, Earl. *Jim Crow America*. New York: Duell, Sloan and Pearce, 1947.

Cook, Fred J. *The Nightmare Decade, The Life and Times of Senator Joe McCarthy*. New York: Random House, 1971.

Cranston, Earl. *Breaking Down the Walls, A Contribution to Methodist Unification*. New York: Methodist Book Concern, 1915.

Crum, Mason. *The Negro in the Methodist Church*. New York: Board of Missions and Church Extension, The Methodist Church, 1951.

Culver, Dwight W. *Negro Segregation in the Methodist Church*. New Haven: Yale University Press, 1953.

Davis, James H. and Woodie W. White. *Racial Transition in the Church*. Nashville: Abingdon Press, 1980.

Denny, Collins, and Collins Denny, Jr. *An Appeal to Men of Reason and Religion Concerning Methodist Unification*. Richmond, VA: n.p., n.d.

Downs, Karl E. *Meet the Negro*. Pasadena: The Login Press, [1943]. Published by the Methodist Youth Fellowship, Southern California-Arizona Annual Conference, The Methodist Church.

Downs, Mary Isabelle Gray. *Brothers All*. Nashville, TN: Board of Missions, Methodist Episcopal Church, South, 1930.

DuBois, W. E. B. *The Negro Artisan*. Atlanta University: Pub. No. 7, 1902.

_____. *The Souls of Black Folk, Essays and Sketches*. Chicago: A. C. McClurg and Company, 1903.

Dunbar, Anthony P. *Against the Grain, Southern Radicals and Prophets, 1929–1959*. Charlottesville: University Press of Virginia, 1981.

Dykeman, Wilma, and James Stokely. *Seeds of Southern Change, The Life of Will Alexander*. Chicago: University of Chicago Press, 1962.

Eleazer, Robert B. *Reason, Religion and Race*. New York: Abingdon-Cokesbury Press, 1950.

Embree, Edwin R. *13 Against the Odds*. New York: The Viking Press, 1945.

Farmer, James. *Lay Bare the Heart, An Autobiography of The Civil Rights Movement*. New York: New American Library, 1985.

Flexner, Eleanor. *Century of Struggle: The Woman's Rights Movement in the United States*. Cambridge, MA: The Belknap Press of Harvard University Press, 1959. Revised Edition, 1975. Seventh Printing 1982.

Fox-Genovese, Elizabeth. *Within the Plantation Household: Black and White Women of the Old South*. Chapel Hill: The University of North Carolina Press, 1988.

Franklin, John Hope and August Meier, eds. *Black Leaders of the Twentieth Century*. Urbana: University of Illinois Press, 1982.

Gallagher, Buell Gordon. *Color and Conscience: The Irrepressible Conflict*. New York: Harper and Brothers, Publishers, 1946.

Garner, C. C., J. F. McLeod, Jr., J. B. Nichols, A. S. Turnipseed, and J. A. Zellner. *Making Methodism Methodist*. N.p.: Stone and Pierce, 1946, 1947.

Gavins, Raymond. *The Perils and Prospects of Southern Black Leadership: Gordon Blaine Hancock, 1884–1970*. Durham, NC: Duke University Press, 1977.

Giddings, Paula. *When and Where I Enter, the Impact of Black Women on Race and Sex in America*. New York: Bantam Books, 1984.

Goddard, Oscar Elmo, and Mrs. R. W. [Tochie] MacDonnell. *Making America Safe, A Study of the Home Missions of the Methodist Episcopal Church, South*. Nashville, TN: Centenary Commission of the Methodist Episcopal Church, South, [1918].

Gorrell, Donald K., ed. "Woman's Rightful Place," *Women in United Methodist History*. Dayton, OH: United Theological Seminary, 1980.

Gossett, Thomas F. *Race: The History of an Idea in America*. Dallas: Southern Methodist University Press, 1963.

Graham, John H. *Black United Methodism: Retrospect and Prospect*. First edition. New York: Vantage Press, 1979.

Gravely, William B. "Methodist Preachers, Slavery and Caste: Types of Social Concern in Antebellum America." *Duke Divinity Review*. Vol. 34, August 1969.

Green, Donald Ross, James A. Jordan, W. J. Bridgeman, and Clay V. Brittain. *Black Belt Schools: Beyond Desegregation*. Atlanta: Southern Regional Council, 1965.

Hagood, Lewis Marshall. *The Colored Man in the Methodist Episcopal Church*. Westport, CT: Negro Universities Press, [1970] Reprint of the 1890 edition.

Hall, Jacquelyn Dowd. *Revolt Against Chivalry: Jessie Daniel Ames and the Woman's Campaign Against Lynching*. New York: Columbia University Press, 1979.

Hancock, Gordon B. "Writing a 'New Charter of Southern Race Relations.'" *New South*. January 1964.

Harding, Vincent. *The Other American Revolution*. Los Angeles: Center for Afro-American Studies, University of California, and Atlanta, GA: Institute of the Black World, 1980.

Hartmann, Susan M. *The Home Front and Beyond, American Women in the 1940s*. Boston: Twayne Publishers, 1982.

Haygood, Atticus G. *Our Brother in Black: His Freedom and His Future*. Nashville: Southern Methodist Publishing House, 1887.

Hill, Patricia R. *The World Their Household, The American Woman's Foreign Mission Movement and Cultural Transformation, 1870–1920*. Ann Arbor: The University of Michigan Press, 1985.

Hill, Samuel S., Jr. *Southern Churches in Crisis*. New York: Holt, Rinehart and Winston, 1966.

Hill, Samuel S., Jr., Edgar T. Thompson, Anne Firor Scott, Charles Hudson, and Edwin S. Gaustad. *Religion and the Solid South*. Nashville: Abingdon Press, 1972.

Hilton, Bruce. *The Delta Ministry*. London: The Macmillan Co. Collier-Macmillan Ltd., 1969.

Holder, Ray. *The Mississippi Methodists 1799–1983, A Moral People "Born of Conviction."* N.p.: Maverick Prints, 1984.

Holifield, E. Brooks. *Gentlemen Theologians: American Theology in Southern Culture, 1775–1860*. Durham, NC: Duke University Press, 1978.

Holt, Rackham. *Mary McLeod Bethune, A Biography*. Garden City, NY: Doubleday and Company, Inc., 1964.

hooks, bell. *Ain't I A Woman: Black Women and Feminism*. Boston: South End Press, 1981.

Hoover, Theressa. *With Unveiled Face, Centennial Reflections on Women and*

Men in the Community of the Church. New York: Women's Division, General Board of Global Ministries, The United Methodist Church, 1983.

Hughes, Langston. *Fight for Freedom, The Story of the NAACP.* New York: W. W. Horton and Company, Inc., 1962.

Jacobson, Julius. *The Negro and the American Labor Movement.* Garden City, NY: Anchor Books, Doubleday & Company, Inc., 1968.

Jezer, Marty. *The Power of the People: Active Nonviolence in the United States.* Culver City, CA: Peace Press, Inc., 1977.

Johnson, Charles S. *A Preface to Racial Understanding.* New York: Friendship Press, 1936.

_____. *To Stem This Tide, A Survey of Racial Tension Areas in the United States.* Boston: The Pilgrim Press, 1943.

Jones, Donald G. *The Sectional Crisis and Northern Methodism: A Study in Piety, Political Ethics, and Civil Religion.* Metuchen, NJ: Scarecrow Press, 1979.

Jones, Lewis and Stanley Smith. *Field Reports on Desegregation in the South. Tuskegee, Alabama: Voting Rights and Economic Pressure.* New York: Anti-Defamation League of B'nai B'rith with the cooperation of the National Council of Churches of Christ in the United States of America, 1958.

Kapur, Sudarshan. *Raising Up a Prophet: The African-American Encounter with Gandhi.* Boston: Beacon Press, 1992.

Keller, Rosemary Skinner, Louise L. Queen, and Hilah F. Thomas, eds. *Women in New Worlds, Historical Perspectives on Wesleyan Tradition.* Nashville: Abingdon Press, 1982.

Kelsey, George D. *Racism and the Christian Understanding of Man.* New York: Charles Scribner's Sons, 1965.

King, Martin Luther, Jr. *Stride Toward Freedom.* New York: Harper & Row, 1958.

_____. *The Trumpet of Conscience.* New York: Harper & Row, 1967.

_____. *Where Do We Go From Here: Chaos or Community?* Boston: Beacon Press, 1967.

_____. *Why We Can't Wait.* New York: The New American Library, 1962, 1964.

King, Mary. *Freedom Song, A Personal Story of the 1960s Civil Rights Movement.* New York: Quill, William Morrow, 1987.

Kneebone, John T. *Southern Liberal Journalists and the Issue of Race, 1920–1944.* Chapel Hill: The University of North Carolina Press, 1985.

Knepper, Jeanne G. "Radicals in Conservative Times: An Investigation of the Strategies and Decisions of MFSS During the Periods 1915–1920 and 1939–1948." Unpublished paper, 1984.

_____. "Sacred Rights, Holy Liberties: The Methodist Federation for Social Action." Unpublished paper.

Knotts, Alice. "Race Relations in the 1920s: A Challenge to Southern Methodist Women." *Methodist History.* July 1988.

Knudson, Albert C. *The Principles of Christian Ethics.* New York: Abingdon-Cokesbury Press, 1943.

Lakey, Othal Hawthorne. *The History of the CME Church.* Memphis, TN: The CME Publishing House, 1985.

Lebsock, Suzanne. *The Free Women of Petersburg, Status and Culture in a Southern Town: 1784–1860.* New York: W. W. Norton and Company, 1985.

Lerner, Gerda. *Black Women in White America, A Documentary History.* New York: Vintage Books, 1973.

_____. *The Majority Finds Its Past: Placing Women in History.* New York: Oxford University Press, 1979.

Lewis, Anthony and the *New York Times. Portrait of a Decade, The Second American Revolution.* New York: Random House, 1964.

Logan, Rayford W. *The Betrayal of the Negro from Rutherford B. Hayes to Woodrow Wilson.* New York: Collier Books, 1954.

McClain, William B. *Black People in the Methodist Church, Whither Thou Goest?* Cambridge, MA: Schenkman Publishing Company, 1984.

McDowell, John Patrick. *The Social Gospel in the South.* Baton Rouge: Louisiana State University Press, 1982.

McGill, Ralph. *A Church, A School.* New York: Abingdon Press, 1959.

_____. *The South and the Southerner.* Boston: Little, Brown and Company, 1959, 1963.

McGovern, James R. *Anatomy of a Lynching: The Killing of Claude Neal.* Baton Rouge: Louisiana State University Press, 1982.

McNeil, Genna Rae. *Charles Hamilton Houston and the Struggle for Civil Rights.* Philadelphia: University of Pennsylvania Press, 1983.

Magalis, Elaine. *Conduct Becoming to a Woman: Bolted Doors and Burgeoning Missions.* Women's Division, Board of Global Ministries, The United Methodist Church, c. 1971.

Mathews, Donald G. *Religion in the Old South.* Chicago: University of Chicago Press, 1977.

Meeker, Ruth Esther. *Six Decades of Service: A History of the Woman's Home Missionary Society of the Methodist Episcopal Church.* Cincinnati, OH: Steinhauser, Inc., 1969.

Meier, August and Elliott M. Rudwick. *CORE, A Study in the Civil Rights Movement 1942–1968.* New York: Oxford University Press, 1973.

_____. *From Plantation to Ghetto, An Interpretive History of American Negroes.* New York: Hill and Wang, 1966.

Meier, August, Elliott Rudwick, and Francis L. Broderick, eds. *Black Protest Thought in the Twentieth Century*. Indianapolis: Bobbs-Merrill Educational Publishing, 1965, 1971. Second Edition, Eighth Printing, 1980.

Meier, August. *Negro Thought in America, 1880–1915, Racial Ideologies in the Age of Booker T. Washington*. Ann Arbor: The University of Michigan Press, 1963.

Morris, Alden D. *The Origins of the Civil Rights Movement, Black Communities Organizing for Change*. New York: The Free Press, A Division of Macmillan, Inc., 1984.

Morrow, Ralph Ernest. *Northern Methodism and Reconstruction*. East Lansing: Michigan State University Press, 1956.

Murray, Peter Carlisle. "Christ and Caste in Conflict: Creating a Racially Inclusive Methodist Church." Ph.D. Dissertation. Indiana University, 1985.

Muse, Benjamin. *The American Negro Revolution; from Nonviolence to Black Power, 1963–1967*. Bloomington: Indiana University Press [1968].

Myrdal, Gunnar. *An American Dilemma, The Negro Problem and Modern Democracy*. New York: Harper & Row, Publishers, 1944, 1962.

Nash, Gary B. *Red, White and Black*. Englewood Cliffs, NJ: Prentice-Hall, Inc., 1982.

Nelson, William Stuart, ed. *The Christian Way in Race Relations*. New York: Harper and Brothers Publishers, 1948.

Newberry, Anthony Lake. "Without Urgency or Ardor: The South's Middle-of-the-Road Liberals and Civil Rights, 1945–1960." Ph.D. Dissertation. Ohio University. 1982.

Newsome, Clarence G. "Mary McLeod Bethune in Religious Perspective: A Seminal Essay." Dissertation, Graduate School of Duke University. 1982.

Norrell, Robert J. *Reaping the Whirlwind: The Civil Rights Movement in Tuskegee*. New York: Alfred A. Knopf, 1985.

North Georgia Conference United Methodist Women. *The Journey: United Methodist Women in North Georgia, 1878–1983*. North Georgia Conference United Methodist Women, 1984.

Oldham, J. H. *Christianity and the Race Problem*. New York: Association Press, 1924.

Peterson, Thomas Virgil. *Ham and Japheth*. Metuchen, NJ: Scarecrow Press, 1978.

Rauschenbusch, Walter. *Christianity and the Social Crisis*. New York: The Macmillan Company, 1907.

Read, Frank T. and Lucy S. McGough. *Let Them Be Judged: The Judicial Integration of the Deep South*. Metuchen, NJ: Scarecrow Press, 1978.

Richardson, Harry Van Buren. *Dark Salvation: The Story of Methodism as It Developed Among Blacks in America*. First edition. Garden City, NY: Anchor Press, 1976.

Richey, Russell E. and Kenneth E. Rowe, eds., *Rethinking Methodist History, a Bicentennial Historical Consultation* (Nashville: Kingswood Books, 1985) 75–88.

Root, Robert. *Progress Against Prejudice, The Church Confronts the Race Problem*. New York: Friendship Press, 1957.

Rorrence, Ridgely. *The Story of John Hope*. New York: Macmillan, 1948.

Rose, Arnold M., ed. *Assuring Freedom to the Free, A Century of Emancipation in the U.S.A.* Detroit: Wayne State University Press, 1964.

Rosenberg, Rosalind. *Beyond Separate Spheres, Intellectual Roots of Modern Feminism*. New Haven: Yale University Press, 1982.

Rothman, Sheila M. *Woman's Proper Place, A History of Changing Ideals and Practices, 1870 to the   Present*. New York: Basic Books, Inc., Publishers, 1978.

Sangster, W. E. *Methodism, Her Unfinished Task*. London: The Epworth Press, 1947.

Schmidt, Jean Miller. "Toward a New History." Cassette tape. The Iliff Week of Lectures. 25 January 1984.

Scott, Anne Firor. *Making the Invisible Woman Visible*. Urbana: University of Illinois Press, 1984.

_____. *The Southern Lady, From Pedestal to Politics, 1830–1930*. Chicago: University of Chicago Press, 1970.

Sellers, James. *The South and Christian Ethics*. New York: Association Press, 1962.

Shaw, Daniel W. *Should the Negroes of the Methodist Episcopal Church Be Set Apart in a Church by Themselves?* New York: Eaton and Mains, 1912.

Shriver, Donald W. Jr., ed. *The Unsilent South, Prophetic Preaching in Racial Crisis*. Richmond, VA: John Knox Press, 1965.

Sitkoff, Harvard. *The Struggle for Black Equality 1954–1980*. New York: Hill and Wang, 1981. Fourth printing 1983.

Sledge, Robert Watson. *Hands on the Ark: The Struggle for Change in the Methodist Episcopal Church, South, 1914–1939*. Lake Junaluska, NC: United Methodist Commission on Archives and History, 1975.

Smith, H. Shelton. *In His Image, But . . . : Racism in Southern Religion 1780–1910*. Durham, NC: Duke University Press, 1972.

Smith, Lillian. *Killers of the Dream*. Garden City, NY: Anchor Books, 1963. Originally published by W. W. Norton & Co., Inc., 1949.

_____. *Now Is the Time*. New York: Dell Publishing Company, Inc., 1955.

_____. *One Hour*. New York: Harcourt, Brace and Co., 1959.

_____. *The Winner Names the Age, A Collection of Writings by Lillian Smith*. Michelle Cliff, ed. New York: W. W. Norton and Co., 1978.

Sosna, Morton. *In Search of the Silent South, Southern Liberals and the Race Issue*. New York: Columbia University Press, 1977.

"Southern Methodist Women Ask Searching Questions." *Christian Century*. 54, 21 April 1937.

Stampp, Kenneth M. *The Era of Reconstruction, 1865–1877*. New York: Vintage Books, 1965.

Stowell, Jay Samuel. *Methodist Adventures in Negro Education*. New York: The Methodist Book Concern, 1922.

Straughn, James H. *Inside Methodist Union*. Nashville: The Methodist Publishing House, 1958.

Thomas, Hilah F., and Rosemary Skinner Keller, eds. *Women in New Worlds, Historical Perspectives on Wesleyan Tradition*. Nashville: Abingdon, 1981.

Thurman, Howard. *The Luminous Darkness, A Personal Interpretation of the Anatomy of Segregation and the Ground of Hope*. New York: Harper & Row, Publishers, 1965.

Tilson, Everett. *The Conscience of Culture*. Nashville: National Methodist Student Movement, The Board of Education of The Methodist Church, 1953.

_____. *Segregation and the Bible*. New York: Abingdon Press, 1958.

Tomkinson, Laura E. *Twenty Years' History of the Woman's Home Missionary Society of the Methodist Episcopal Church, 1880–1900*. Cincinnati: The Woman's Home Missionary Society, the Methodist Episcopal Church, 1903.

Toppin, Edgar A. *Blacks in America: Then and Now*. Boston: The Christian Science Publishing Society, 1969.

van der Bent, Ans J., ed. *World Council of Churches' Statements and Actions on Racism, 1948–1979*. Geneva: Programme to Combat Racism, World Council of Churches, 1980.

White, Ronald Cedric, Jr. "Social Christianity and the Negro in the Progressive Era, 1890–1920." Princeton University, Ph.D. diss., 1972.

White, Ronald Cedric, Jr., and C. Howard Hopkins. *The Social Gospel, Religion and Reform in Changing America*. Philadelphia: Temple University Press, 1976.

Wilkins, Josephine. "An Answer When Negro Southerners Spoke." *New South*. January 1964.

Williams, Juan. *Eyes on the Prize: America's Civil Rights Years, 1954–1965*. New York: Viking Penguin Inc., 1987.

Wilson, Robert L. *The Effect of Racially Changing Communities on Methodist*

Churches in Thirty-two Cities in the Southeast. New York: Department of Research and Survey, National Division, Board of Missions of The Methodist Church, 1968.

_____. *The Northern Negro Looks at the Church.* New York: Department of Research and Survey, National Division, Board of Missions of The United Methodist Church, 1968.

Wogaman, J. Philip. *A Christian Method of Moral Judgment.* Philadelphia: The Westminster Press, 1976.

_____. *Methodism's Challenge in Race Relations, A Study of Strategy.* Boston: Boston University Press, 1960.

Woodward, C. Vann. *The Strange Career of Jim Crow.* New York: Oxford University Press, 1957.

Index

LaVergne, TN USA
25 March 2010
177078LV00003B/7/P